D1102340

Bolivia

Ben Box, Robert & Daisy Kunstaetter

Credits

Footprint credits

Editor: Felicity Laughton
Production and layout: Emma Bryers
Maps: Kevin Feeney

Managing Director: Andy Riddle
Content Director: Patrick Dawson
Publisher: Alan Murphy
Publishing Managers: Felicity Laughton, Jo Williams, Nicola Gibbs
Marketing and Partnerships Director: Liz Harper
Marketing Executive: Liz Eyles
Trade Product Manager: Diane McEntee
Account Managers: Paul Bew, Tania Ross
Advertising: Renu Sibal, Elizabeth Taylor
Trade Product Co-ordinator: Kirsty Holmes

Photography credits
Front and back cover: Dreamstime

Printed in Great Britain by CPI Antony Rowe, Chippenham, Wiltshire

MIX
Paper from responsible sources
FSC® C013604
www.fsc.org

Every effort has been made to ensure that the facts in this guidebook are accurate. However, travellers should still obtain advice from consulates, airlines, etc, about travel and visa requirements before travelling. The authors and publishers cannot accept responsibility for any loss, injury or inconvenience however caused.

Publishing information

Footprint *Focus Bolivia*
1st edition
© Footprint Handbooks Ltd
June 2012

ISBN: 978 1 908206 72 5
CIP DATA: A catalogue record for this book is available from the British Library

® Footprint Handbooks and the Footprint mark are a registered trademark of Footprint Handbooks Ltd

Published by Footprint
6 Riverside Court
Lower Bristol Road
Bath BA2 3DZ, UK
T +44 (0)1225 469141
F +44 (0)1225 469461
footprinttravelguides.com

Distributed in the USA by Globe Pequot Press, Guilford, Connecticut

The content of Footprint *Focus Bolivia* has been taken directly from Footprint's *South American Handbook* which was researched and written by Ben Box, Robert & Daisy Kunstaetter.

Contents

On Bolivia's Altiplano you are so far up it will make your head spin. Every day in La Paz, the highest seat of government in the world transforms itself from a melée of indigenous markets and modern business into a canyon of glittering stars as the lights come on at nightfall.

Bolivia has some of the most bio-diverse conservation areas in South America: Madidi, Amboró and Noel Kempff Mercado all have an incredible range of habitats and variety of flora and fauna, and you should visit at least one on your journey. If you fancy a trek, there are adventurous trails within a day of the capital, while anyone nostalgic for the revolutionary days of the 1960s can retrace the final steps of Che Guevara. For an exhilarating bike ride, try one of the most dangerous roads in the world, from mountain heights to the lush Yungas valleys, through waterfalls and round hairpin bends – but do go with an expert.

In Bolivia you learn to expect the unexpected. On the largest salt flat on earth, a vast blinding-white expanse, you lose track of what is land and what is sky. At Carnival in Oruro, dancers wear masks of the scariest monsters you could ever dream of. To visit the mines at Potosí, once the silver lode for the Spanish Empire, you buy coca leaves and other gifts for the miners. In the surreal Reserva Eduardo Avaroa, volcanoes overlook lakes of blue, white, green and red, where flamingos feed, and Dalí-esque rock structures dot the Altiplano. In the Bolivian Amazon you can swim with pink river dolphins or fish for piranhas.

Before you go home, you can fill your bags with everything from the beautiful autumnal colours of the textiles, to packs of dried llama foetuses. The latter are said to protect homes from evil spirits but are unlikely to ingratiate you with first-world customs and agriculture officers.

Planning your trip

Where to go

La Paz is a good place to start, as many international flights land here and it is closest to the well-travelled overland routes from Peru and Chile. The city is easy to explore, but you do need time to adjust to the altitude. This is, after all, the highest seat of government in the world (Sucre, not La Paz, is Bolivia's official capital). There are some good museums and churches in La Paz, and many indigenous market areas. Daytrips include the pre-Inca city of **Tiwanaku**, which is close to beautiful **Lake Titicaca**, where a night or more on its shores is recommended. Northeast of La Paz, over the cordillera, are the **Yungas**, subtropical valleys rich in vegetation, where a town like **Coroico** can provide welcome relief from the chill of the Altiplano. Equally pleasant and also lower than La Paz is **Sorata**, a good base for climbing, trekking and biking.

South of La Paz is the mining city of **Oruro**, which hosts famous carnival celebrations, including the **Diablada** devil-dance, usually held in mid- to late February. Southeast are the colonial cities of **Potosí**, where Spain garnered much of its imperial wealth from abundant silver deposits and present-day miners scour the mountain for meagre pickings; and **Sucre**, one of Bolivia's finest colonial cities and a centre for language study and volunteering. **Uyuni** and **Tupiza**, further south again, are the jumping-off places for trips to high-altitude puna with salt flats, coloured lakes, flamingos and volcanoes. **Tarija**, southeast of Potosí, is best known for its fruits and wine, and delightful climate.

East of La Paz is **Cochabamba**, Bolivia's fourth largest city and centre of one of the country's main agricultural zones. Reached from Cochabamba, **Parque Nacional Torotoro**, with its dinosaur tracks, rock paintings, canyons and waterfalls, is a tough but excellent excursion. Further east is **Santa Cruz de la Sierra**, Bolivia's largest city, from where you can visit **Amboró**, **Noel Kempff Mercado** and other unique national parks, as well as follow in the footsteps of Che Guevara. Also reached from Santa Cruz, **Samaipata** is a particularly pleasant resort town with an important archaeological site. In the far east of the country, don't miss the fabulous **Jesuit missions** of Chiquitania, or the lovely **Reserva Tucavaca** along the road and railway to Brazil.

From La Paz you can fly or ride (when roads are passable) into the Beni region, in the heart of the Bolivian Amazon. **Rurrenabaque** is the chief destination and starting point for **Parque Nacional Madidi**, which claims a greater bio-diversity than anywhere else on earth. Outside of Rurrenabaque, the further north you go the fewer tourists you will meet. The dry season (May to September) is the best time to visit.

National parks Administered by the **Servicio Nacional de Areas Protegidas (SERNAP)** ① *Francisco Bedregal 2904 y Victor Sanjinés, Sopocachi, T02-242 6268, www.sernap.gob. bo*, an administrative office with limited tourist information. Better are Sernap's regional offices, addresses given in the travelling text. Involved NGOs include: **Fundación para el Desarrollo del Sistema Nacional de Areas Protegidas** ① *Prolongación Cordero 127, across from US Embassy, La Paz, T02-211 3364, www.fundesnap.org*; **Fundación Amigos de la Naturaleza (FAN)** ① *Km 7.5 Vía a La Guadria, Santa Cruz, T03-355 6800, www.fan-bo.org*; **Probioma** ① *Calle 7 Este 29, Equipetrol, Santa Cruz, T03-343 1332, www.probioma.org.bo*.

Don't miss...

Numbers relate to map on page 4.

Best time to visit Bolivia

The dry season is May to September, July and August see the most tourists, while some of the best festivals, eg Carnival and Holy Week, fall during the wet season – generally December to March. The country has four climatic zones: (1) The Puna and Altiplano; average temperature, 10°C, but above 4000 m may drop as low as -30°C at night from June to August. By day, the tropical sun raises temperatures to above 20°C. Rainfall on the northern Altiplano is 400-700 mm, much less further south. Little rain falls upon the western plateau between May and November, but the rest of the year can be wet. (2) The Yungas north of La Paz and Cochabamba, among the spurs of the Cordillera; altitude, 750-1500 m; average temperature 24°C. Rainfall in the Yungas is 700-800 mm a year, with high humidity.(3) The Valles, or high valleys and basins gouged out by the rivers of the Puna; average temperature 19°C. (4) The tropical lowlands; altitude 150m to 750 m; rainfall is high but seasonal (heaviest November to March, but can fall at any time); large areas suffer from alternate flooding and drought. The climate is hot, ranging from 23° to 25°C in the south and to 30°C in the north. Occasional cold winds from the south, the *surazos*, can lower the temperature suddenly and considerably.

Getting to Bolivia

Air

Most South American countries have direct flights from **Europe**. In many cases, though, the choice of departure point is limited to Madrid and one or two other cities (Paris or Amsterdam, for instance). Argentina, Brazil and Venezuela have the most options: France, Germany, Italy, Spain and the UK (although the last named not to Venezuela). Brazil also has flights from Lisbon to a number of cities. Where there are no direct flights connections can be made in the USA (Miami, or other gateways), Buenos Aires, Rio de Janeiro or São Paulo. **Main US gateways** are Miami, Houston, Dallas, Atlanta and New York. On the west coast, Los Angeles has flights to several South American cities. If buying airline tickets routed through the USA, check that US taxes are included in the price. Flights from **Canada** are mostly via the USA, although there are direct flights from Toronto to Bogotá and Santiago. Likewise, flights from **Australia** and **New Zealand** are best through Los Angeles, except for the Qantas/LAN route from Sydney and Auckland to Santiago, and **Qantas'** non-stop route Sydney-Santiago, from where connections can be made. From **Japan** and from **South Africa** there are direct flights to Brazil. Within **Latin America** there is plenty of choice on local carriers and some connections on US or European airlines.

Prices and discounts

Most airlines offer discounted fares on scheduled flights through agencies who specialize in this type of fare. If you buy discounted air tickets always check the reservation with the airline concerned to make sure the flight still exists. Also remember the IATA airlines' schedules change in March and October each year, so if you're going to be away a long time it's best to leave return flight coupons open. Peak times are 7 December-15 January and 10 July-10 September. If you intend travelling during those times, book as far ahead as possible. Between February and May and September and November special offers may be available.

Transport in Bolivia

Air

All of the following offer internal air services. **AeroSur**, *www.aerosur.com*; also has various international flights, including Cuzco two to three times a week. **Boliviana de Aviación (BoA)**, *www.boa.bo*; also flies to São Paulo and Buenos Aires. **TAM**, *www.tam.bo*, the military airline, flies to main cities as well as several smaller and more remote destinations. **Aerocon** *www.aerocon.bo*, based in Trinidad, serves mostly the northen jungle. **Amaszonas** *www.amaszonas.com* flies between La Paz, Rurrenabaque and other lowland destinations; as well as La Paz and Uyuni. Many flights radiate from La Paz, Santa Cruz or Cochabamba. Make sure you have adequate baggage insurance.

Bus

Buses ply most of the roads. Inter-urban buses are called *flotas*, urban ones *micros* or *minibuses* (vans); *trufis* are shared taxis. Larger bus companies run frequent services and offer a/c, TV and other mod cons. You can usually buy tickets with reserved seats a day or two in advance. Alternatively, savings may sometimes be obtained by bargaining for fares at the last minute, although not at peak travel times like national holidays. A small charge is made for use of bus terminals; payment is before departure.

In the wet season, bus travel is subject to long delays and detours, at extra cost, and cancellations are not uncommon. On all journeys, take some food, water and toilet paper. It is best to travel by day, not just to enjoy the scenery and avoid arriving at night, but also for better road safety (also see Road Safety, page 13). Bus companies are responsible for any items packed in the luggage compartment or on the roof, but only if they give you a ticket for each bag.

Train

The western highland railway is operated by **Ferroviaria Andina** (FCA, www.fca.com.bo). There are passenger trains to the Argentine border at Villazón from Oruro, via Uyuni and Tupiza. The eastern lowland line is run by **Ferroviaria Oriental** (www.ferroviariaoriental. com), with services from Santa Cruz to the Brazilian border. There are also several other minor but potentially interesting train routes

Maps

Good maps of Bolivia are few and far between, and maps in general can be hard to find. **Instituto Geográfico Militar**. Many IGM maps date from the 1970s and their accuracy is variable; prices also vary, US$4.50-7 a sheet. **Walter Guzmán Córdova** makes several travel and trekking maps, available from some bookshops in La Paz. The **German Alpine**

Price codes

Where to stay

$$$$ over US$150   **$$$** US$66-151

$$ US$30-65   **$** under US$30

Price of a double room in high season, including taxes.

Restaurants

$$$ over US$12   **$$** US$7-12   **$** US$6 and under

Prices for a two-course meal for one person, excluding drinks or service charge.

Club (**Deutscher Alpenverein**, www.alpenverein.de) produces two maps of Sorata-Ancohuma-Illampu and Illimani, but these are not usually available in La Paz.

Where to stay in Bolivia → *See our hotel grade price guide above.*

Hotels and hostales

Hotels must display prices by law. The number of stars awarded each hotel is also regulated and is fairly accurate. The following terms likewise reflect the size and quality of an establishment (from largest and best, to smallest and simplest): *hotel, hostal, residencial,* and *alojamiento*. A *pensión* is a simple restaurant, not a place to sleep.

Camping

Camping is best suited to the wilderness areas of Bolivia, away from towns, and people. Organized campsites, car or trailer camping does not exist here. Because of the abundance of cheap hotels you should never have to camp in populated areas

Youth hostels

Youth hostels or self-styled 'backpackers' are not necessarily cheaper than hotels. A number of mid-range *residenciales* are affiliated to **Hostelling International (HI)**, www.hostellingbolivia.org; some others just say they are. Another website listing hostels is www.boliviahostels.com, but they are not necessarily affiliated to HI.

Food and drink in Bolivia → *See our restaurants price guide above.*

Restaurants in Bolivia

Most restaurants do not open early but many hotels include breakfast, which is also served in markets (see below). In *pensiones* and cheaper restaurants a basic lunch (*almuerzo* – usually finished by 1300) and dinner (*cena*) are normally available. The *comida del día* is the best value in any class of restaurant. Breakfast and lunch can also be found in markets, but eat only what is cooked in front of you. Dishes cooked in the street are not safe. Llama meat contains parasites, so make sure it has been properly cooked, and be especially careful of raw salads as many tourists experience gastrointestinal upsets.

Food

Bolivian highland cooking is usually tasty and *picante* (spicy). Recommended local specialities include *empanadas* (cheese pasties) and *humintas* (maize pies); *pukacapas* are *picante* cheese pies. Recommended main dishes include *sajta de pollo*, hot spicy chicken with onion, fresh potatoes and *chuño* (dehydrated potatoes), *parrillada* (mixed grill), *fricase* (juicy pork with *chuño*), *silpancho* (very thin fried breaded meat with eggs, rice and bananas), and *ají de lengua*, ox-tongue with hot peppers, potatoes and *chuño* or *tunta* (another kind of dehydrated potato). *Pique macho*, roast meat, sausage, chips, onion and pepper is especially popular with Bolivians and travellers alike. Near Lake Titicaca fish becomes an important part of the local diet and trout, though not native, is usually delicious. Bolivian soups are usually hearty and warming, including *chairo* made of meat, vegetables and *chuño*. *Salteñas* are very popular meat or chicken pasties eaten as a mid-morning snack, the trick is to avoid spilling the gravy all over yourself.

In the lowland Oriente region, the food usually comes with cooked banana, yucca and rice. This area also has good savoury snacks, such as *cuñapés* made with manioc flour. In the northern lowlands, many types of wild meat are served in tourist restaurants and on jungle tours. Bear in mind that the turtles whose eggs are eaten are endangered and that other species not yet endangered soon will be if they stay on the tourist menu.

Ají is hot pepper, frequently used in cooking. *Rocoto* is an even hotter variety (with black seeds), sometimes served as a garnish and best avoided by the uninitiated. *Llajua* is a hot pepper sauce present on every Bolivian table. It's potency varies greatly so try a little bit before applying dollops to your food.

Bolivia's temperate and tropical fruits are excellent and abundant. Don't miss the luscious grapes and peaches in season (February-April). Brazil nuts, called *almendras* or *castañas*, are produced in the northern jungle department of Pando and sold throughout the country.

The popular tourist destinations have a profusion of cafés and restaurants catering to the gringo market. Some offer decent international cuisine at reasonable prices, but many seem convinced that foreigners eat only mediocre pizza and vegetarian omelettes. There must be a hundred 'Pizzería Italianas' in Bolivia's tourist towns.

Drink The several makes of local lager-type **beer** are recommendable; *Paceña* and *Huari* are the best-known brands. There are also micro-brews in La Paz. *Singani*, the national spirit, is distilled from grapes, and is cheap and strong. *Chuflay* is *singani* and a fizzy mixer, usually 7-Up. Good **wines** are produced by several vineyards near Tarija (tours are available, see page 93). *Chicha* is a fermented maize drink, popular in Cochabamba. The hot maize drink, *api* (with cloves, cinnamon, lemon and sugar), is good on cold mornings. **Bottled water** is readily available. Tap, stream and well water should never be drunk without first being purified.

Essentials A-Z

Accident and emergency

Police T110. Ambulance T118.
Robberies should be reported to the
Policía Turística, they will issue a report for
insurance purposes. In La Paz: Calle Hugo
Estrada 1354, Plaza Tejada Sorzano frente al
estadio, Miraflores, next to Love City Chinese
restaurant, T222 5016. In cities which do not
have a Policía Turística report robberies to
the *Fuerza Especial de Lucha Contra el Crimen*
(FELCC), Departamento de Robos.

Electricity

220 volts 50 cycles AC. Sockets usually
accept both continental European (round)
and US-type (flat) 2-pin plugs. Also some
110 volt sockets, when in doubt, ask.

Embassies and consulates

For all Bolivian embassies abroad and all
foreign embassies and consulates in Bolivia,
see http://embassy.goabroad.com.

Festivals

2 Feb: Virgen de la Candelaria, in rural
communities, Copacabana, Santa Cruz.
Carnaval, especially famous in Oruro, is
celebrated throughout the country in Feb
or Mar. There are parades with floats and
folkloric dances, parties, much drinking
and water throwing even in the coldest
weather and nobody is spared. Many related
festivities take place around the time of
Carnaval. Two weeks beforehand is **Jueves
de Compadres** followed by **Jueves de
Comadres**. Shrove Tuesday is celebrated as
Martes de Challa, when house owners make
offerings to Pachamama and give drinks
to passers-by. **Carnaval Campesino** usually
begins in small towns on Ash Wednesday,
when regular Carnaval ends, and lasts for
5 days, until **Domingo de Tentación**. Palm
Sun (**Domingo de Ramos**) sees parades to
the church throughout Bolivia; the devout
carry woven palm fronds, then hang them

outside their houses. **Semana Santa** in the
eastern Chiquitania is very interesting, with
ancient processions, dances, and games not
found outside the region. **Corpus Christi**
is also a colourful festival. **3 May**: Fiesta
de la Invención de la Santa Cruz, various
parts. **2 Jun**: Santísima Trinidad in Beni
Department. **24 Jun**: San Juan, all Bolivia.
29 Jun: San Pedro y San Pablo, at Tiquina,
Tihuanaco and throughout Chiquitania.
25 Jul: Fiesta de Santiago (St James),
Altiplano and lake region. **14-16 Aug**:
Virgen de Urkupiña, Cochabamba. Is a
3-day Catholic festivity mixed with quechua
rituals and parades with folkloric dances.
16 Aug: San Roque, patron saint of dogs; the
animals are adorned with ribbons and other
decorations. **1** and **2 Nov**: All Saints and
All Souls, any local cemetery. **18 Nov**: Beni's
Departmental anniversary, especially in
Trinidad. Cities may be very quiet on national
holidays, but celebrations will be going on in
the villages. Hotels are often full at the most
popular places, for instance Copacabana on
Good Fri; worth booking in advance.
Public holidays Some dates may be
moved to the nearest weekend. 1 Jan,
New Year's Day; 22 Jan, Día del Estado
Plurinacional; Carnival Week, Mon, Shrove
Tuesday, Ash Wednesday; Holy Week: Thu,
Fri and Sat; 1 May, Labour Day; Corpus Christi
(movable May-Jun); 16 Jul, La Paz Municipal
Holiday; 5-7 Aug, Independence; 24 Sep,
Santa Cruz Municipal Holiday; 2 Nov, Day
of the Dead; Christmas Day.

Money → *US$1 = Bs6.86. 1 euro = Bs8.70 (May 2012)*

The currency is the boliviano (Bs), divided
into 100 centavos. There are notes for 200,
100, 50, 20 and 10 bolivianos, and 5, 2 and 1
boliviano coins, as well as 50, 20 and (rare)
10 centavos. Bolivianos are often referred to
as pesos; expensive items, including hotel
rooms, may be quoted in dollars.

Many *casas de cambio* and street changers (but among banks only **Banco Nacional de Bolivia**, BNB, www.bnb.com.bo) accept cash euros as well as dollars. Large bills may be hard to use in small villages, always carry some 20s and 10s. ATMs (**Enlace** network T800-103060) are common in all departmental capitals and some other cities but not in all small towns, including several important tourist destinations. Samaipata, Sorata and Rurrenabaque, among others, have no ATM. **Banco Unión**, has most ATMs in small towns, see www.bancounion.com.bo for locations. ATMs are not always reliable and, in addition to plastic, **you must always carry some cash**. Most ATMs dispense both Bs and US$. Debit cards and Amex are generally less reliable than Visa/MC credit cards at ATMs. Note that Bolivian ATMs dispense cash first and only a few moments later return your card. Many tourists forget to take their card. In small towns without banks or ATMs, look for **Prodem**, which changes US$ cash at fair rates, and gives cash advances at tellers on Visa/MC for about 5% commission. (Prodem ATMs do not accept international cards.) **Banco Fie** is also found throughout the country, changes US$ cash at all branches and gives cash advances at some locations. ATM scams are worst in La Paz, but may occur elsewhere. For lost Visa cards T800-100188, MasterCard T800-100172.

Travellers' cheques (TCs) are of limited use in Bolivia. Most tourist establishments will not accept payment with TCs, or they may impose a surcharge of up to 20%. **Banco Ganadero**, www.bg.com.bo, branches in most larger cities, will exchange US$ TCs to US$ cash or Bolivianos, 2% commission; likewise **Banco Bisa**, www.bisa.com, US$6 fee plus 1% commission (maximum 5 TCs); also Casa de cambio **Sudamer**, Camacho y Colón, La Paz, about 1.5% commission for Bs, 2% for US$ cash.

Cost of travelling Bolivia is cheaper to visit than most neighbouring countries. Budget travellers can get by on US$15-20 per person per day for two travelling together. A basic hotel in small towns costs as little as US$5 per person, breakfast US$1, and a simple set lunch (*almuerzo*) around US$2-3. For around US$35, though, you can find much better accommodation, more comfortable transport and a wider choice in food. Prices are higher in the city of La Paz; in the east, especially Santa Cruz and Tarija; and in Pando and the upper reaches of the Beni. The average cost of using the internet is US$0.50 per hr.

Opening hours
Business hours Shops: Mon-Fri 0830-1230, 1430-1830 and Sat 0900-1200. Opening and closing in the afternoon are later in lowland provinces. Banks and offices normally open Mon-Fri 0900-1600, Sat 0900-1300, but may close for lunch.

Safety
Violent crime is less common in Bolivia than some other parts of South America. Tricks and scams abound however. Fake police, narcotics police and immigration officers – usually plain-clothed but carrying forged ID – have been known to take people to their 'office' and ask to see documents and money; they then rob them. Legitimate police do not ask people for documents in the street unless they are involved in an accident, fight, etc. If approached, walk away and seek assistance from as many bystanders as possible. Never get in a vehicle with the 'officer' nor follow them to their 'office'. Many of the robberies are very slick, involving taxis and various accomplices. Take only radio taxis, identified by their dome lights and phone numbers. Always lock the doors, sit in the back and never allow other passengers to share your cab. If someone else gets in, get out at once. Also if smeared or spat-on, walk away, don't let the good Samaritan clean you up, they will clean you out instead.

The largest cities call for the greatest precautions. The countryside and small towns are generally safe. Note however that civil disturbance, although less frequent in recent years, remains part of Bolivian life. It can take the form of strikes, demonstrations in major cities and roadblocks (*bloqueos*), some lasting a few hrs, others weeks. Try to be flexible in your plans if you encounter disruptions and make the most of nearby attractions if transport is not running. You can often find transport to the site of a roadblock, walk across and get onward transport on the other side. Check with locals to find out how tense the situation is.

Road safety

Precarious roads, poorly maintained vehicles and frequently reckless drivers combine to cause many serious, at times fatal, accidents. Choose your transport judiciously and don't hesitate to pay a little more to travel with a better company. Look over the vehicle before you get on; if it doesn't feel right, look for another. If a driver is drunk or reckless, demand that he stop at the nearest village and let you off. Also note that smaller buses, although less comfortable, are often safer on narrow mountain roads.

Tax

Airport tax International departure tax of US$24 is payable in dollars or bolivianos, cash only. Airport tax for domestic flights, US$2. **IVA/VAT** 13%.

Telephone → *Country code +591.*

Equal tones with long pauses: ringing. Equal tones with equal pauses: engaged. IDD prefix: 00. Calls from public *cabinas* are expensive.

Time

GMT-4 all year.

Tipping

Up to 10% in restaurants is very generous, Bolivians seldom leave more than a few coins. Tipping is not customary for most services (eg taxi driver) though it is a reward when service has been very good.

Guides expect a tip as does someone who has looked after a car or carried bags.

Tourist information and tour operators

InfoTur offices are found in most departmental capitals (addresses given under each city), at international arrivals in El Alto airport (La Paz) and Viru Viru (Santa Cruz). In La Paz at Mariscal Santa Cruz y Colombia, T265 1778, www.turismolapaz.travel. **HighLives**, 48 Fernthorpe Rd, London, SW16 6DR, T020-8696 9097, www.highlives. co.uk. Fully organized, luxury, tailor-made tours in Latin America.

Useful websites

www.bolivia.com (Spanish) News, tourism, entertainment and information on regions.
www.boliviaweb.com
English-language portal.
www.bolivia-online.net (Spanish, English and German) Travel information about La Paz, Cochabamba, Santa Cruz and Sucre.
http://ande-mesili.com (multilingual) The site of climbing guide and author Alain Mesili, with lots of interesting links.
www.presidencia.gob.bo
Presidential website.
http://lanic.utexas.edu/la/sa/ bolivia Excellent database on various topics indigenous to Bolivia, maintained by the University of Texas, USA.
www.noticiasbolivianas.com All the Bolivian daily news in one place.
www.chiquitania.com Detailed information in English about all aspects of Chiquitania.

Visas and immigration

A passport only, valid for 6 months beyond date of visit, is needed for citizens of almost all Western European countries, Israel, Japan, Canada, South American countries, Australia and New Zealand. Nationals of all other countries require a visa. US citizens may obtain a visa either in advance at a

Bolivian consulate, or directly on entry to the country at airports and land borders. Requirements include a fee of US$135 cash (subject to change), proof of sufficient funds (eg showing a credit card) and a yellow fever vaccination certificate. Only the fee is universally enforced. Some nationalities must gain authorization from the Bolivian Ministry of Foreign Affairs, which can take 6 weeks. Other countries that require a visa do not need authorisation (visas in this case take 1-2 working days). It is best to check current requirements before leaving home. Tourists are usually granted 90 days stay on entry at airports, less at land borders. You can apply for a free extension (*ampliación*) at immigration offices in all departmental capitals, up to a maximum stay of 90 days per calendar year (180 days for nationals of Andean nations). If you overstay, the current fine is US$3 per day. Be sure to keep the green paper with entry stamp inside your passport, you will be asked for it when you leave.

Weights and measures

Metric, but some old Spanish measures are used for produce in markets.

Wildlife, conservation and sustainable development

www.armonia-bo.org The Asociación Civil Armonía promotes conservation of birds and their habitat in Bolivia.
www.redesma.org Site of the Red de Desarrollo Sostenible y Medio Ambiente (in Spanish and English) has lots of links to sustainable development topics and organizations.
www.wcs.org/international/latinamerica/amazon_andes World Conservation Society site with information on the Gran Chaco and on Northwestern Bolivia.
See also National Parks, page 6.

Contents

Bolivia

Footprint features

La Paz and around

The minute you arrive in La Paz, the highest seat of government in the world, you realize this is no ordinary place. El Alto airport is at a staggering 4000 m above sea level. The sight of the city, lying 400 m below, at the bottom of a steep canyon and ringed by snow-peaked mountains, takes your breath away – literally. For at this altitude breathing can be a problem.

The Spaniards chose this odd place for a city on 20 October 1548, to avoid the chill winds of the plateau, and because they had found gold in the Río Choqueyapu, which runs through the canyon. The centre of the city, Plaza Murillo, is at 3636 m, about 400 m below the level of the Altiplano and the sprawling city of El Alto, perched dramatically on the rim of the canyon.

Arriving in La Paz → *Phone code: 02. Population: La Paz, 855,000, El Alto, 882,000.*

Getting there La Paz has the highest commercial **airport** in the world, at El Alto, high above the city at 4058 m; T281 0240. A taxi from the airport to the centre takes about 30 minutes, US$7, to the Zona Sur US$9. There are three main **bus terminals**; the bus station at Plaza Antofagasta, the cemetery district for Sorata, Copacabana and Tiwanaku, and Villa Fátima for the Yungas, including Coroico, and northern jungle. ►► *See also Transport, page 36.*

Getting around There are two types of city bus: *micros* (small, old buses), which charge US$0.20 a journey; and the faster, more plentiful minibuses (small vans), US$0.15-0.30 depending on the journey. *Trufis* are fixed-route collective taxis, with a sign with their route on the windscreen, US$0.40 pp in the centre, US$0.50 outside. Taxis are often, but not always, white. There are three types: regular honest taxis which may take several passengers at once (US$0.85-1.10 for short trips), fake taxis which have been involved in robberies (see below), and radio taxis which take only one group of passengers at a time. Since it is impossible to distinguish between the first two, it is best to pay a bit more for a radio taxi which has a dome light and number and can be ordered by phone; note the number when getting in. Radio taxis charge US$1.10-1.40 in the centre, more to the suburbs.

Orientation The city's main street runs from **Plaza San Francisco** as Avenida Mariscal Santa Cruz, then changes to Avenida 16 de Julio (more commonly known as El Prado) and ends at **Plaza del Estudiante**. The business quarter, government offices, central university (UMSA) and many of the main hotels and restaurants are in this area. Banks and exchange houses are clustered on Calle Camacho, between Loayza and Colón, not far from **Plaza Murillo**, the traditional heart of the city. From the Plaza del Estudiante, Avenida Villazón splits into Avenida Arce, which runs southeast towards the wealthier residential districts of **Zona Sur**, in the valley, 15 minutes away; and Avenida 6 de Agosto which runs through **Sopocachi**, an area full of restaurants, bars and clubs. Zona Sur has shopping centres, supermarkets with imported items and some of the best restaurants and bars in La Paz (see page 30). It begins after the bridge at La Florida beside the attractive Plaza Humboldt. The main road, Avenida Ballivián, begins at Calle 8 and continues up the hill to San Miguel on Calle 21 (about a 20-minute walk).

Sprawled around the rim of the canyon is **El Alto**, Bolivia's second-largest city (after Santa Cruz, La Paz is a close third). Its population of almost one million is mostly indigenous migrants from the countryside and its political influence has grown rapidly. El Alto is connected to La Paz by motorway (toll US$0.25) and by a road to Obrajes and the Zona Sur. Minibuses from Plaza Eguino leave regularly for Plaza 16 de Julio, El Alto, more leave from Plaza Pérez Velasco for La Ceja, the edge of El Alto. Intercity buses to and from La Paz always stop at El Alto in an area called *terminal*, off Avenida 6 de Marzo, where transport companies have small offices. If not staying in La Paz, you can change buses here and save a couple of hours. There is accommodation nearby, but the area is not safe, especially at night.

Best time to visit La Paz Because of the altitude, nights are cold the year round. In the day, the sun is strong, but the moment you go into the shade or enter a building, the temperature falls. From December-March, the summer, it rains most afternoons, making it feel colder than it actually is. Temperatures are even lower in winter, June-August, when the sky is always clear. The two most important festivals, when the city gets particularly busy, are **Alasitas** (last week of January and first week of February) and **Festividad del Señor del Gran Poder** (end May/early June). See Festivals, page 32.

Tourist offices The **Gobierno Municipal de La Paz** ① *www.turismolapaz.travel* has information centres at: Plaza del Estudiante ① *at the lower end of El Prado between 16 de Julio and México, T237 1044, Mon-Fri 0830-1200, 1430-1900, Sat-Sun 0900-1300*, very helpful, English and French spoken. El Prado InfoTur ① *Mariscal Santa Cruz y Colombia, T265 1778, Mon-Fri 0830-1900, Sat-Sun 0930-1300*. Bus terminal ① *T228 5858, Mon-Fri 0600-2200, Sat 0800-1500, Sun 1400-2200, holidays 0800-1200, 1600-2000*. Angelo Colonial ① *C Linares y Sagárnaga (at the restaurant), T215 9632*, and Plaza Pérez Velasco ① *opposite San Francisco, under the pedestrian walkway*. Tourist office for **El Alto**: **Dirección de Promoción Turística** ① *C 5 y Av 6 de Marzo, Edif Vela, p 5, also at arrivals in airport, T282 9281, Mon-Fri 0800-1200, 1400-1800*; the municipality is trying to attract visitors.

Health Travellers arriving in La Paz, especially when flying directly from sea level, may experience mild altitude sickness. If your symptoms are severe, consult a physician. See Health in Essentials.

Safety The worst areas for crime are around Plaza Murillo and the Cemetery neighbourhood where local buses serve Copacabana and Tiwanaku. Tourist police (T222 5016) now patrol these bus stops during the daytime, making them safer than in the past, but caution is still advised. Other areas, particularly Sopocachi, are generally safer. **Warning for ATM users**: scams to get card numbers and PINs have flourished, especially in La Paz. The tourist police post warnings in hotels. ►► *See also Safety, page 12.*

1 La Paz

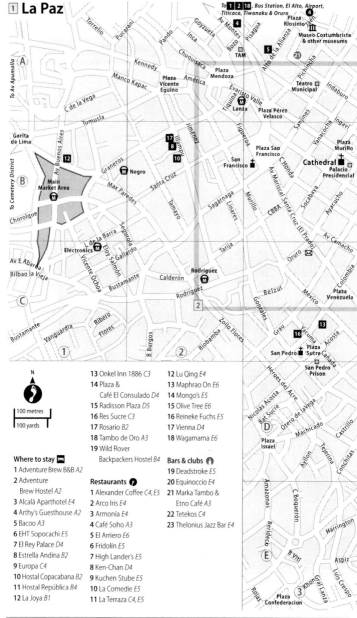

Where to stay 🛏
1 Adventure Brew B&B *A2*
2 Adventure Brew Hostel *A2*
3 Alcalá Aparthotel *E4*
4 Arthy's Guesthouse *A2*
5 Bacoo *A3*
6 EHT Sopocachi *E5*
7 El Rey Palace *D4*
8 Estrella Andina *B2*
9 Europa *C4*
10 Hostal Copacabana *B2*
11 Hostal República *B4*
12 La Joya *B1*
13 Onkel Inn 1886 *C3*
14 Plaza & Café El Consulado *D4*
15 Radisson Plaza *D5*
16 Res Sucre *C3*
17 Rosario *B2*
18 Tambo de Oro *A3*
19 Wild Rover Backpackers Hostel *B4*

Restaurants 🍴
1 Alexander Coffee *C4, E5*
2 Arco Iris *E4*
3 Armonía *E4*
4 Café Soho *A3*
5 El Arriero *E6*
6 Fridolín *E5*
7 High Lander's *E5*
8 Ken-Chan *D4*
9 Kuchen Stube *E5*
10 La Comedie *E5*
11 La Terraza *C4, E5*
12 Lu Qing *E4*
13 Maphrao On *E6*
14 Mongo's *E5*
15 Olive Tree *E6*
16 Reineke Fuchs *E5*
17 Vienna *D4*
18 Wagamama *E6*

Bars & clubs 🍸
19 Deadstroke *E5*
20 Equinoccio *E4*
21 Marka Tambo & Etno Café *A3*
22 Tetekos *C4*
23 Thelonius Jazz Bar *E4*

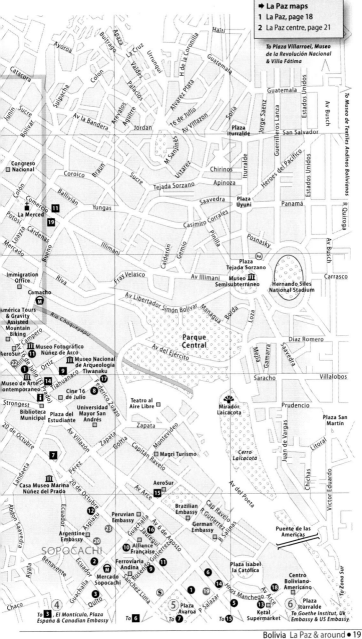

➡ La Paz maps
1 La Paz, page 18
2 La Paz centre, page 21

To Plaza Villarroel, Museo
de la Revolución Nacional
& Villa Fátima

Haití

Ayoroa
Catacora

Buitrago
Apaza
La Cruz de la Coronilla
Urrungui
Guatemala

Colón
Valdés
Palacios
Alvarez Plata

Junín
Sulpacha
Arévalos
Aguirre
Té de Julio
Jordán
Soria
Av Villazón
Guatemala
Estados Unidos
Av Busch

Sucre
Bolívar
Av la Bandera
Plaza
Iturralde
Jorge Sáenz
San Salvador

To Museo de Textiles Andinos Bolivianos

Congreso
Nacional
Coroico
Braun
Sucre
M Sanjinés
Ustárez
Chirinos
Iturralde
Guerrilleros Lanza
Estados Unidos

Colón
Ballivián
Yungas
Tejada Sorzano
Apinoza
Saavedra
Plaza
Uyuni
Panamá
Héroes del Pacífico

Comercio
La Merced
Pojosi
Loaiza
Cárdenas
Illimani
Casimiro Corrales
Posnasky
Av Busch
R Quiroga

Mercado
Bueno
Riva
Calderón
Gemio
Pinilla
Plaza
Tejada Sorzano

Immigration
Office
Camacho
Río Choqueyapu
Fray Velasco
Av Illimani
Museo
Semisubterráneo
Av Libertador Simón Bolívar
Managua
Borda
Hernando Siles
National Stadium
Carrasco

M
América Tours
& Gravity
Assisted
Mountain
Biking
Loza
Díaz Romero
Villalobos

AeroSur
Campero
Ortiz
Museo Fotográfico
Núñez de Arco
Museo Nacional
de Arqueología
Tiwanaku
Parque
Central
Av del Ejército
Melia
Gamarra
Saavedra

Museo de Arte
contemporáneo
Trihuanaco
Federico Zuazo
Saracho
Villalobos

Strongest
Biblioteca
Municipal
Cine 16
de Julio
Plaza del
Estudiante
Universidad
Mayor San
Andrés
Zapata
Teatro al
Aire Libre
Mirador
Laicacota
Prudencio
Plaza San
Martín

20 de Octubre
Av Villazón
Zapata
Golfia
Capitán Ravelo
Montevideo
Magri Turismo
Cerro
Laicacota
Juan de Vargas
Litoral

Casa Museo Marina
Núñez del Prado
Landaeta
Pérez
20 de Octubre
AeroSur
Av del Poeta
Victor Eduardo

Ecuador
Aspiazu
Peruvian
Embassy
Guachalla
Jáuregui
Av 6 de Agosto
Brazilian
Embassy
Cap Ravelo
R Gutiérrez
Salinas
German
Embassy
Puente de las
Américas

SOPOCACHI
Argentine
Embassy
Ecuador
Alliance
Française
Ferroviaria
Andina
Rosendo Gutiérrez

Abdón Saavedra
Benavente
Guachalla
Quito
Sánchez Lima
Plaza Isabel
la Católica
Centro
Boliviano-
Americano

Ayala
Chaco
④
To ③, El Montículo, Plaza
España & Canadian Embassy
Mercado
Sopocachi
⑤ Plaza
Avaroa
P Salazar
Hnos Manchego
Ketal
Supermarket
⑥ Plaza
Iturralde
To Goethe Institut, Uk
Embassy & US Embassy

Places in La Paz

There are few colonial buildings left in La Paz; probably the best examples are in **Calle Jaén** (see below). Late 19th-, early 20th-century architecture, often displaying European influence, can be found in the streets around Plaza Murillo, but much of La Paz is modern. The **Plaza del Estudiante** (Plaza Franz Tamayo), or a bit above it, marks a contrast between old and new styles, between the commercial and the more elegant. The **Prado** itself is lined with high-rise blocks dating from the 1960s and 1970s.

Around Plaza Murillo

Plaza Murillo, three blocks north of the Prado, is the traditional centre. Facing its formal gardens are the **Cathedral**, the **Palacio Presidencial** in Italian renaissance style, known as the **Palacio Quemado** (burnt palace) twice gutted by fire in its stormy 130-year history, and, on the east side, the **Congreso Nacional**. In front of the Palacio Quemado is a statue of former President Gualberto Villarroel who was dragged into the plaza by a mob and hanged in 1946. Across from the Cathedral on Calle Socabaya is the **Palacio de los Condes de Arana** (built 1775), with beautiful exterior and patio. It houses the **Museo Nacional de Arte** ① *T240 8542, www.mna.org.bo, Tue-Fri 0900-1230, 1500-1900, Sat 1000-1700, Sun 0900-1330, US$1.50.* It has a fine collection of colonial paintings including many works by Melchor Pérez Holguín, considered one of the masters of Andean colonial art, and which also exhibits the works of contemporary local artists. Calle Comercio, running east-west across the Plaza, has most of the stores and shops. West of Plaza Murillo, at Ingavi 916, in the palace of the Marqueses de Villaverde is the **Museo Nacional de Etnografía y Folklore** ① *T240 8640, Mon-Fri 0900-1230, 1500-1900, Sat 0900-1630, Sun 0900-1430, free.* Various sections show the cultural richness of Bolivia by region through textiles and other items. It has a *videoteca*.

Northwest of Plaza Murillo is **Calle Jaén**, a picturesque colonial street with a restaurant/ peña, a café, craft shops, good views and four museums (known as Museos Municipales) housed in colonial buildings ① *Tue-Fri 0930-1230, 1500-1900, Sat 1000-1700, Sun 0900-1330, US$0.15 each.* **Museo Costumbrista** ① on Plaza Riosinio, at the top of Jaén, T228 0758, US$0.60, has miniature displays depicting incidents in the history of La Paz and well-known Paceños, as well as miniature replicas of reed rafts used by the Norwegian Thor Heyerdahl, and the Spaniard Kitin Muñoz, to prove their theories of ancient migrations. **Museo del Litoral Boliviano** (T228 0758), has artefacts of the War of the Pacific, and interesting selection of old maps. **Museo de Metales Preciosos** (T228 0329), is well set out with Inca gold artefacts in basement vaults, also ceramics and archaeological exhibits, and **Museo Casa Murillo** (T228 0553), the erstwhile home of Pedro Domingo Murillo, one of the martyrs of the La Paz independence movement of 16 July 1809, has a good collection of paintings, furniture and national costumes. In addition to the Museos Municipales is the **Museo de Instrumentos Musicales** ① *Jaén 711 e Indaburo, T240 8177, daily 0930-1300, 1430-1830, US$0.75,* in a refurbished colonial house. **Museo Tambo Quirquincho** ① *C Evaristo Valle, south of Jaén, Plaza Alonso de Mendoza, T239 0969, Tue-Fri, 0930-1230, 1500-1900, Sat-Sun, 0900-1300, US$0.15,* displays modern painting and sculpture, carnival masks, silver, early 20th century photography and city plans, and is recommended.

Plaza San Francisco up to the cemetery district

At the upper end of Avenida Mcal Santa Cruz is the **Plaza San Francisco** with the **church and monastery of San Francisco** ① *open for Mass at 0700, 0900, 1100 and 1900, Mon-Sat, and also at 0800, 1000 and 1200 on Sun.* Dating from 1549, this is one of the finest examples of colonial religious architecture in South America and well worth seeing. The **Centro Cultural Museo San Francisco** ⓘ *Plaza San Francisco 503, T231 8472, Mon-Sat 0900-1800, US$2.80, allow 1½-2 hrs, free guides available but tip appreciated, some speak English and French*, offers access to various areas of the church and convent including the

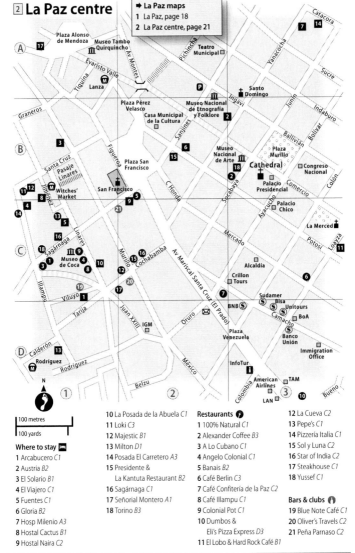

2 La Paz centre

➜ **La Paz maps**
1 La Paz, page 18
2 La Paz centre, page 21

100 metres
100 yards

Where to stay 🛏
1 Arcabucero C1
2 Austria B2
3 El Solario B1
4 El Viajero C1
5 Fuentes C1
6 Gloria B2
7 Hosp Milenio A3
8 Hostal Cactus B1
9 Hostal Naira C2
10 La Posada de la Abuela C1
11 Loki C3
12 Majestic B1
13 Milton D1
14 Posada El Carretero A3
15 Presidente &
   La Kantuta Restaurant B2
16 Sagárnaga C1
17 Señorial Montero A1
18 Torino B3

Restaurants 🍴
1 100% Natural C1
2 Alexander Coffee B3
3 A Lo Cubano C1
4 Angelo Colonial C1
5 Banais B2
6 Café Berlin C3
7 Café Confitería de la Paz C2
8 Café Illampu C1
9 Colonial Pot C1
10 Dumbos &
   Eli's Pizza Express D3
11 El Lobo & Hard Rock Café B1
12 La Cueva C2
13 Pepe's C1
14 Pizzería Italia C1
15 Sol y Luna C2
16 Star of India C2
17 Steakhouse C1
18 Yussef C1

Bars & clubs 🍸
19 Blue Note Café C1
20 Oliver's Travels C2
21 Peña Parnaso C2

Tiny treats

One of the most intriguing items for sale in Andean markets is *Ekeko*, the god of good fortune and plenty and one of the most endearing of the Aymara folk legends. He is a cheery, avuncular little chap, with a happy face, a pot belly and short legs. His image, usually in plaster of Paris, is laden with various household items, as well as sweets, confetti and streamers, food, and with a cigarette dangling cheekily from his lower lip. Believers say that these statues only bring luck if they are received as gifts. The *Ekeko* occupies a central role in the festival of Alacitas, the Feast of Plenty, which takes place in La Paz at the end of January. Everything under the sun can be bought in miniature: houses, trucks, buses, suitcases, university diplomas; you name it, you'll find it here. The idea is to have your mini-purchase blessed by a *Yatiri*, an Aymara priest, and the real thing will be yours within the year.

choir, crypt (open 1400-1730), roof, various chapels and gardens. Fine art includes religious paintings from the 17th, 18th and 19th centuries, plus visiting exhibits and a hall devoted to the works of Tito Yupanqui, the indigenous sculptor of the Virgen de Copacabana. There is a pricey but good café at entrance. Behind the San Francisco church a network of narrow cobbled streets rise steeply up the canyon walls. Much of this area is a street market. Handicraft shops, travel agencies, hotels and restaurants line the lower part of **Calle Sagárnaga** (here you find the highest concentration of tourists and pick-pockets). The **Mercado de Brujas**, 'witchcraft market', on Calles Melchor Jiménez and Linares, which cross Santa Cruz above San Francisco, sells charms, herbs and more gruesome items like llama foetuses. The excellent **Museo de la Coca** ① *Linares 914, T231 1998, daily 1000-1900, US$1.50, www.cocamuseum.com, shop with coca products for sale*, is devoted to the coca plant, its history, cultural significance, medical values and political implications, with explanations in five languages. Nearby is the recommended **Museo de Arte Texil Andino Boliviano** ① *Linares 906, daily 1000-1900, Sun 1000-1700, US$1.20*, a small collection of old traditional weavings (not to be confused with the larger **Museo de Textiles Andinos Bolivianos** in Miraflores, see below).

Further up, from Illampu to Rodríguez and in neighbouring streets, is the produce-based **Rodríguez market** ① *daily, but best on Sun morning*. Turning right on Max Paredes, heading north, is **Avenida Buenos Aires**, where small workshops turn out the costumes and masks for the Gran Poder festival, and with great views of Illimani, especially at sunset. Continuing west along Max Paredes towards the **cemetery district**, the streets are crammed with stalls selling every imaginable item. Transport converges on the Cemetery district (for more information see page 37). See also Safety, page 17.

The Prado, Sopocachi, Miraflores and Zona Sur

Museo de Arte Contemporáneo Plaza ① *Av 16 de Julio 1698, T233 5905, daily 0900-2100, US$2*. In a 19th-century house which has been declared a national monument, there is a selection of contemporary art from national and international artists. Just off the Prado (down the flight of stairs by the Hotel Plaza) is **Museo Nacional de Arqueología** or **Tiahuanaco** (Tiwanaku) ① *Tiwanacu 93 entre Bravo y F Zuazo, T231 1621, www.bolivian. com/arqueologia, closed for renovation in 2012*. It contains good collections of the arts and crafts of ancient Tiwanaku and items from the eastern jungles. It also has an exhibition of gold statuettes and objects found in Lake Titicaca. On Avenida Libertador Simón Bolívar, from where there are views of Mt Illimani, is the modern **Mercado Camacho** produce market. In Sopocachi district, by Plaza España, is **El Montículo**, a park with great views of the city and Illimani. In the residential district of Miraflores, east of the centre, on Plaza Tejada Sorzano, outside the Hernán Siles national football stadium is the **Museo Semisubterráneo**, a sunken garden full of replicas of statues and artefacts from Tiwanaku, but difficult to get to because of the traffic. Further north, at Plaza Benito Juárez, is **Museo de Textiles Andinos Bolivianos** ① *Guatemala y Cuba, T224 3601, www.museodetextiles. org, Mon-Sat 0930-1200, 1500-1800, Sun 1000-1230, US$1.25*, with displays of textiles from around the country. At the north end of Av Busch are Plaza Villarroel and **Museo del la Revolución Nacional** ① *Tue-Fri 0930-1200, 1500-1800, Sat-Sun 1000-1200, US$0.15*, a memorial of the 1952 revolution and a mausoleum with tombs of former presidents.

Around La Paz

South of La Paz
To the south of the city are dry hills of many colours, topped by the **Muela del Diablo**, a striking outcrop. Here is the **Valle de la Luna**, or 'Valley of the Moon' (US$2.10), with impressive eroded hills; the climate in this valley is always much warmer than in the city. For transport details see page 38. About 3 km from the bridge at Calacoto the road forks, get out of the minibus at the turning and walk a few minutes east to the Valle entrance, or get out at the football field which is by the entrance. Take good shoes and water, but do not go alone, armed robbery has occurred. Just past the Valle de la Luna is **Mallasa** where there are several small roadside restaurants and cafés and the **Hotel Oberland** (see page 28). The **zoo** ① *on the road to Río Abajo, entrance just past Mallasa, daily 0900-1700, US$0.50 adults, US$0.25 children*, in a beautiful, wide open park-like setting, conditions for the animals and birds are relatively good.

Tiwanaku
① *The site is open 0900-1700, US$11, including entry to museums. Allow 4 hrs to see the ruins and village. See also Transport, page 38.*
This remarkable archaeological site, 72 km west of La Paz, near the southern end of Lake Titicaca, takes its name from one of the most important pre-Columbian civilizations in South America. It is the most popular excursion from La Paz, with facilities being improved as a result. Many archaeologists believe that Tiwanaku existed as early as 1600 BC, while the complex visible today probably dates from the eight to the 10th centuries AD. The site may have been a ceremonial complex at the centre of an empire which covered almost half Bolivia, southern Peru, northern Chile and northwest Argentina. It was also a hub of trans-Andean trade. The demise of the Tiwanaku civilization, according to studies by Alan Kolata of the University of Illinois, could have been precipitated by the flooding of the area's extensive system of raised fields (*Sukakollu*), which were capable of sustaining a population of 20,000. The Pumapunku section, 1 km south of the main complex may have been a port, as the waters of the lake used to be much higher than they are today. The raised field system is once again being used in parts of the Titicaca area.

One of the main structures is the **Kalasasaya**, meaning 'standing stones', referring to the statues found in that part: two of them, the Ponce monolith (centre of inner patio) and the Fraile monolith (southwest corner), have been re-erected. In the northwest corner is the Puerta del Sol, originally at Pumapunku. Its carvings, interrupted by being out of context, are thought to be either a depiction of the creator god, or a calendar. The motifs are exactly the same as those around the Ponce monolith. The **Templo Semisubterráneo** is a sunken temple whose walls are lined with faces, all different, according to some theories depicting states of health, the temple being a house of healing; another theory is that the faces display all the ethnicities of the world. The **Akapana**, originally a pyramid (said to have been the second largest in the world, covering over 28,000 sq m), still has some ruins on it. Plastering of the Akapana's walls was halted in 2009 when UNESCO, among others, declared it inappropriate. At **Pumapunku**, some of whose blocks weigh between 100 and 150 tonnes, a natural disaster may have put a sudden end to the construction before it was finished. There is a small **Museo Lítico** at the ticket office, with several large stone pieces and, at the site, the **Museo Regional Arqueológico**, containing a well-illustrated explanation of the raised field system of agriculture. Many other artefacts are in the **Museo Nacional de Arqueología** in La Paz.

Written guide material is difficult to come by; hiring a guide costs US$8 for two hours, some speak English but don't be bullied into taking one if you prefer to go on your own. Locals sell copies of Tiwanaku figures; cheaper here than in La Paz.

Nearby **Tiwanaku village**, with several basic hotels and eateries, still has remnants from the time of independence and the 16th-century church used pre-Columbian masonry. In fact, Tiwanaku for a long while was the 'quarry' for the altiplano. For the **Willkakuti**, winter solstice festival on 21 June, there is an all-night vigil and colourful dances. There is also a colourful local festival on the Sunday after Carnival.

By road to Chile

The main route to Chile is via Tambo Quemado (see page 59), but an alternative route, on which there are no trucks, is to go by good road direct from La Paz via Viacha to **Santiago de Machaco** (130 km, petrol); then 120 km on a very bad road to the border at **Charaña** (basic **Alojamiento Aranda**; immigration behind railway station). From Visviri, on the Chilean side of the frontier (no services), a regular road runs to Putre.

Trekking and climbing near La Paz

Four so-called 'Inca Trails' link the Altiplano with the Yungas, taking you from the high Andes to the sub-tropics, with dramatic changes in weather, temperature and vegetation. Each has excellent sections of stonework and they vary in difficulty from relatively straightforward to quite hard-going. In the rainy season going can be particularly tough. For details of how to reach the starting point of each trail, see Transport sections on page 39.

Takesi Trail Start at **Ventilla** (see below), walk up the valley for about three hours passing the village of Choquekhota until the track crosses the river and to the right of the road, there is a falling-down brick wall with a map painted on it. The Takesi and Alto Takesi trails start here, following the path to the right of the wall. The road continues to Mina San Francisco. In the first hour's climb from the wall is excellent stone paving which is Inca or pre-Inca, depending on who you believe, either side of the pass at 4630 m. There are camping possibilities at *Estancia Takesi* and in the village of Kakapi you can sleep at the simple **Kakapi Tourist Lodge**, 10 beds with good mattresses, solar shower and toilet. It is run by the local community and sponsored by Fundación Pueblo. It is also possible to camp. You also have to pass the unpleasant mining settlement of Chojlla, between which and Yanakachi is a gate where it is necessary to register and often pay a small 'fee'. Yanakachi has a number of good places to stay, several good hikes and an orphanage you can help at. The Fundación Pueblo office on the plaza has information. Buy a minibus ticket on arrival in Yanakachi or walk 45 minutes down to the La Paz-Chulumani road for transport. The trek can be done in one long day, especially if you organize a jeep to the start of the trail, but is more relaxing in two or three. If you take it slowly, though, you'll have to carry camping kit. Hire mules in Choquekhota for US$8 per day plus up to US$8 for the muleteer. A 2-3 day alternative is from Mina San Francisco to El Castillo and the village of Chaco on the La Paz-Chulumani road. This trek is called La Reconquistada and has the distinction of including a 200 m disused mining tunnel.

Choro Trail (La Cumbre to Coroico) Immediately before the road drops down from La Cumbre to start the descent to Las Yungas, there is a good dirt road leading up to the *apacheta* (narrow pass) where the trail starts properly. Cloud and bad weather are normal at La Cumbre (4660 m): you have to sign in at the Guardaparque post on the way to the pass. The trail passes Samaña Pampa (small shop, sign in again, camping US$0.60), Chucura (pay US$1.20 fee, another shop, camping), Challapampa (camping possible, US$0.60, small shop), the Choro bridge and the Río Jacun-Manini (fill up with water at both river crossings). At Sandillani it is possible to stay at the lodge or camp in the carefully tended garden of a Japanese man, Tamiji Hanamura, who keeps a book with the names of every passing traveller. He likes to see postcards and pictures from other countries. There is good paving down to Villa Esmeralda, after which is Chairo (lodging and camping), then to Yolosa. It takes three days to trek from La Cumbre to Chairo, from where you can take a truck to Puente Yolosita, the turn-off for Cocoico on the new road. From Puente Yolosita trucks run uphill to Coroico when they fill, US$0.70, 15 minutes. The Choro Trail has a reputation for unfriendliness and occasional robbery, take care.

Yunga Cruz (Chuñavi to Chulumani) The best, but hardest of the four 'Inca' trails, it has seen little use in recent years and may be badly overgrown; enquire in advance. From Chuñavi (3710 m) follow the path left (east) and contour gently up. Camping possible after two hours. Continue along the path staying on left hand side of the ridge to reach Cerro Khala Ciudad (literally, Stone City Mountain, you'll see why). Good paving brings you round the hill to join a path coming from Quircoma (on your right); continue, heading north, to Cerro Cuchillatuca and then Cerro Yunga Cruz, where there is water and camping is possible. After this point water and camping are difficult and normally impossible until you get down to Sikilini. The last water and camping possibilities are all within the next hour, take advantage of them. Each person should have at least two litres of water in bottles. Colectivos run from Sikilini to Chulumani. Starting in Chuñavi the trek takes three days. An alternative route is from Chuñavi to Irupana.

Huayna Potosí Huayna Potosí (6088 m) is normally climbed in two days, with one night in a basic shelter at 5300 m or camped on a glacier at 5600 m. Acclimatization and experience on ice are essential, and the mountain is dangerous out of season. There are four shelters: a community-run shelter 10 minutes up from the pass, one by the lake, very cold; *Refugio Huayna Potosí* at 4780 m, with toilets and shower, run by the tour operator of the same name, and a basic shelter at 5300 owned by the same operator. Average cost is US$100 per person for two-day tour for three people (US$200 for one) including all equipment except sleeping bag. The starting point for the normal route is at Zongo. A three-day trek in the area is also offered. See Climbing, hiking and trekking, page 34, for tour operators.

La Paz and around listings

For hotel and restaurant price codes and other relevant information, see pages 9-10.

🛏 Where to stay

Around Plaza Murillo *p20,*
maps p18 and p21

$$$ Gloria, Potosí 909, T240 7070, www.hotelgloria.com.bo. Modern, central, includes buffet breakfast, 2 restaurants (1 is vegetarian), good food and service, cable TV, internet, run Gloria Tours (www.gloriatours.com.bo). Recommended.

$$$ Presidente, Potosí 920 y Sanjines, T240 6666, www.hotelpresidente-bo.com. The 'highest 5-star in the world'. Includes buffet breakfast, gym and sauna, pool, all open to non-residents, internet, Wi-Fi, a/c, excellent service, comfortable, heating, good food.

$$ Señorial Montero, Av América 120, esq Plaza Alonso de Mendoza 120, T245 7300. Includes breakfast, heating in rooms, cable TV, popular with tour groups; big, old-fashioned, comfortable hotel.

$$-$ Hostal República, Comercio 1455, T220 2742, www.hostalrepublica.com. Old house of former president, includes breakfast, more expensive in apartment, cheaper with shared bath, hot water, luggage stored, good café, quiet garden, Wi-Fi, book ahead and ask for room on upper floor.

$ Adventure Brew Bed & Breakfast, Av Montes 533, T246 1614, mostly private rooms with bath, cheaper in dorms for 8, includes pancake breakfast, Wi-Fi, use of kitchen, free beer from microbrewery every night, rooftop bar with great views and spa, nightly bbqs, good value, popular meeting place.

$ Adventure Brew Hostel, Av Montes 504, T291 5896, www.theadventurebrewhostel.com. More economical than B&B above, 8 to 12-bed dorms, with shared hot showers, includes pancake breakfast and a free beer every night, rooftop terrace with great views of the city and Illimani, basement bar, travel agency and bank, lively young crowd,

convenient to the bus station, associated with **Gravity Assisted Mountain Biking** (see What to do).

$ Arthy's Guesthouse, Montes 693, T228 1439, http://arthyshouse.tripod.com. Shared bath, warm water, kitchen facilities, safe, helpful, popular with bikers, English spoken, 2400 curfew.

$ Austria, Yanacocha 531, T240 8540. Very economical, shared bath, cheaper in shared room, basic, hot water but only 3 showers, safe deposit, laundry, TV lounge, use of kitchen, internet, luggage storage, no English spoken.

$ Bacoo, Calle Alto de la Alianza 693, T228 0679, infobacoo@gmail.com. Some rooms with private bath, cheaper in dorm, includes breakfast, Wi-Fi, jacuzzi, restaurant and bar, garden, ping pong and pool, arrange tours.

$ Hosp Milenio, Yanacocha 860, T228 1263, hospedajemilenio@hotmail.com. Economical, shared bath, electric shower, basic, family house, homely and welcoming, popular, helpful owner, quiet, kitchen, breakfast extra, security boxes, internet, great value.

$ Loki, Loayza 420, T211 9024, www.loki hostel.com. Old Hotel Vienna renovated as member of this chain of popular party hostels. Cheaper in 14-bed dorms (one dorm is girl-only), kitchen, includes breakfast, TV room, computer room and Wi-Fi, bar (serves dinner). Has tour operator.

$ Posada El Carretero, Catacora 1056, entre Yanacocha y Junín, T228 5271. Very economical single and double rooms (cheaper with shared bath), also dorms, hot showers, kitchen, helpful staff, good atmosphere and value.

$ Tambo de Oro, Armentia 262, T228 1565. Near bus station, cheaper with shared bath, hot showers, good value if a bit run down, safe for luggage.

$ Torino, Socabaya 457, T240 6003, www.hoteltorino.com.bo. Ask for better rooms in new section, older ones are run-down, cheaper without bath. Popular with backpackers, free book exchange, cultural centre, travel agency, good service. Restaurant next door for breakfast and good-value lunch (Mon-Fri 1200-1500).

$ Wild Rover Backpackers Hostel, Comercio 1476, T211 6903, www.wildrover hostel.com. Party hostel in renovated colonial-style house with courtyard and high-ceilings, dorms with 6-10 beds and doubles with shared bath, bar, TV room, book exchange, internet, serve dinner and breakfast, helpful staff speak English.

Plaza San Francisco up to the cemetery district *p20, maps p18 and p21*

$$$ Rosario, Illampu 704, T245 1658, www.hotelrosario.com. Includes good buffet breakfast, sauna, laundry, internet café (free for guests, great view), Wi-Fi, good restaurant, stores luggage, no smoking, very helpful staff. Highly recommended. **Turisbus** travel agency downstairs (see Tour operators, page 36), Cultural Interpretation Centre explains items for sale in nearby 'witches' market'.

$$ Estrella Andina, Illampu 716, T245 6421. Includes breakfast, cheaper in low season, all rooms have a safe and are decorated individually, English spoken, family run, comfortable, tidy, helpful, Wi-Fi, roof terrace, heaters, money exchange, very nice. Also owns **$ Cruz de los Andes**, Aroma 216, T245 1401, same style but shares premises with a car garage.

$$ Hostal Naira, Sagárnaga 161, T235 5645, www.hostalnaira.com. Hot water, comfortable but pricey, rooms around courtyard, some are dark, price includes good buffet breakfast in **Café Banais**, safety deposit boxes.

$$ La Posada de la Abuela, C Linares 947, T233 2285. Very pleasant inn, includes continental breakfast and Wi-Fi.

$ Arcabucero, C Viluyo 307 y Linares, T231 3473. Price rises in high season, pleasant new rooms in converted colonial house, excellent value but check the beds, breakfast extra.

$ El Solario, Murillo 776, T236 7963. Central, shared bath, luggage store, kitchen, internet, international phone calls, laundry and medical services, taxi and travel agency, good value, gets crowded.

$ El Viajero, Illampu 807, T245 1640. Reasonable hostel, decorated with plants, cheaper without bath and in dorm which has lockers.

$ Fuentes, Linares 888, T231 3966, www.hotelfuentesbolivia.com. Cheaper without bath, hot water, variety of rooms and prices, includes breakfast, nice colonial style, comfortable, TV, internet, sauna, good value, family run.

$ Hostal Cactus, Jiménez 818 y Santa Cruz, T245 1421. Very economical, shared electric showers, kitchen facilities, luggage store, poor beds and plumbing, don't leave valuables unattended, but peaceful, quiet, helpful, nice communal feel. **Coca Travels** agency downstairs, good.

$ Hostal Copacabana, Illampu 734, T245 1626, www.hostalcopacabana.com. Hot water, good showers, soft beds, includes breakfast, internet, fading but OK.

$ La Joya, Max Paredes 541, T245 3841, www.hotelajoya.com. Cheaper without bath, breakfast included, modern and comfy, lift, area unsafe at night but provides transfers.

$ Majestic, Santa Cruz 359, T245 1628. Simple rooms with bath, cable TV, breakfast included, restaurant, comfortable, laundry, safe.

$ Milton, Illampu 1126-1130, T236 8003, www.hotelmiltonbolivia.com. Hot water, includes breakfast, psychedelic 1970s style wallpaper in many rooms, restaurant, expensive laundry, luggage store, excellent views from roof, popular.

$ Onkel Inn 1886, Colombia 257, T249 0456. Hostel in a remodelled 19th-century house, rooms with and without bath, doubles, triples and bunks, with breakfast. Jacuzzi, laundry facilities, internet, café and bar, HI affiliated.

$ Res Sucre, Colombia 340, on Plaza San Pedro, T249 2038. Cheaper without bath,

quiet area, hot water, big rooms, kitchen and laundry facilities, luggage stored, helpful.
$ Sagárnaga, Sagárnaga 326, T235 0252, www.hotel-sagarnaga.com. Cheaper in plain rooms without TV, includes breakfast, solar hot water, Wi-Fi, 2 ATMs, English spoken, *peña*.

The Prado, Sopocachi, Miraflores and Zona Sur *p22, map p21*
$$$$ Casa Grande, Av Ballivián 1000 y C 17, Calacoto, T279 5511, www.casa-grande. com.bo. Beautiful, top quality apartments, includes buffet breakfast, Wi-Fi, airport pickup, restaurant, very good service, US$3150 per month.
$$$$ Europa, Tiahuanacu 64, T231 5656, www.hoteleuropa.com.bo. Next to the Museo Nacional de Arqueología. Excellent facilities and plenty of frills, health club, Wi-Fi, several restaurants, parking. Recommended.
$$$$-$$$ Radisson Plaza, Av Arce 2177, T244 1111, www.radisson.com/lapazbo. 5-star hotel with all facilities, includes breakfast, gym, pool and sauna (also for guests of Plaza Hotel), Wi-Fi, excellent buffet in restaurant (see Restaurants, below).
$$$ Alcalá Aparthotel, Sanjinés 2662 at Plaza España, Sopocachi, T241 2336, www. alcalapartamentos.com. Comfortable, spacious, furnished apartments, includes breakfast, internet, 20% discount per month.
$$$ El Rey Palace, Av 20 de Octubre 1947, T241 8541, www.hotelreypalace. com. Includes breakfast, large suites with heating, a/c and cable TV, internet, excellent restaurant, stylish.
$$$ Plaza, Av 16 de Julio 1789, T237 8311. Excellent hotel with good value restaurant (see below), includes breakfast, Wi-Fi, pool.
$$ A La Maison, Pasaje Muñoz Cornejo15, Sopocachi, T241 3704, www.alamaison-lapaz.com. Apart-hotel, breakfast, laundry service, Wi-Fi, TV, kitchens in the larger flats, meals and tourist services can be arranged, daily and monthly rates available.
$$ EHT Sopocachi, Macario Pinilla 580 at the base of El Montículo, T241 0312.

Spacious furnished apartments with kitchenette, good location and views, gym.

El Alto *p17*
$$ Alexander, Av Jorge Carrasco 61 y C 3, Ceja, Zona 12 de Octubre, T282 3376. Modern, with breakfast, **$** pp in dorm, parking, disco, cable TV.
$ Orquídea, C Dos 22 y Av 6 de Marzo, Villa Bolívar A, near bus terminals, T282 6487. Includes breakfast, comfortable heated rooms, cheaper with shared bath, electric showers, good value. Better than others in the area.

South of La Paz *p23*
$$$ Gloria Urmiri, Potosí 909, Urmiri, T240 7070, www.hotelgloria.com.bo. At hot springs 2 hrs from La Paz, price for 2 days, 1 night (price varies according to type of room), includes entry to pools, sauna and all facilities as well as 4 meals, lunch to lunch. Transport US$7.25 pp return. Massage available, reservations required.
$$ Allkamari, near Valle de las Animas, 30 mins from town on the road to Palca, T279 1742, www.casalunaspa.com. Reservations required, cabins for up to 8 in a lovely valley between the Palca and La Animas canyons, a retreat with nice views of Illimani and Mururata, a place to relax and star-gaze, **$** pp in dorm, solar heating, jacuzzi included, meals on request, use of kitchen, horse and bike rentals, massage, shamanic rituals, taxi from Calacoto US$7, bus No 42 from the cemetery to Uni (7 daily weekdays, hourly weekends), get off at Iglesia de las Animas and walk 1 km.
$$ Oberland, Mallasa, El Agrario 3118, near main road, 12 km from La Paz centre, T274 5040, www.h-oberland.com. A Swiss-owned, chalet-style restaurant (excellent, not cheap) and hotel (also good) with older resort facilities, includes buffet breakfast, Wi-Fi, lovely gardens, spa, sauna, covered pool (open to public – US$2 – very hot water), volleyball, tennis. Permit camping with vehicle, US$4 pp. Recommended.

🍴 Restaurants

Around Plaza Murillo *p20, maps p18 and p21*

$$ La Kantuta, in *Hotel Presidente*, Potosí 920, T240 6666. Excellent food, good service. **La Bella Vista** on the top floor is fancier.

Cafés

Alexander Coffee, Potosí 1091. Part of a chain, sandwiches, salads, coffee, pastries.
Café Berlin, Mercado 1377 y Loayza, and at Av Montenegro 708, San Miguel, 0800-2300. Coffee, omelettes, breakfast, popular with locals and smoky.
Café Confitería de la Paz, Camacho 1202, on the corner where Ayacucho joins Av Mcal Santa Cruz. Good if expensive tea room, traditional, great coffee and cakes but very smoky.
Café Soho, Jaén 747. Cosy café with small courtyard, inside and outside seating, local artwork, open Mon-Sun 0930-2300.

Plaza San Francisco up to the cemetery district *p20, maps p18 and p21*

$$$-$$ Steakhouse, Tarija 243B, T231 0750, www.4cornerslapaz.com, daily 1500-2300. Good cuts of meat, large variety of sauces and a great salad bar in a modern environment.
$$ La Cueva, Tarija 210B, T231 4523, www.4cornerslapaz.com, daily 1130-late. Small cosy mexican restaurant, quick service, wide selection of tequilas.
$$ Pizzería Italia, Illampu 840, T246 3152, and 809, 2nd floor, T245 0714. Thin-crust pizza, and pasta.
$$-$ A Lo Cubano, Sagárnaga 357, entre Linares y Illampu, T245 1797. Open Mon-Sat 1200-2200. *Almuerzo* for US$3.65, but it runs out fast, also other choices of good Cuban food, good value.
$$-$ Angelo Colonial, Linares 922, T215 9633. Vegetarian options, good music, internet, open early for breakfast, can get busy with slow service. Has a hostal at Av Santa Cruz 1058.

$$-$ Colonial Pot, Linares 906 y Sagárnaga. Bolivian dishes and a variety of main courses including vegetarian, set meal US$4.35 and à-la-carte, pastries, snacks, hot and cold drinks, quiet, homey, music, exceptional value.
$$-$ Sol y Luna, Murillo 999 y Cochabamba, T211 5323, www.solyluna-lapaz.com. Mon-Fri 0900-0100, Sat-Sun 1700-0100. Dutch run, breakfast, *almuerzo* and international menu, coffees and teas, full wine and cocktail list, live music Mon and Thu, movies, Wi-Fi, guide books for sale, book exchange, salsa lessons.
$$-$ Star of India, Cochabamba 170, T211 4409. British-run Indian curry house, will deliver, including to hotels. Recommended.
$$-$ Tambo Colonial, in Hotel Rosario (see above). Excellent local and international cuisine, good salad bar, buffet breakfast, peña at weekend.
$$-$ Yussef, Sagárnaga 380, 2nd floor. Lebanese, mezze, good for vegetarians, good value and relaxed atmosphere.
$ 100% Natural, Sagárnaga 345. Range of healthy, tasty fast foods ranging from salads to burgers and llama meat, good breakfasts.
$ El Lobo, Illampu y Santa Cruz. Israeli dishes, good meeting place, noticeboard, popular.

Cafés

Banais, Sagárnaga 161, same entrance as Hostal Naira. Coffee, sandwiches and juices, buffet breakfast, set lunch, laid-back music and computer room.
Café Illampu, Linares 940, upstairs. Mon-Sat 0800-2000, Sun 0930-1700. La Paz branch of the Swiss-run Sorata café known for its sandwiches, bread and cakes. Also salads, llama sausages, and European specialties like *roesti* and *spaetzle*. Recommended.
Hard Rock Café, Santa Cruz 399 e Illampu, T211 9318, www.hardrockcafebolivia.lobo pages.com. Serves Hard Rock fair, turns into nightclub around 2400, popular with locals and tourists.
Pepe's, Pasaje Jiménez 894, off Linares. All-day breakfasts, sandwiches, omelettes, tables outside, cards and dominoes, magazines and guidebooks.

The Prado, Sopocachi, Miraflores and Zona Sur *p22, map p21*

$$$ Chalet la Suisse, Av Muñoz Reyes 1710, Cota Cota, T279 3160, www.chaletlasuisse. com. Open 1900-2400, booking is essential on Fri. Serves excellent fondue, steaks.

$$$-$$ El Arriero, Av 6 de Agosto 2525 (Casa Argentina), Sopocachi, T243 5060, also Av Montenegro entre C 17 y 18, San Miguel, T279 1907. The best Argentine *parrilla* in the city, also daily *almuerzo* from US$7.50. Not backpacker friendly.

$$$-$$ La Comedie, Pasaje Medinacelli 2234, Sopocachi, T242 3561. Mon-Fri 1200-1500, 1900-2300, Sat-Sun 1900-2300. 'Art café restaurant', contemporary, French menu, good salads, wine list and cocktails.

$$$-$$ Utama, in Plaza hotel, Av 16 de Julio 1789, T237 8311. 2 restaurants: **Utama** on the top floor, with the views, 1700-2300, à la carte, and **Uma**, on the ground floor, for breakfast and lunch, buffet lunch US$6.15.

$$$-$$ Wagamama, Pasaje Pinilla 2557, T243 4911. Open Mon-Sat 1200-1400, 1900-2130 (closed Sun). Serves sushi, excellent service, popular with ex-pats.

$$ El Consulado, Bravo 299 (behind Plaza Hotel), T211 7706, http://cafeelconsulado. com. Open 0900-2000. Serves lunch and coffee and drinks in the evening. In gorgeous setting with outdoor seating and covered terrace, includes high-end handicraft store, book exchange, Wi-Fi, photo gallery, organic coffee and food, pricey but worth it.

$$ High Lander's, Final Sánchez Lima 2667, Sopocachi, T243 0023. Mon-Fri 1200-1500, 1700-2300, Sat 1900-2330, happy hour Mon-Fri 1700-1900. Variable Tex-Mex fare, nice atmosphere, good views from the end of the street.

$$ La Quebecoise, 20 de Octubre 2387, Sopocachi. Good upmarket international cuisine.

$$ La Tranquera, Capitán Ravelo 2123 next to Hotel Camino Real, T244 1103; also at Hotel Camino Real, Calacoto, T279 2323. Daily 1200-1600, 1900-2300. International food, grill and salad bar.

$$ Maphrao On, Hnos Manchego 2586, near Plaza Isabela la Católica, T243 4682. Open 1200-1400, 1900-2400. Thai and South East Asian food, warm atmosphere, good music.

$$ Reineke Fuchs, Pje Jáuregui 2241, Sopocachi, T244 2979, and Av Montenegro y C 18, San Miguel, T277 2103, www.reineke fuchs.com, Mon-Fri 1200-1430 and from 1900, Sat from 1900 only. German-style bar/ restaurant, many imported German beers, also set lunch from US$5.

$$ Suma Uru, Av Arce 2177 in Radisson Plaza Hotel, T244 1111. *Almuerzo* Mon-Fri for US$8 and excellent buffet, in 5-star setting on Sun 1200-1500, US$11.60. Friendly to backpackers.

$$-$ Eli's Pizza Express, Av 16 de Julio 1400 block. English spoken, open daily including holidays (also at Comercio 914 and Av Montenegro y C 19, Zona Sur), very popular, maybe not the best pizza in La Paz, but certainly the largest omelettes.

$$-$ Ken-Chan, Bat Colorado 98 y F Suazo, p 2 of Japanese Cultural Center, T244 2292. Open 1800-2300. Japanese restaurant with wide variety of dishes, popular.

$$-$ Mongo's, Hnos Manchego 2444, near Plaza Isabela la Católica, T244 0714. Open 1830-0300, live music Tue, excellent Mexican fare and steaks, open fires, bar (cocktails can be pricey), club after midnight, popular with gringos and locals.

$$-$ Vienna, Federico Zuazo 1905, T244 1660, www.restaurantvienna.com. Mon-Fri 1200-1400, 1830-2200, Sun 1200-1430. Excellent German, Austrian and local food, great atmosphere and service, live music.

$ Armonía, Ecuador 2286 y Quito. Mon-Sat 1200-1400. Nice vegetarian buffet lunch.

$ Como en Casa, Av del Ejercito 1115, on the road through the Parque Urbano towards Miraflores. Open1100-1500. Good value set meals, meat and vegetable options, good service and atmosphere.

$ Lu Qing, 20 de Octubre 2090 y Aspiazu, T242 4188. Mon-Sat 1130-1500, 1830-2300, Sun 1100-1530. Chinese food, large choice of dishes, set meals on weekdays.

$ Olive Tree, Campos 334, Edificio Iturri, T243 1552. Mon-Fri 1100-2200, Sat 1100-1500. Good salads, soups and sandwiches, attentive service.

Cafés
Alexander Coffee (Café Alex), Av 16 de Julio 1832, also at 20 de Octubre 2463 Plaza Avaroa, Av Montenegro 1336, Calacoto, and the airport. Open 0730-2400.Excellent coffee, smoothies, muffins, cakes and good salads and sandwiches, Wi-Fi. Recommended.
Arco Iris, F Guachalla 554 y Sánchez Lima, Sopocachi. Also in Achumani, C 16 by the market. Bakery and handicraft outlet of Fundación Arco Iris (www.arcoirisbolivia. org), which works with street children, good variety of breads, pastries, meats and cheeses.
Dumbos, Av 16 de Julio, near *Eli's* and Cinema. Daily 0600-2400. For meat and chicken *salteñas*, ice creams, snacks, look for the dancing furry animals outside.
Fridolín, Av 6 de Agosto 2415; and Prolongación Montenegro, San Miguel. Daily 0800-2200. *Empanadas*, *tamales*, savoury and sweet (Austrian) pastries, coffee, breakfast, Wi-Fi.
Kuchen Stube, Rosendo Gutiérrez 461, Sopocachi. Mon-Fri 0800-2000, Sat-Sun 0800-1900. Excellent cakes, coffee and German specialities, also *almuerzo* Mon-Fri.
La Terraza, 16 de Julio 1615, 0630-0030; 20 de Octubre 2171 y Gutiérrez; and Av Montenegro 1576 y C 8, Calacoto, both 0730-2400. Excellent sandwiches and coffee, pancakes, breakfasts, Wi-Fi.

🎵 Bars and clubs

The epicentre for nightlife in La Paz is currently Plaza Avaroa in Sopocachi. Clubs are clustered around here and crowds gather Fri and Sat nights.

Around Plaza Murillo *p20,*
maps p18 and p21
Etno Café, Jaén 722, T228 0343. Open Mon-Sat 1930-0300. Small café/bar with cultural programmes including readings, concerts,

movies, popular, serves artisanal and fair trade drinks (alcoholic or not).

San Francisco up to the cemetery district *p20, maps p18 and p21*
Blue Note Café, Viluyo esq Plaza Gastón Velasco. Mon-Sat 1200-2400. Wine bar with light food, interesting hat collection, good place to hang out for a coffee or glass of wine in relaxed atmosphere.
Oliver's Travels, Murillo y Tarija, T231 1574. Fake English pub serving breakfasts, curries, fish and chips, pasta, sports channels, music, travel agency.

The Prado, Sopocachi, Miraflores and Zona Sur *p22, map p21*
Deadstroke, Av 6 de Agosto 2460, Sopocachi, T243 3472. Bar/pool hall, café and billiards bar, food, drinks (good value for beer), billiards, pool and other games, opens 1700 (1900 on Sat).
Equinoccio, Sánchez Lima 2191, Sopocachi. Top venue for live rock music and bar, Thu-Sat, cover charge US$2.10, or more for popular bands.
Tetekos, C México 1553. Loud music, cheap drinks, popular with locals and backpackers.
Thelonius Jazz Bar, 20 de Octubre 2172, Sopocachi, T242 4405. Wed-Sat shows start at 2200. Renowned for jazz (what else?), cover charge US$1.40-2.80.

🎵 Entertainment

For current information on cinemas and shows, check *La Prensa* or *La Razón* on Fri, or visit www.la-razon.com. Also look for *Bolivian Express* (in English), *Kaos* and *Mañana*, all free monthly magazines with listings of concerts, exhibits, festivals, etc.

Around Plaza Murillo *p20,*
maps p18 and p269
Bocaisapo, Indaburo 654 y Jaén. Live music in a bar; no cover charge, popular, open Thu-Fri 1900-0300.

Marka Tambo, Jaén 710, T228 0041. Thu-Sat 2100-0200, also Mon-Sat 1230-1500 for lunch. US$6 for evening show, food and drinks extra, live shows with traditional dancing and music (peña), touristy but recommended.

Plaza San Francisco up to the cemetery district *p20, maps p18 and p21*

Peña Parnaso, Sagárnaga 189, T231 6827. Daily starting at 2030, meals available, purely for tourists but a good way to see local costumes and dancing.

Cinemas Films mainly in English with Spanish subtitles cost around US$3.50. Near Sopocachi is **Multicine**, Av Arce 2631, 11 modern cinemas, food court, gym, arcades; also **Megacenter** in the Zona Sur (see Shopping Malls, below). **Cinemateca Boliviana**, Oscar Soria (prolong Federico Zuazo) y Rosendo Gutiérrez, T244 4090, info@cinematecaboliviana.org. Municipal theatre with emphasis on independent productions.

Theatre Teatro Municipal Alberto Saavedra Pérez has a regular schedule of plays, opera, ballet and classical concerts, at Sanjinés e Indaburo, T240 6183. The National Symphony Orchestra is very good and gives inexpensive concerts. Next door is the **Teatro Municipal de Cámara**, which shows dance, drama, music and poetry. **Casa Municipal de la Cultura 'Franz Tamayo'**, almost opposite Plaza San Francisco, hosts a variety of exhibitions, paintings, sculpture, photography, etc, mostly free. Free monthly guide to cultural events at information desk at entrance. The **Palacio Chico**, Ayacucho y Potosí, in old Correo, operated by the Secretaría Nacional de Cultura, also has free exhibitions (good for modern art), concerts and ballet, Mon-Fri 0900-1230, 1500-1900.

✹ Festivals

La Paz *p16, maps p18 and p21*
Starting **24 Jan** Alasitas, in Parque Central up from Av del Ejército, also in Plaza Sucre/San Pedro, recommended. **Carnaval** in **Feb**
or **Mar**. **End May/early Jun** Festividad del Señor del Gran Poder, the most important festival of the year, with a huge procession of costumed and masked dancers on the 3rd Sat after Trinity. **Jul** Fiestas de Julio, a month of concerts and performances at the Teatro Municipal, with a variety of music, including the University Folkloric Festival. **8 Dec**, festival around Plaza España, colourful and noisy. On **New Year's Eve** there are fireworks displays; view from higher up. See page 11 for national holidays and festivals outside La Paz.

🛒 Shopping

La Paz *p16, maps p18 and p21*
Bookshops Los Amigos del Libro, Av Ballivián 1275, also Av Montenegro 1410, San Miguel and the airport, www.librosbolivia.com. Large stock of English, French and German books; also a few maps, expensive. **Gisbert**, Comercio 1270, and in San Miguel on a small lane opposite Café Alexander. Books, maps, stationery. **The Spitting Llama**, Linares 947 (inside Hostal La Posada de la Abuela), T7039 8720, www.thespittingllama.com. Issue ISIC cards, sell used books, guidebooks and camping gear including GPS units, English spoken, helpful; branches in Cochabamba and Copacabana. **Yachaywasi**, Pasaje Trigo 1971 y Av Villazón, on lane between Plaza del Estudiante and the university. Large selection, popular with students.

Camping equipment Kerosene for pressure stoves is available from a pump in Plaza Alexander, Pando e Inca. **Ayni Sport Bolivia**, Jiménez 806, open Mon-Sun 1030-2100. Rents and sometimes sells camping equipment and mountain gear (trekking shoes, fleeces, climbing equiment etc). **Caza y Pesca**, Edif Handal Center, No 9, Av Mcal Santa Cruz y Socabaya, T240 9209. English spoken. **Tatoo Bolivia**, Illampu 828, T245 1265, www.tatoo.ws. Tatoo clothing plus outdoor equipment including backpacks, shoes, etc. English and Dutch spoken. For camping stove fuel enquire at **Emita Tours** on Sagárnaga.

Handicrafts Above Plaza San Francisco (see page 20), up Sagárnaga, by the side of San Francisco church (behind which are many handicraft stalls in the Mercado Artesanal), are booths and small stores with interesting local items of all sorts. The lower end of Sagárnaga is best for antiques. **Galería Dorian**, Sagárnaga 177, is an entire gallery of handicraft shops; includes **Tejidos Wari**, unit 12, for high-quality alpaca goods, will make to measure, English spoken. On Linares, between Sagárnaga and Santa Cruz, high quality alpaca goods are priced in US$. Also in this area are many places making fleece jackets, gloves and hats, but shop around for value and service. **Alpaca Style**, C 22 No 14, T271 1233, Achumani. Upmarket shop selling alpaca and leather clothing. **Artesanía Sorata**, Linares 900, T245 4728, and Sagárnaga 363. Specializes in dolls, sweaters and weavings. **Ayni**, Illampu 704, www.aynibolivia.com. Fair trade shop in Hotel Rosario, featuring Aymara work. **Comart Tukuypaj**, Linares 958, T231 2686, and C 21, Galería Centro de Moda, Local 4B, San Miguel, www.comart-tukuypaj. com. High-quality textiles from an artisan community association. **Incapallay**, Linares 958, p 2, www.incapallay.org. A weavers' cooperative from Tarabuco and Jalq'a communities, near Sucre. **Jiwitaki Art Shop**, Jaén 705, T7725 4042. Run by local artists selling sketches, paintings, sculptures, literature, etc. Open Mon-Fri 1100-1300, 1500-1800. **LAM** shops on Sagárnaga. Good quality alpaca goods. **Millma**, Sagárnaga 225, T231 1338, and Claudio Aliaga 1202, Bloque L-1, San Miguel, closed Sat afternoon and Sun. High-quality alpaca knitwear and woven items and, in the San Miguel shop, a permanent exhibition of ceremonial 19th and 20th century Aymara and Quechua textiles (free). **Mother Earth**, Linares 870, T239 1911. 0930-1930 daily. High-quality alpaca sweaters with natural dyes. **Toshy** on Sagárnaga. Top-quality knitwear.

Jewellery Good jewellery stores include **Joyería King's**, Loayza 261, between Camacho and Mercado, T220 1331. Also at Torre Ketal, C 15, Calacoto, T277 2542.

Maps IGM: head office at Estado Mayor, Av Saavedra 2303, Miraflores, T214 9484, Mon-Thu 0900-1200, 1500-1800, Fri 0900-1200, take passport to buy maps. Also office in Edif Murillo, Final Rodríguez y Juan XXIII, T237 0116, Mon-Fri 0830-1230, 1430-1830, some stock or will get maps from HQ in 24 hrs. **Librería IMAS**, Av Mcal Santa Cruz entre Loayza y Colón, Edif Colón, T235 8234. Ask to see the map collection. Maps are also sold in the Post Office on the stalls opposite the Poste Restante counter.

Markets In addition to those mentioned in the Plaza San Francisco section (page 22), the 5-km sq **Feria 16 de Julio, El Alto** market is on Thu and Sun (the latter is bigger). Take any minibus that says La Ceja and get off at overpass after toll booth (follow crowd of people or tell driver you're going to La Feria), or take 16 de Julio minibus from Plaza Eguino. Arrive around 0900; most good items are sold by 1200. Goods are cheap, especially on Thu. Absolutely everything imaginable is sold here. Be watchful for pickpockets, just take a bin liner to carry your purchases. **Mercado Sopocachi**, Guachalla y Ecuador, a well-stocked covered market selling foodstuffs, kitchen supplies, etc.

Musical instruments Many shops on Pasaje Linares, the stairs off C Linares, also on Sagárnaga/Linares, for example **Walata 855**.

Shopping malls and supermarkets
Megacenter, Av Rafael Pabón, Irpavi, huge food court, 18 cinemas, bowling, banks, ATMs. **Shopping Norte**, Potosí y Socabaya. Mall with restaurants and expensive merchandise. **Supermercado Ketal**, Av Arce y Pinillo, near Plaza Isabel la Católica, Sopocachi, Av Busch y Villalobos, Miraflores, C 21, San Miguel, and Av Ballivián y C 15, Calacoto. Well-stocked supermarket.

La Paz *p16, maps p18 and p21*
City tours
Sightseeing, T279 1440, city tours on a double-decker bus, 2 circuits, downtown and Zona Sur with Valle de la Luna (1 morning and 1 afternoon departure to each), departs from Plaza Isabel la Católica and can hop on at Plaza San Francisco, tour recorded in 7 languages, US$6 for both circuits, Mon-Fri at 0830 and 1430, Sat-Sun at 0900 and 1430.

Climbing, hiking and trekking
Guides must be hired through a tour company. There is a mountain rescue group, **Socorro Andino Boliviano**, Calle 40 Villa Aérea, T246 5879, www.socorroandino.org.
Alberth Bolivia Tours, Illampu 713, T245 8018, www.hikingbolivia.com. Good for climbing and trekking, helpful, equipment rental.
Andean Summits, Muñoz Cornejo 1009 y Sotomayor, Sopocachi, T242 2106, www.andeansummits.com. For mountaineering and other trips off the beaten track, contact in advance.
Bolivian Mountains, Rigoberto Paredes 1401 y Colombia, p 3, San Pedro, T249 2775, www.bolivianmountains.com (in UK T01273-746545). High-quality mountaineering with experienced guides and good equipment, not cheap.
Climbing South America, Murillo 1014 y Rodríguez, Ed Provenzal PB, of 1, T215 2232, www.climbingsouthamerica.com. Climbing and trekking in Bolivia, Argentian and Chile, equipment rental, Australian run.
Refugio Huayna Potosí, Sagárnaga 308 e Illampu, T245 6717, www.huayna-potosi.com. Climbing and trekking tours, run 2 mountain shelters on Huayna Potosí and climbing school.
The Adventure Climbing Company, Av Jaimes Freyre 2950, Plaza Adela Zamudio, Sopocachi, T241 4197. Climbing, trekking and other adventures, equipment rental and sales, experienced guides.

Trek Bolivia, Sagárnaga 392, T231 7106. Organizes expeditions in the Cordillera.
For trekking Maps, see Essentials (page 8) and Shopping, above.

Football
Popular and played on Wed and Sun at the **Siles Stadium** in Miraflores (Micro A), which is shared by both La Paz's main teams, Bolívar and The Strongest. There are reserved seats.

Golf
Mallasilla is the world's highest golf course, at 3318 m. Non-members can play here on weekdays; no need to book. Club hire, green fee, balls and a caddy also costs US$37. There is also a course at Los Pinos in the Zona Sur.

Snooker/pool/other
Picco's, Edif 16 de Julio, Av 16 de Julio 1566. Good tables and friendly atmosphere.
YMCA sportsground and gym: opposite the UMSA University, Av Villazón, and clubhouse open to the public (table tennis, billiards, etc).

Tour operators
America Tours, Av 16 de Julio 1490 (El Prado), Edificio Avenida pb, No 9, T237 4204, www.america-ecotours.com. Cultural and ecotourism trips to many parts of the country, rafting, trekking and horse-riding, English spoken. Highly recommended.
Andean Base Camp, Illampu 863, T246 3782. Overland tours throughout Bolivia, Swiss staff, good reports.
Andean Epics, T7127 6685, www.andeanepics.com. Innovative multi-day cycling trips, eg Sorata to Rurrenabaque, which include bike, boat and 4WD combinations. Owner Travis Gray is very knowledgeable and helpful.
Andean Secrets, General Gonzales 1314 y Almirante Grau, San Pedro (Mon-Fri 1500-1900, Sat 0900-1730, Sun 1000-1400), T7729 4590, quimsacruz_bolivia@hotmail.com, www.andean-secrets.com. Female mountain guide Denys Sanjines specializes in the Cordillera Quimsa Cruz.

Barracuda Biking Company, Illampu 750, inside Hostal Gloria, of 4, T245 9950, info@barracudabiking.com. Bike trips to Coroico at a lower price than the upmarket companies.

Bolivian Journeys, Sagárnaga 363, p 2, T235 7848, www.bolivianjourneys.org. Camping, mountain bike tours, equipment rental, maps, English and French spoken, helpful.

B-Side Adventures, Linares 943, T211 4225. Good for cycling to Coroico and other rides.

Colibrí, Alberto Ostria 1891 y J M Cáceres, Edif Isabelita p 4, Sopocachi Alto, T242 3246, www.colibri-adventures.com. Climbing, trekking, adventure tours, helpful guides.

Crillon Tours, Camacho 1223, T233 7533, www.titicaca.com. A company with over 50 years experience. Joint scheduled tours with Lima arranged. Fixed departures to Salar de Uyuni, trips throughout Bolivia, including the Yungas, Sajama and Lauca, community and adventure tourism and much more. ATM for cash. Recommended. Full details of their Lake Titicaca services on page 49. See www.alwa.travel for their deluxe overlanding scheme.

Deep Rainforest, Galería Dorian, Sagárnaga 189, of. 9A, T215 0385, www.deep-rainforest. com. Off the beaten track trekking, climbing, canoe trips from Guanay to Rurrenabaque, rainforest and pampas trips.

Detour, Av Mcal Santa Cruz 1392, esq Colombia, T236 1626. Good for flight tickets.

Enjoy Bolivia, Plaza Isabel la Católica, Edif Presidente Bush, of 2, T243 5162, www.njboltravel.com. Wide selection of tours and transport service. Airport and bus terminal transfers, van service to Oruro (US$13 pp shared, US$90 private).

Fremen Creative Tours, Bernardo Trigo 447, p 2, Plaza del Estudiante, T244 2777, www.salar-amazon.com. Large well-established operator offering tours throughout Bolivia, including **Tayka** hotels around Salar de Uyuni, **El Puente Jungle Lodge** at Villa Tunari and *Reina de Enín* riverboat.

Gloria Tours/Hotel Gloria, Potosí 909, T240 7070, www.gloriatours.com.bo. Good service, see Where to stay, pages 26 and 28.

Gravity Bolivia, Av 16 de Julio 1490, Edif Avenida, PB, No 10, T231 3849, www.gravity bolivia.com. A wide variety of mountain biking tours throughout Bolivia, including the world-famous downhill ride to Coroico. Also offer a zipline at the end of the ride, or independently (www.ziplinebolivia.com); and rap jumping from buildings in La Paz. Also bike rides more challenging than Coroico, including single-track and high-speed dirt roads, with coaching and safety equipment. Sells guidebooks. Book on website in advance or by phone until 2200, T7065 2678.

Kanoo Tours, Illampu 832 entre Sagarnaga y Santa Cruz, T246 0003, www.kanootours. com. Also at Adventure Brew Hostel and Loki Hostel. Sells Gravity Bolivia tours (see above), plus Salar de Uyuni, Rurrenabaque jungle trips and Perú.

La Paz On Foot, Prol Posnanski 400, Miraflores, T224 8350/7154 3918, www.lapazonfoot.com. Walking city tours, walking and sailing trips on Titicaca, tours to Salar de Uyuni and multi-day treks in the Yungas and Apolobamba. Recommended.

Lipiko Tours, Av Mariscal Santa Cruz, corner of Sagarnaga No 918, Galeria La República, T214 5129, www.travel-bolivia.co.uk. Tailor-made tours for all budgets, 4WD tours, trekking, climbing and adventure sport, trips to Amazon and national parks. Also cover Peru, Chile and Argentina.

Magri Turismo, Capitán Ravelo 2101, T244 2727, www.magriturismo.com. Recommended for tours throughout Bolivia, flight tickets. Own **La Estancia** hotel on the Isla del Sol.

Moto Andina, Urb La Colina N°6 Calle 25, Calacoto, T7129 9329, www.moto-andina. com (in French). Motorcycle tours of varying difficulty in Bolivia, contact Maurice Manco.

Mundo Quechua, Av Circunvalación 43, Achumani, Zona Sur, T279 6145, www.mundoquechua.com. Custom made climbing, trekking and 4WD tours throughout Bolivia. Also extrensions to Peru and Argentina. English and French spoken, good service.

Peru Bolivian Tours, Calle Capitán Ravelo 2097, esquina Montevideo, Edif Paola Daniela, 1st piso, oficina 1-A, T244 5732, www.perubolivian.com. More than 20 years' experience, arranges special programmes throughout Bolivia and Peru.

Queen Travel, Calle 18 7802, Calacoto, T279 5450, www.boliviatravel-queen.com. Offers a wide range of tours all over Bolivia, including Lake Titicaca, Salar de Uyuni, Northern Jungle and Eastern lowlands.

Topas Travel, Carlos Bravo 299 (behind Hotel Plaza), T211 1082, www.topas.bo. Joint venture of Akhamani Trek (Bolivia), Topas (Denmark) and the Danish embassy, offering trekking, overland truck trips, jungle trips, biking and climbing, English spoken, restaurant and *pensión*.

Transturin, Av Arce 2678, Sopocachi, T242 2222, www.transturin.com. Full travel services with tours in La Paz and throughout Bolivia. Details of their Lake Titicaca services on page 49.

Tupiza Tours, Villalobos 625 y Av Saavedra, Edif Girasoles, pb, Miraflores, T224 5254, www.tupizatours.com. La Paz office of the Tupiza agency. Specialize in the Salar and southwest Bolivia, but also offer tours around La Paz and throughout the country.

Turisbus, Av Illampu 704, T245 1341, www.turisbus.com. Lake Titicaca and Isla del Sol, Salar de Uyuni, Rurrenbaque, trekking and Bolivian tours. Also tours and tickets to Puno and Cuzco.

Turismo Balsa, Av 6 de Agosto 3 y Pinilla, T244 0620, www.turismobalsa.com. City and tours throughout Bolivia, see also under Puerto Pérez, page 46. Also international flight deals.

⊖ Transport

La Paz *p16, maps p18 and p21*
Air
Cotranstur minibuses, T231 2032, white with 'Cotranstur' and 'Aeropuerto' written on the side and back, go from Plaza Isabel La Católica, stopping all along the Prado and Av Mcal Santa Cruz to the airport, 0615-2300, US$0.55 (allow about 1 hr), best to buy an extra seat for your luggage, departures every 4 mins. Shared transport from Plaza Isabel La Católica, US$3.50 pp, carrying 4 passengers, also private transfers from **Enjoy Bolivia**, see Tour operators, page 34. Radio-taxi is US$7 to centre, US$9 to Zona Sur. Prices are displayed at the airport terminal exit. There is an **Info Tur** office in arrivals with a *casa de cambio* next to it (dollars, euros cash and TCs, poor rates; open 0530-1300, 1700-0300, closed Sun evening – when closed try the counter where departure taxes are paid). Several ATMs in the departures hall. The international and domestic departures hall is the main concourse, with all check-in desks. There are separate domestic and international arrivals. Bar/restaurant and café upstairs in departures. For details of air services, see under destinations.

Bus
For information, T228 5858. Buses to: **Oruro**, **Potosí**, **Sucre**, **Cochabamba**, **Santa Cruz**, **Tarija** and **Villazón**, leave from the main terminal at Plaza Antofagasta (micros 2, M, CH or 130), see under each destination for details. Taxi to central hotels, US$1.10. The terminal (open 0400-2300) has a tourist booth by the main entrance, ATMs, internet, a post office, **Entel**, restaurant, luggage store and travel agencies. Touts find passengers the most convenient bus and are paid commission by the bus company. To **Oruro** van service with **Enjoy Bolivia**, see page 35, US$13 pp shared, US$90 private.

To **Copacabana**, several bus companies (tourist service) pick-up travellers at their hotels (in the centre) and also stop at the main terminal, tickets from booths at the terminal (cheaper) or agencies in town. They all leave about 0800 (Titicaca Bolivia also at 1400), 3½ hrs, US$3.60-4.50 one way, return from Copacabana about 1330. When there are not enough passengers for each company, they pool them. **Diana Tours** T228 2809, **Titicaca Bolivia**, T246

2655, **Turisbus** T245 1341 (more expensive), many others. You can also book this service all the way to Puno, US$7.

Public buses to **Copacabana, Tiwanaku, Desaguadero** (border with Peru) and **Sorata**, leave from the Cemetery district. To get there, take any bus or minibus marked 'Cementerio' going up C Santa Cruz (US$0.15-0.20). On Plaza Reyes Ortiz are **Manco Capac**, and **2 de Febrero** for **Copacabana** and **Tiquina**. From the Plaza go up Av Kollasuyo and at the 2nd street on the right (Manuel Bustillos) is the terminal for minibuses to **Achacachi, Huatajata** and **Huarina**, as well as Trans Unificada and **Flor del Illampu** minibuses for **Sorata**. Several micros (20, J, 10) and minibuses (223, 252, 270, 7) go up Kollasuyo. Taxi US$1 from downtown. Buses to **Coroico, the Yungas and northern jungle** leave from Villa Fátima (25 mins by micros B, V, X, K, 131, 135, or 136, or *trufis* 2 or 9, which pass Pérez Velasco coming down from Plaza Mendoza,

and get off at the *ex-gasolinera* YPFB, C Yanacachi 1434). See Safety, page 17.

International buses From main bus terminal: to **Buenos Aires**, US$75, 2 a week with **Ormeño**, T228 1141, 54 hrs via Santa Cruz and Yacuiba; via Villazón with **Río Paraguay**, 3 a week, US$75, or **Trans Americano**, US$85. Alternatively, go to Villazón and change buses in Argentina. To **Arica** via the frontier at Tambo Quemado and Chungará **Pullmanbus** at 0630 (good), **Cuevas** at 0700, **Zuleta** at 0600, **Nuevo Continente** at 1230 except Sat, **Litoral**, T228 1920, Sun-Thu 1230, US$14-18. Connecting service for Iquique or Santiago. To **Cuzco**: agencies to **Puno** where you change to a different company, most easily booked through travel agencies, US$14-22, but cheaper paying for each segment at a time. For luxury and other services to Puno see under Lake Titicaca below. Direct to Cuzco, 12 hrs with **Litoral**, US$14 via Desaguadero

and Puno (5 hrs, US$8.40). To **Lima**, **Ormeño** daily at 1430, US$70, 27 hrs; **Nuevo Continente** at 0830, US$55, 26 hrs, via Desaguadero, change to **Cial** in Puno.

Car hire
Imbex Rent a Car, Calacoto 11 No 7896, T212 1012, www.imbex.com. Wide range of well-maintained vehicles; Suzuki jeeps from US$60 per day, including 200 km free for 4-person 4WD. Recommended. **Kolla Motors**, Rosendo Gutierrez 502 y Ecuador, Sopocachi, T241 9141, www.kollamotors.com. 6-seater 4WD Toyota jeeps, insurance and gasoline extra. **Petita Rent-a-car**, Valentín Abecia 2031, Sopocachi Alto, T242 0329, www.rentacarpetita.com. Swiss owners Ernesto Hug and Aldo Rezzonico. Recommended for personalized service and well-maintained 4WD jeeps, minimum rental 1 week. Their vehicles can also be taken outside Bolivia. Also offer adventure tours (German, French, English spoken). Ernesto has a highly recommended garage for VW and other makes, Av Jaimes Freyre 2326, T241 5264.

Taxi
Standard taxis charge US$0.85-1.70 pp for short trips within city limits. A *trufi* US$0.40-0.50 pp in the centre. Taxi drivers are not tipped. At night, for safety, only take **radio taxis** (radio móvil), which are named as such, have a unique number and radio communication (eg **Gold** T241 1414 in the centre, 272 2722 in Zona Sur, **Servisur** T271 9999). They charge US$0.85-2.15 in centre, more to suburbs and at night. Also good value for tours for 3 people. **Oscar Vera**, Simón Aguirre 2158, Villa Copacabana, La Paz, T223 0453, specializes in trips to the Salar de Uyuni and the Western Cordillera.

Train
Ferroviaria Andina (FCA), Sánchez Lima 2199 y Fernando Guachalla, Sopocachi, T241 9770, www.fca.com.bo, Mon-Fri 0800-1600. Sells tickets for the **Oruro-Uyuni-Tupiza-Villazón** line; see schedule and fares under

Oruro Transport (page 63). Tickets for *ejecutivo* class sold up to 2 weeks in advance, for *salón* 1 week. Must show passport to buy tickets. Also operate a **tourist train** from **El Alto** station, C 8, Villa Santiago I, by Cuartel Ingavi, the 2nd Sun of each month at 0800, to **Guaqui** via Tiwanaku; returning from Guaqui at 1500; US$6 *ejecutivo*, US$1.50 *popular*, confirm all details in advance.

South of La Paz *p23*
For Valle de la Luna, Minibuses 231, 273 and 902 can be caught on C México, the Prado or Av 6 de Agosto. Alternatively take Micro 11 ('Aranjuez' large, not small bus) or ones that say 'Mallasa' or 'Mallasilla' along the Prado or Av 6 de Agosto, US$0.65, and ask driver where to get off. Most of the travel agents organize tours to the Valle de la Luna. There are brief, 5-min stops for photos in a US$15 tour of La Paz and surroundings; taxis cost US$6, US$10 with a short wait.

Tiwanaku *p23*
To get to Tiwanaku, tours booked through agencies cost US$12 (not including entry fee or lunch). Otherwise take any **Micro** marked 'Cementerio' in La Paz, get out at Plaza Félix Reyes Ortiz, on Mariano Bautista (north side of cemetery), go north up Aliaga, 1 block east of Asín to find Tiwanaku micros, US$2, 1½ hrs, every 30 mins, 0600 to 1500. Tickets can be bought in advance. **Taxi** costs about US$25-55 return (shop around), with 2 hrs at site. Some **buses** go on from Tiwanaku to Desaguadero; virtually all Desaguadero buses stop at the access road to Tiwanaku, 20-min walk from the site. Return buses (last back 1700) leave from south side of the Plaza in village. Minibuses (vans) to **Desaguadero**, from José María Asín y P Eyzaguirre (Cemetery district) US$2, 2 hrs, most movement on Tue and Fri when there is a market at the border. **Note** When returning from Tiwanaku (ruins or village) to La Paz, do not take an empty minibus. We have received reports of travellers being taken to El Alto and robbed

at gun point. Wait for a public bus with paying passengers in it.

Takesi Trail *p24*
Take a **Líneas Ingavi** bus from C Gral Luis Lara esq Venacio Burgoa near Plaza Líbano, San Pedro going to **Pariguaya** (see Yunga Cruz below), daily at 0800, US$1, 2 hrs. On Sun, also mini-buses from C Gral Luis Lara y Boquerón, hourly 0700-1500. To **Mina San Francisco**: hire a **jeep** from La Paz; US$85, takes about 2 hrs. **Veloz del Norte** (T02-221 8279) leaves from Ocabaya 495 in Villa Fátima, T221 8279, 0900 daily, and 1400 Thu-Sun, US$2.10, 3½ hrs, continuing to Chojlla. From Chojlla to La Paz daily at 0500, 1300 also on Thu-Sun, passing **Yanakachi** 15 mins later.

Choro Trail *p25*
To the *apacheta* pass beyond **La Cumbre**, take a **taxi** from central La Paz for US$15, 45 mins, stopping to register at the Guardaparque hut. Buses from Villa Fátima to Coroico and Chulumani pass La Cumbre. Tell driver where you are going, US$2.10. The trail is signed.

Yunga Cruz Trail *p25*
Take the **bus** to **Pariguaya** (2 hrs past Chuñavi, see Takesi above), at 0800 Mon-Sat, 6 hrs to Chuñavi, US$2.25; 6½ hrs to Lambate (3 km further on). It's not possible to buy tickets in advance, be there at 0700. Also **Trans Río Abajo** to **Lambate** from C Gral Luis Lara y Romualdo Herrera, San Pedro, daily 0700-0800.

Huayna Potosí *p25*
The mountain can be reached by transport arranged through tourist agencies (US$100) or the refugio, **taxi** US$45. **Minibus Trans Zongo**, Av Chacaltaya e Ingavi, Ballivián, El Alto, daily 0600, 2½ hrs, US$1.80 to Zongo, check on return time. Also minibuses from the Ballivián area that leave when full; (few on Sun). If camping in the Zongo Pass area, stay at the site near the white house above the cross.

⊙ Directory

La Paz *p16, maps p18 and p21*
Airline offices Aerolíneas Argentinas, Edif Petrolero, 16 de Julio 1616, Mezanine, of 13, T235 1360. **AeroSur**, Av Arce 2177, Hotel Radisson, p 5, T244 4930; also Av 16 de Julio 1616, T231 3233. **Amazonas**, Av Saavedra 1649, Miraflores, T222 0848. **American Airlines**, Av 16 de Julio 1440, Edif Hermann and Galería Tellería, of 203, San Miguel, T237 2009, 800-100229. **Boliviana de Aviación (BoA)**, Camacho 1413 y Loayza, T211 7993, T901-105010. **Iberia**, Ayacucho 378, Edif Credinform p 5, T220 3911. **LAN**, Av 16 de Julio 1566, p 1, T235 8377, toll free T800-100521. **Lufthansa**, Av 6 de Agosto 2512 y P Salazar, T243 1717. **Sky Airline**, 16 de Julio 1459, Edif Avenida, p1, T211 0440, fly to northern Chile. **TACA**, Edif Petrolero, 16 de Julio 1616 PB, and Av Montenegro 1420, San Miguel, T215 8200, toll free T800-108222.
Cultural centres Alliance Française, Guachalla 399 esq Av 20 de Octubre T242 5005, http://lapaz.alianzafrancesa.org.bo. French-Spanish library, videos, newspapers, and cultural gatherings information. Call for opening hours. **Centro Boliviano Americano (CBA)**, Parque Zenón Iturralde 121, T244 0650 (10 mins walk from Plaza del Estudiante down Av Arce), www.cba. edu.bo. Has public library and recent US papers. **Goethe-Institut**, Av Arce 2708 esq Campos, T243 1916, www.goethe. de/lapaz. Excellent library, recent papers in German, CDs, cassettes and videos free on loan, German books for sale. **Cycle spares** See Gravity Bolivia, page 35, very knowledgeable, www.gravitybolivia. com. **Embassies and consulates** For all foreign embassies and consulates in La Paz, see http://embassy.goabroad.com.
Language schools Alliance Française (see also above). Instituto Exclusivo, Av 20 de Octubre 2315, Edif Mechita, T242 1072, www.instituto-exclusivo.com. Spanish lessons for individual and groups,

accredited by Ministry of Education. **Instituto de La Lengua Española**, María Teresa Tejada, C Aviador esq final 14, No 180, Achumani, T279 6074, T7155 6735. One-to-one lessons US$7 per hr. Recommended. **Speak Easy Institute**, Av Arce 2047, between Goitía and Montevideo, T244 1779, speakeasyinstitute@yahoo. com. US$6 for one-to-one private lessons, cheaper for groups and couples, Spanish and English taught, very good. **Private Spanish lessons** from: **Isabel Daza**, Murillo 1046, p 3, T231 1471, T7062 8016. US$4 per hr. **Enrique Eduardo Patzy**, Méndez Arcos 1060, Sopocachi, T241 5501 or 776-22210, epatzy@hotmail.com. US$6 an hr one-to-one tuition, speaks English and Japanese. Recommended. **Medical services** For hospitals, doctors and dentists, contact your consulate or the tourist office for recommendations. **Health and hygiene: Ministerio de Desarollo Humano, Secretaría Nacional de Salud**, Av Arce,

near **Radisson Plaza**, yellow fever shot and certificate, rabies and cholera shots, malaria pills, bring own syringe. **Centro Piloto de Salva**, Av Montes y Basces, T245 0026, 10 mins walk from Plaza San Francisco, for malaria pills, helpful. **Laboratorios Illimani**, Edif Alborada p 3, of 304, Loayza y Juan de la Riva, T231 7290, open 0900-1230, 1430-1700, fast, efficient, hygienic. Tampons may be bought at most *farmacias* and supermarkets. Daily papers list pharmacies on duty (de turno). For contact lenses, **Optalis**, Comercio 1089. **Useful addresses Immigration**: to renew a visa go to **Migración Bolivia**, Camacho 1468, T211 0960. Mon-Fri 0830-1230, 1430-1830, go early. Allow 48 hrs for visa extensions. **Tourist Police**: C Hugo Estrada 1354, Plaza Tejada Sorzano frente al estadio, Miraflores, next to **Love City** Chinese restaurant, T222 5016, toll free T800-108687. Open 0830-1800, for police report for insurance claims after theft.

Lake Titicaca

Lake Titicaca is two lakes joined by the Straits of Tiquina: the larger, northern lake (Lago Mayor, or Chucuito) contains the Islas del Sol and de la Luna; the smaller lake (Lago Menor, or Huiñamarca) has several small islands. The waters are a beautiful blue, reflecting the hills and the distant cordillera in the shallows of Huiñamarca, mirroring the sky in the rarified air and changing colour when it is cloudy or raining. A boat trip on the lake is a must.

Arriving at Lake Titicaca

Getting there A paved road runs from La Paz to the southeastern shore of the lake. One branch continues north along the eastern shore, another branch goes to the Straits of Tiquina (114 km El Alto-San Pablo) and Copacabana. A third road goes to Guaqui and Desaguadero on the southwestern shore. ▸▸ *See also Transport, page 50.*

La Paz to Copacabana

Puerto Pérez The closest point to the capital on Lake Titicaca, Puerto Pérez, 72 km from La Paz, was the original harbour for La Paz. It was founded in the 19th century by British navigators as a harbour for the first steam boat on the lake (the vessel was assembled piece by piece in Puno). Colourful fiestas are held on New Year's Day, Carnival, 3 May and 16 July (days may change each year). There are superb views of the lake and mountains.

Huatajata Further north along the east shore of the lake is Huatajata, with Yacht Club Boliviano (restaurant open to non-members, Saturday, Sunday lunch only, sailing for members only) and **Crillon Tours' International Hydroharbour** and **Inca Utama Hotel** (see below). Reed boats are still built and occasionally sail here for the tourist trade. There are several small but interesting exhibits of reed boats that were used on long ocean voyages. Beyond here is **Chúa**, where there is fishing, sailing and **Transturin's** catamaran dock (see below).

Islands of Lake Huiñamarca

On **Suriqui** (one hour from Huatajata) in Lake Huiñamarca, a southeasterly extension of Lake Titicaca, you can see reed *artesanías*. The late Thor Heyerdahl's *Ra II*, which sailed from Morocco to Barbados in 1970, his *Tigris* reed boat, and the balloon gondola for the Nazca (Peru) flight experiment, were also constructed by the craftsmen of Suriqui. Reed boats are still made on Suriqui, probably the last place where the art survives. On **Kalahuta** there are *chullpas* (burial towers), old buildings and the uninhabited town of Kewaya. On **Pariti** there is Inca terracing and the **Museo Señor de los Patos**, with weavings and Tiwanku-era ceramics.

From Chúa the main road reaches the east side of the Straits at **San Pablo** (clean restaurant in blue building, with good toilets). On the west side is San Pedro, the main Bolivian naval base, from where a paved road goes to Copacabana and the border. Vehicles are transported across on barges, US$5. Passengers cross separately, US$0.20 (not included in bus fares) and passports may be checked. Expect delays during rough weather, when it can get very cold.

Copacabana → *Phone code: 02. Population: 15,400. Altitude: 3850 m.*

A popular little resort town on Lake Titicaca, 158 km from La Paz by paved road, Copacabana is set on a lovely bay and surrounded by scenic hills. **Municipal tourist office** ① *16 de Julio y 6 de Agosto, Wed-Sun 0800-1200, 1400-1800.* There is only one ATM in town, best bring some cash.

Red de Turismo Comunitario ① *6 de Agosto y 16 de Julio, T7729 9088, www. titicacaturismo.com, Mon-Sat 0800-1230, 1300-1900,* can arrange tours to nearby communities. At major holidays (Holy Week, 3 May, and 6 August), the town fills with visitors; beware of thieves at these times.

Copacabana has a heavily restored, Moorish-style **basilica**. ① *open 0700-2000; minimum 5 people at a time to visit museum, Tue-Sat 1000-1100, 1500-1600, Sun 1000-1100, US$1.50, no photos allowed.* It contains a famous 16th century miracle-working Virgen Morena (Dark Lady), also known as the Virgen de Candelaria, one of the patron saints of Bolivia. The basilica is clean, white, with coloured tiles decorating the exterior arches, cupolas and chapels. It is notable for its spacious atrium with four small chapels; the main chapel has one of the finest gilt altars in Bolivia. There are 17th- and 18th-century paintings and statues in the sanctuary. Vehicles decorated with flowers and confetti are blessed in front of the church.

On the headland which overlooks the town and port, **Cerro Calvario**, are the Stations of the Cross (a steep 45-minute climb – leave plenty of time if going to see the sunset). On the hill behind the town is the **Horca del Inca**, two pillars of rock with another laid across them; probably a sun clock, now covered in graffiti. There is a path marked by arrows, boys will offer to guide you: fix price in advance if you want their help.

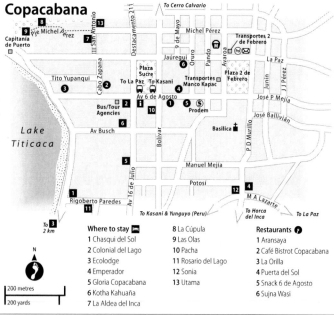

Copacabana

Where to stay
1 Chasqui del Sol
2 Colonial del Lago
3 Ecolodge
4 Emperador
5 Gloria Copacabana
6 Kotha Kahuaña
7 La Aldea del Inca
8 La Cúpula
9 Las Olas
10 Pacha
11 Rosario del Lago
12 Sonia
13 Utama

Restaurants
1 Aransaya
2 Café Bistrot Copacabana
3 La Orilla
4 Puerta del Sol
5 Snack 6 de Agosto
6 Sujna Wasi

200 metres
200 yards

There are many great hikes in the hills surrounding Copacabana. North of town is the **Yampupata Peninsula**. It is a beautiful 17 km (six hours) walk to the village of Yampupata at the tip of the peninsula, either via Sicuani on the west shore or Sampaya on the east shore, both picturesque little towns. There are also minibuses from Copacabana to Yampupata, where you can hire a motorboat or rowboat to Isla del Sol or Isla de la Luna; boats may also be available from Sampaya to Isla de la Luna.

Isla del Sol

The site of the main Inca creation myth (there are other versions) is a place of exceptional natural beauty and spiritual interest. Legend has it that Viracocha, the creator god, had his children, Manco Kapac and Mama Ocllo, spring from the waters of the lake to found Cuzco and the Inca dynasty. A sacred rock at the island's northwest end is worshipped as their birthplace. Near the rock are the impressive ruins of **Chincana**, the labyrinth. At the south end of the island are the **Fuente del Inca**, a spring reached by Inca steps leading up from the lake, and the ruins of **Pilcocaina**, a two storey building with false domes and nice views over the water. Several restored pre-Columbian roads cross the island from north to south.

There are three communities on Isla del Sol: Challapampa, Challa and Yumani, from north to south. All have electricity (Yumani also has Internet), accommodation and simple places to eat. All charge visitors fees, US$0.75-$1.50, which allow entry to small museums or nearby archaeologic sites (keep tickets at hand). The island is heavily touristed and gets crowded in high season. Touts and beggars can be persistent, especially in Yumani. Tour operators in Copacabana offer half- and full-day 'tours' (many are just transport, see page 50) but at least an overnight stay is recommended to appreciate fully the island and to enjoy the spectacular walk from north to south (or vice-versa) at a comfortable pace. Note that it is a steep climb from the pier to the town of Yumani. Local guides are available in Challapampa and Yumani.

Southeast of Isla del Sol is the smaller **Isla de la Luna**, which may also be visited. The community of Coati is located on the west shore, an Inca temple and nunnery on the east shore.

Border with Peru

West side of Lake Titicaca The road goes from La Paz 91 km west to the former port of **Guaqui** (at the military checkpoint here, and other spots on the road, passports may be inspected). The road crosses the border at **Desaguadero** 22 km further west and runs along the shore of the lake to Puno. (There are three La Paz-Puno routes.) Bolivian immigration is just before the bridge, open 0830-2030 (Peru is one hour earlier than Bolivia). Get exit stamp, walk 200 m across the bridge then get entrance stamp on the other side. Get Peruvian visas in La Paz. There are a few hotels and restaurants on both sides of the border; very basic in Bolivia, slightly better in Peru. Money changers on Peruvian side give reasonable rates. Market days are Friday and Tuesday: otherwise the town is dead.

Via Copacabana From Copacabana a paved road leads 8 km south to the frontier at Kasani, then to Yunguyo, Peru. Do not photograph the border area. For La Paz tourist agency services on this route see International buses, page 37, and What to do, page 49. The border is open 0730-1930 Bolivian time (one hour later than Peruvian time). International tourist buses stop at both sides of the border; if using local transport walk 300 m between the two posts. Do not be fooled into paying any unnecessary charges to police or immigration. Going to Peru, money can be changed at the Peruvian side of the border. Coming into Bolivia, the best rates are at Copacabana.

East side of Lake Titicaca

From Huarina, a road heads northwest to Achacachi (market Sunday; fiesta 14 September). Here, one road goes north across a tremendous marsh to **Warisata**, then crosses the altiplano to Sorata (see below). At Achacachi, another road runs roughly parallel to the shore of Lake Titicaca, through **Ancoraimes** (Sunday market, the church hosts a community project making dolls and alpaca sweaters, also has dorms), **Carabuco** (with colonial church), **Escoma**, which has an Aymara market every Sunday morning, to **Puerto Acosta**, 10 km from the Peruvian border. It is a pleasant, friendly town with a large plaza and several simple places to stay and eat. The area around Puerto Acosta is good walking country. From La Paz to Puerto Acosta the road is paved as far as Escoma, then good until Puerto Acosta (best in the dry season, approximately May to October). North of Puerto Acosta towards Peru the road deteriorates and should not be attempted except in the dry season. An obelisk marks the international frontier at Cerro Janko Janko, on a promontory high above the lake with magnificent views. Here are hundreds of small stone storerooms, deserted except during the busy Wednesday and Saturday smugglers' market, the only days when transport is plentiful. You should get an exit stamp in La Paz before heading to this border (only preliminary entrance stamps are given here). There is a Peruvian customs post 2 km from the border and 2 km before Tilali, but Peruvian immigration is in Puno.

Sorata → *Phone code: 02. Population: 8500. Altitude: 2700 m.*

Sorata, 163 km from La Paz (paved but for the last 15 km), is a beautiful colonial town nestled at the foot of Mount Illampu; all around it are views over steep lush valleys. The climate is milder and more humid compared to the altiplano. Nearby are some challenging long-distance treks as well as great day-hikes. The town has a charming plaza, with views of the snow-capped summit of Illampu on a clear day. **Tourist office** ① *in Alcaldía, Mon-Fri 0800-1200, 1400-1800, Sat 0830-1200*. The main fiesta is 14 September. There is no ATM in Sorata, take cash.

A popular excursion is to **San Pedro cave** ① *0800-1700, US$2, toilets at entrance*, beyond the village of San Pedro. The cave has an underground lake (no swimming allowed) and is lit. It is reached either by road, a 12 km walk (three hours each way), or by a path high above the the Río San Cristóbal (about four hours, impassable during the rainy season and not easy at any time). Get clear directions before setting out and take sun protection, food, water, etc. Taxis and pickups from the plaza, 0600-2200, US$7-8 with a 30-minute wait. **The Mirador del Iminiapi** (Laripata)offers excellent views of town and the Larecaja tropical valleys. It is a nice day-walk or take a taxi, US$7-8 return.

Trekking and climbing from Sorata

Sorata is the starting point for climbing **Illampu** and **Ancohuma**. All routes out of the town are difficult, owing to the number of paths in the area and the very steep ascent. Experience and full equipment are necessary. You can hire trekking guides and mules (see What to do, page 50). The 3-4 day trek to **Lagunas Chillata and Glaciar** is the most common and gets busy during high season. Laguna Chillata can also be reached by road or on a long day-hike with light gear, but mind the difficult navigation and take warm clothing. Laguna Chillata has been heavily impacted by tourism (remove all trash, do not throw it in the pits around the lake) and groups frequently camp there. The **Illampu Circuit**, a 6-7 day high-altitude trek (three passes over 4000 m, one over 5000 m) around Illampu, is excellent. It can get very cold and it is a hard walk, though very beautiful with nice campsites on the way. Some food can be bought in Cocoyo on the third day. You must be acclimatized before setting out. Another option is the Trans-Cordillera Trek, 10-12 days from Sorata to Huayna Potosí, or longer all the way to Illimani at the opposite (south) end of the Cordillera Real. Some communities charge visitors fees along the way and there have in the past been armed holdups near Laguna San Francisco but no incidents reported in recent years.

Cordillera Apolobamba

The Area Protegida Apolobamba forms part of the Cordillera Apolobamba, the north extension of the Cordillera Real. The range itself has many 5000 m-plus peaks, while the conservation area of some 483,744 ha protects herds of vicuña, huge flocks of flamingos and many condors. The area adjoins the Parque Nacional Madidi (see page 104). This is great trekking country and the 4-6-day **Charazani to Pelechuco** (or vice versa) mountain trek is one of the best in the country (see Footprint's *Bolivia Handbook* for details). It passes traditional villages and the peaks of the southern Cordillera Apolobamba.

Sorata

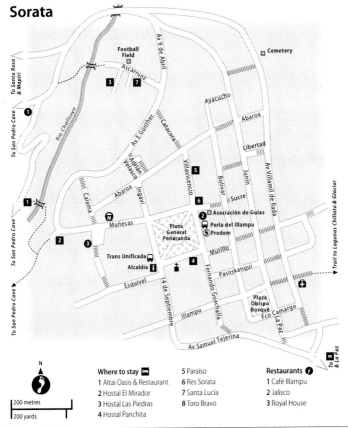

N
200 metres
200 yards

Where to stay 🛏
1 Altai Oasis & Restaurant
2 Hostal El Mirador
3 Hostal Las Piedras
4 Hostal Panchita
5 Paraíso
6 Res Sorata
7 Santa Lucía
8 Toro Bravo

Restaurants 🍴
1 Café Illampu
2 Jalisco
3 Royal House

Charazani is the biggest village in the region (3200 m), with hot springs (US$0.75). Its three-day fiesta is around 16 July. There are some cheap *alojamientos*, restaurants and shops. Pelechuco (3600 m) is a smaller village, also with cheap *alojamientos*, cafés and shops. The road to Pelechuco goes through the Area Protegida, passing the community of Ulla Ulla, 5 km outside of which are the reserve's HQ at La Cabaña. Visitors are welcome to see the orphaned vicuñas. There are economical community hostels at the villages of Lagunillas and Agua Blanca. Basic food is available in the communities. For information, contact SERNAP in La Paz (page 6).

Lake Titicaca listings

For hotel and restaurant price codes and other relevant information, see pages 9-10.

⊙ Where to stay

La Paz to Copacabana *p41*
Puerto Pérez
$$$ Hotel Las Balsas, run by Turismo Balsa (see page 36, or T02-289 5147). In beautiful lakeside setting, views of the cordillera, all rooms have balcony over the lake, negotiate out of season, fitness facilities including pool, jacuzzi, sauna. Excellent restaurant with fixed price lunch or dinner.
$ Hostería Las Islas, nearby on the Plaza. Shared bath, hot water, heated rooms, comfortable but it can get crowded at times. There's a **Blue Note** jazz bar next door.

Huatajata
$$ Hotel Titicaca, between Huatajata and Huarina, Km 80 from La Paz, T289 5180 (in La Paz T220 3666). Beautiful views, sauna, pool, good restaurant. It's very quiet during the week.
$ Máximo Catari's Inti Karka hotel, on the lakeshore, T7197 8959, erikcatari@hotmail. com. Economical rooms, cheaper with shared bath. Also restaurant, open daily, average prices.

Copacabana *p42, map p42*
$$ Ecolodge, 2 km south along the lakeshore, T862 2500 (or 245 1626 Hostal Copacabana, La Paz). Small comfortable cabins in a quiet out-of-the way location, nice grounds. Includes breakfast (other

meals not available), solar hot water, helpful owner.
$$ Gloria Copacabana, 16 de Julio y Manuel Mejía, T862 2094, La Paz T240 7070, www.hotelgloria.com.bo. Includes buffet breakfast, full board available, bar, café and restaurant with international and vegetarian food, Wi-Fi, gardens, parking. Same group as Gloria in La Paz.
$$ Las Olas, lake-end of Pje Michel Pérez past La Cúpula, T862 2112, www. hostallasolas.com. Tastefully decorated suites, each in its own style. All have kitchenettes, heaters, lovely grounds and views, outdoor solar-heated jacuzzi, a special treat. Warmly recommended.
$$ Rosario del Lago, Rigoberto Paredes y Av Costanera, T862 2141, reservations La Paz T244 1756, www.hotelrosario.com/ lago. Includes buffet breakfast, Wi-Fi, comfortable rooms with lake views, beautifully furnished, good restaurant, small museum, handicraft shop, **Turisbus** office (see Transport below), parking. Efficient and attentive service.
$$-$ La Cúpula, Pje Michel Pérez 1-3, 5 mins' walk from centre, T862 2029, www.hotelcupula.com. Variety of rooms and prices, cheaper with shared bath, reliable hot water, sitting room with TV and video, fully equipped kitchen, library, book exchange, attentive service, excellent restaurant (**$$** with vegetarian options, great breakfast). Popular, advance booking advised. Highly recommended.
$ Chasqui del Sol, Av Costanera 55, T862 2343, www.chasquidelsol.com. Includes

breakfast, lakeside hotel, café/breakfast room has great views, trips organized, video room, parking.

$ Colonial del Lago, Av 6 de Agosto y Av 16 de Julio, T862 2270. Economical, some roms with lake view, cheaper without bath, hot water, garden, restaurant and *peña*.

$ Emperador, C Murillo 235, T862 2083. Very economical, even cheaper without bath, electric showers, newer rooms at the back, popular, helpful, tours arranged.

$ Kotha Kahuaña, Av Busch 15, T862 2022. Very economical, cheaper without bath, simple kitchen facilities, quiet, hospitable, basic but clean and good value.

$ La Aldea del Inca, San Antonio 2, T862 2452, www.aldeadelinca.com. Includes breakfast, electric shower, snack bar, ample grounds, parking.

$ Sonia, Murillo 253, T862 2019. Economical, cheaper without bath, good beds, big windows, roof terrace, laundry and kitchen facilities, breakfast in bed on request, very helpful, good value. Recommended.

$ Utama, Michel Pérez, T862 2013, www.utamahotel.com. Comfortable rooms, includes breakfast, hot water, good showers, restaurant, book exchange.

Isla del Sol *p43*
Yumani

Most of the *posadas* on the island are here. Quality varies; ignore the touts and shop around for yourself. Please conserve water, it is hauled up the steep hill by donkeys.

$$ Palla Khasa, 600 m north of town on the main trail to Challapampa, T7321 1585, pallakhasa@gmail.com. Includes good breakfast, large rooms, good beds, restaurant with fine views, nice location and grounds, family run, solar electricity, changes US$ and other currencies. Book in advance.

$ Hostal Comunitario, half-way up the hill on the right, T7354 9898. Economical with electric shower, simple rooms, pleasant common area, back yard.

$ Inti Kala, at the top of the hill, T7194 4013. Cheaper without bath, electric shower, fantastic views, serves good meals.

$ Templo del Sol, at the top of the hill, T7400 5417. Comfortable economical rooms, cheaper without bath, electric shower, great views, comfy beds, and a good restaurant.

Challa

Located mid-island on the east shore, about 200 m below the main north-south trail. Most hostels are on the beach, the town is uphill.

$ Inca Beach, on the beach, T7353 0309. Simple economical rooms with bath, electric shower, kitchen and laundry facilities, meals available, nice common area, camping possible, good value.

$ Qhumpuri, on hillside above beach, T7472 6525. Simple economical 2-room units with nice views, private toilet, shared electric shower, tasty meals available.

Challapampa

$ Cultural, one block from beach, T7190 0272. Clean economical rooms, cheaper without bath, nice terrace.

$ Manco Kapac, by the dock, T7128 8443. Basic clean economical rooms, shared bath, electric shower, friendly, camping possible.

$ Wipala, 1 km north on trail to Chincana, T7257 0092. Simple economical rooms, electric shower, lovely quiet location.

Tour group accommodation

La Posada del Inca, a restored colonial hacienda, owned by **Crillon Tours**, only available as part of a tour with Crillon, see page 35. **Magri Turismo** also owns a hotel on the island, **La Estancia**, www.ecolodge-laketiticaca.com. See La Paz, Tour operators on page 35. See also **Transturin's** overnight options on page 49.

Sorata *p44, map p45*

$$ Altai Oasis, T213 3895, www.altaioasis.com. At the bottom of the valley in a beautiful setting, 15 min steep downhill walk from town, or taxi US$2. Cabins, rooms with bath (cheaper with shared bath), dorms and camping (US$5 pp). Includes breakfast, very good restaurant (**$$**), bar, lovely grounds, pool, peaceful, very friendly and welcoming, family-run by the Resnikowskis, English and German spoken. Warmly recommended.

$ Hostal El Mirador, Muñecas 400, T7350 5453. Cheaper with shared bath, hot water, kitchen, laundry facilities, terrace.

$ Hostal Las Piedras, just off Ascarrunz, T7191 6341, laspiedras2002@yahoo.de. With private bath, cheaper with shared bath, electric shower, very clean and nice, good breakfast available, basic kitchen facilities, very helpful, English and German spoken. Recommended.

$ Hostal Panchita, on plaza, T213 4242. Simple economical rooms, shared bath, electric shower, sunny courtyard, washing facilities, good value.

$ Paraíso, Villavicencio 117, T7327 5122. With electric shower, basic rooms, terrace, breakfast available.

$ Res Sorata, on plaza, T213 6672. Cheaper without bath, electric shower, restaurant, large but scruffy grounds, poor beds, a bit run down overall but still adequate.

$ Santa Lucía, Ascarrunz, T213 6686. Economical, cheaper with shared bath, electric shower, carpeted rooms, patio, not always open.

$ Toro Bravo, below petrol station at entrance to town, T7197 1836. Economical, with electric shower, ample grounds and rooms (upstairs rooms are better), small pool, restaurant, a bit faded but good value.

🍴 Restaurants

Huatajata *p41*
$$-$ Inti Raymi, next to Inca Utama hotel. With fresh fish and boat trips. There are other restaurants of varying standard, most lively at weekends and in the high season.

Copacabana *p42, map p42*
Excellent restaurants at hotels **Rosario del Lago** and **La Cúpula**. Many touristy places on Av 6 de Agosto toward the lakeshore, all similar.

$$ Café Bistrot Copacabana, Cabo Zapana y 6 de Agosto, upstairs, daily 0730-2100. Varied menu, international dishes, vegetarian options, French and English spoken, friendly owner.

$$-$ La Orilla, Av 6 de Agosto, close to lake. Open daily 1000-2200 (usually), warm, atmospheric, tasty food with local and international choices.

$ Aransaya, Av 6 de Agosto 121. Good restaurant and café.

$ Puerta del Sol, Av 6 de Agosto. Good trout.

$ Snack 6 de Agosto, Av 6 de Agosto, 2 branches. Good trout, big portions, some vegetarian dishes, serves breakfast.

$ Sujna Wasi, Jáuregui 127, daily 0730-2300, serves breakfast, vegetarian lunch, wide range of books on Bolivia, slow service.

Sorata *p44, map p45*
Very good restaurant at **Altai Oasis**, see Where to stay, above. There are several **$$-$** Italian places on the plaza, all quite similar.

$$-$ Café Illampu, 15 min walk on the way to San Pedro cave. Excellent sandwiches, bread and cakes, camping possible. Offers tours with own 4WD vehicle, Swiss-run, English and German spoken. Closed Tue and Dec-Mar.

$$-$ Jalisco, on plaza. Mexican and Italian dishes, sidewalk seating.

$ Royal House, off Muñecas by the market. Decent set lunch, friendly

🎉 Festivals

Copacabana *p42, map p42*
Note: At these times hotel prices quadruple.

1-3 Feb Virgen de la Candelaria, massive procession, dancing, fireworks, bullfights.

Easter, with candlelight procession on Good Friday. **23 Jun**, San Juan, also on Isla del Sol. **4-6 Aug**, La Virgen de Copacabana.

Sorata *p44, map p45*
14 Sep, Fiesta Patronal del Señor de la Columna, is the main festival.

⊙ What to do

Lake Titicaca *p41*
Crillon Tours (address under La Paz, Tour operators, page 35) run a hydrofoil service on Lake Titicaca with excellent bilingual guides. Tours stop at their Andean Roots cultural complex at Inca Utama. Very experienced company. The **Inca Utama Hotel and Spa ($$$)** has a health spa based on natural remedies and Kallawaya medicine; the rooms are comfortable, with heating, electric blankets, good service, bar, restaurant, reservations through **Crillon Tours** in La Paz. Crillon is Bolivia's oldest travel agency and is consistently recommended. Also at **Inca Utama** is an observatory (*alajpacha*) with 2 telescopes and retractable roof for viewing the night sky, an Altiplano Museum, a floating restaurant and bar on the lake (**La Choza Náutica**), a 252-sq m floating island and examples of different Altiplano cultures. Health, astronomical, mystic and ecological programmes are offered. The hydrofoil trips include visits to Andean Roots complex, Copacabana, Islas del Sol and de la Luna, Straits of Tiquina and past reed fishing boats. See Isla del Sol, Where to stay, for *La Posada del Inca*. Crillon has a sustainable tourism project with Urus-Iruitos people from the Río Desaguadero area on floating islands by the Isla Queweya. Trips can be arranged to/from Puno and Juli (bus and hydrofoil excursion to Isla del Sol) and from Copacabana via Isla del Sol to Cuzco and Machu Picchu. Other combinations of hydrofoil and land-based excursions can be arranged (also highland, Eastern lowland, jungle and adventure tours). See www.titicaca.com for full

details. All facilities and modes of transport connected by radio.
Transturin (see also La Paz, Tour operators, page 34) run catamarans on Lake Titicaca, either for sightseeing or on the La Paz-Puno route. The catamarans are more leisurely than the hydrofoils of **Crillon** so there is more room and time for on-board meals and entertainment, with bar, video and sun deck. From their dock at Chúa, catamarans run 2-day/1-night cruises starting either in La Paz or Copacabana. Puno may also be the starting point for trips. Overnight cruises involve staying in a cabin on the catamaran, moored at the Isla del Sol, with lots of activities. On the island, Transturin has the Inti Wata cultural complex which has restored Inca terraces, an Aymara house, the underground Ekeko museum and cultural demonstrations and activities. There is also a 30-passenger totora reed boat for trips to the Pilcocaina Inca palace. All island-based activities are community-led and for catamaran clients only. Transturin runs through services to Puno without many of the formalities at the border. Transturin offers last-minute programmes with 40% discount rates in Puno, Cuzco and La Paz, if booked 6 days prior to departure only. You can book by phone or by email, but ask first, as availability depends on date.
Turisbus (www.turisbus.com, see La Paz, Tour operators page 34 and **Hoteles Rosario**, La Paz, and **Rosario del Lago**, Copacabana) offer guided tours in the fast launches *Titicaca Explorer I* (28 passengers) and *II* (8 passengers) to the Isla del Sol, returning to Copacabana via the Bahía de Sicuani for trips on traditional reed boats. Also La Paz-Puno, with boat excursion to Isla del Sol, boxed lunch and road transport, or with additional overnight at **Hotel Rosario del Lago**.

Copacabana *p42, map p42*
Town is filled with tour agencies, all offering excursions to floating islands on imitation reed vessels, and tours to Isla del Sol (see

Transport, below). Kayak and pedal-boat rentals on the beach, US$3 per hr.

Sorata *p44, map p45*
Mountain biking
Andean Epics, T7127 6685, www.andean epics.com. Biking and other tours, see La Paz Tour operators, page 34.

Trekking guides
It may be cheaper to go to Sorata and arrange for trekking there than to book a trek with an agency in La Paz. Buy specialty foods and supplies in La Paz, Sorata shops have basic items.
Asociación de Guías, Sucre 302 y Guachalla, leave message at **Res Sorata** (T213 6672); hires guides, porters and mules. Prices vary: guides approximately US$30 per day, mules US$15 per day. Porters take maximum 2 mules, remember you have to feed your guide/porter.
Eduardo Chura, T7157 8671, guiasorata@ yahoo.com, is an independent local trekking guide.

⊖ Transport

La Paz to Copacabana *p41*
Puerto Pérez
Bus Regular minibus service from **La Paz** Cementerio district: across from the cemetery, above the flower market, ask for buses to Batallas, US$0.75, but no public transport Batallas-Puerto Pérez.

Huatajata
Bus La Paz-Huatajata, US$1, frequent minibuses from Bustillos y Kollasuyo, Cementerio district, daily 0400-1800, continuing to Tiquina.

Islands of Lago Huiñamarca *p41*
Boat Máximo Catari (see Huatajata, Where to stay, above) and Paulino Esteban (east end of town, T7196 7383) arrange trips to the islands in Lago Huiñamarca for US$15 per hr.

Copacabana *p42, map p42*
If arriving in Bolivia at Copacabana and going to La Paz, be sure to arrive there before dark. See also Safety on page 17.
Bus To/from **La Paz**, US$2 plus US$0.20 for Tiquina crossing, 4 hrs, throughout the day with **Manco Capac, 2 de Febrero**. Both have offices on Copacabana's main plaza (but leave from Plaza Sucre) and in La Paz at Plaza Reyes Ortiz, opposite entrance to cemetery. Buy ticket in advance at weekends and on holidays. **Diana Tours, Milton Tours** and others daily at 1330, from Plaza Sucre, 16 de Julio y 6 de Agosto, US$3.50-4.50, take you to Sagárnaga e Illampu in the tourist district, but will not drop you off at your hotel. (See also Border with Peru via Copacabana, below.)

Isla del Sol *p43*
Boat Andes Amazonía, Unión Marinos and Titicaca Tours run motor boats to the island from Copacabana; offices on Av 6 de Agosto by the beach. These boats leave Copacabana daily at 0830 and 1330 (the latter only go to Yumani), returning at 1530 and arriving back around 1730. Fares vary, confirm all details in advance: US$2 one-way, US$3 if you return the same day; if you stay overnight or longer on the island, it is best to buy a separate ticket when you are ready to return, US$3-3.50. On a full-day tour you can be dropped off at Challapampa around 1100 and picked up at Yumani at 1530 (boats leave punctually, so you will have to walk quickly to see the ruins in the north and then hike south to Yumani). Boats also run from Challa to Copacabana Wed, Sat, Sun at 0700, returning 1300, US$2.

From **Yampupata**: to Yumani by motorboat, US$13 per boat (US$3 pp by rowboat); to Isla de la Luna, US$26 per boat.

Border with Peru *p43*
Via Guaqui and Desaguadero
Bus Road paved all the way to Peru. Buses from La Paz to Guaqui and Desaguadero

depart from J M Asín y P Eyzaguirre, Cementerio, from 0500, US$1.50, shared taxi US$3, 2 hrs. From Desaguadero to **La Paz** buses depart 4 blocks from bridge, last vehicle 2000.

Via Copacabana

Bus Several agencies go from La Paz to **Puno**, with a change of bus and stop for lunch at Copacabana, or with an open ticket for continuing to Puno later. They charge US$7 and depart La Paz 0800, pick-up from hotel. From Copacabana they continue to the Peruvian border at Kasani and on to Puno, stopping for immigration formalities and changing money (better rates in Puno). Both **Crillon Tours** and **Transturin** have direct services to Puno without a change of bus at the border. From Copacabana to Puno, **Trans Titicaca** at 0900, 1330, 1830 and other agencies at 1330, offices on 6 de Agosto, US$3.50-4.50, 3 hrs. Also **Turisbus** (www.turisbus.com) to Puno from Hotel Rosario del Lago at 1330, US$9. To go to **Cuzco**, you will have to change in Puno where the tour company arranges connections, which may involve a long wait, check details. In high season, book at least a day in advance. It is always cheaper, if less convenient, to buy only the next segment of your journey directly from local bus companies and cross the border on your own. *Colectivo* Copacabana (Plaza Sucre)-**Kasani** US$0.50 pp, 15 mins, Kasani-**Yunguyo**, where Peruvian buses start, US$0.20 pp.

East side of Lake Titicaca *p44*

Bus La Paz (Reyes Cardona 772, Cancha Tejar, Cementerio district, T238 2239)-**Puerto Acosta**, 5 hrs, US$4, Tue-Sun 0500. Transport past Puerto Acosta only operates on market days, Wed and Sat, and is mostly cargo trucks. Bus Puerto Acosta-La Paz at about 1500. There are frequent minivans to La Paz from **Escoma**, 25 km from Puerto Acosta; trucks from the border may take you this far.

Sorata *p44, map p45*

Bus Minibuses throughout the day from **La Paz** with Trans Unificada (C Manuel Bustillos 683 y Av Kollasuyo in the Cementerio district, T238 1693); also Perla del Illampu (Manuel Bustillos 615, T238 0548), US$2.50, 3½ hrs. Booking recommended on Fri. To or from **Copacabana** and **Peru**, change buses at Huarina but they are often full so start early and be prepared for a long wait.

Jeeps run from La Paz (C Chorolque y Tarapacá, T245 0296, often full), via Sorata to **Santa Rosa** (US$15, 13 hrs), on the road to **Mapiri** and **Guanay**, a rough route with interesting vegetation and stunning scenery. Onward transport can be found in Santa Rosa. From Guanay private boats may be arranged to **Rurrenabaque** (see page 55), and vehicles run to Caranavi and thence to Coroico. Sorata-Coroico by this route is excellent for offroad motorcycling. If travelling by public trasport it is easier to go La Paz – Coroico – Caranavi – Guanay – Santa Rosa – Sorata – La Paz, than vice versa.

Cordillera Apolobamba *p45*
Charazani

Bus From Calle Reyes Cardona 732, off Av Kollasuyo, Cemetery district, La Paz, daily with **Trans Altiplano**, T283 0859, and **Trans Provincias del Norte** (No 772, T238 2239), 0600-0630, 7 hrs, US$3.50, very crowded. Return to La Paz at 1800; **Altiplano** also has 0900 on Sat and 1200 Mon and Fri.

Pelechuco

Bus From **La Paz** Trans Provincias del Norte leaves daily 0600-0700 from Ex Tranca de Río Seco in El Alto, passing through Qutapampa, Ulla Ulla and Agua Blanca to Pelechuco, 10-12 hrs, US$5, sometimes on sale 24 hrs before departure at the booking office in Calle Reyes Cardona. Return to La Paz between 0300 and 0400 most days.

The Yungas

Only a few hours from La Paz are the subtropical valleys known as the Yungas. These steep, forested slopes, squeezed in between the Cordillera and the Amazon Lowlands, provide a welcome escape from the chill of the capital. The warm climate of the Yungas is also ideal for growing citrus fruit, bananas, coffee and especially coca.

La Paz to the Yungas

All roads from La Paz to the Yungas go via **La Cumbre**, a pass at 4,725 m about one hour northeast of the city. The road out of La Paz circles cloudwards over La Cumbre; all around are towering snowcapped peaks. The first village after the pass is **Unduavi**, where there is a check point, a petrol station, and roadside stalls. Beyond Unduavi an unpaved road branches right 75 km to Chulumani and the Sud-Yungas. The paved road contnues to Cotapata, where it again divides: right is the old unpaved road to Yolosa, the junction 8 km from Coroico (this is the popular cycling route). To the left, the new paved road goes via Chuspipata and Puente Yolosita, where an unpaved road climbs steeply to Coroico. In addition, from Puente Villa on the Unduavi-Chulumani road, an unpaved road runs to Coripata and Coroico. For the La Cumbre-Coroico hike (Choro), see page 25.

All roads to Coroico drop some 3500 m to the green subtropical forest in 70 km. The best views are in May-June, when there is less chance of fog and rain. The old road, the so-called "World's Most Dangerous Road", is steep, twisting, clinging to the side of sheer cliffs, and it is slippery in the wet. It is a breathtaking descent (best not to look over the edge if you don't like heights) and its reputation for danger is more than matched by the beauty of the scenery. Many tourists go on a mountain-bike tour: it is your responsibility to choose top quality bikes (with hydraulic disc brakes) and a reputable company which offers bilingual guides, helmet, gloves, vehicle support throughout the day (see La Paz Tour operators, page 34). Many bike companies take riders back to La Paz the same day, but Coroico is worth more of your time. In Yolosa, at the end of the bike ride, is a three-segment zipline (total 1555 m) operated by Gravity Bolivia; see page 35 and www. ziplinebolivia.com. The road is especially dangerous when it is raining (mid-December to mid-February), be sure the bike is in top shape and be extra cautious.

Coroico → *Phone code: 02. Altitude: 1750 m*

The little town of Coroico, capital of the Nor-Yungas region, is perched on a hill amid beautiful scenery. The hillside is covered with orange and banana groves and coffee plantations. Coroico is a first-class place to relax with several good walks. A colourful four-day festival is held 19-22 October. On 2 November, All Souls' Day, the cemetery is festooned with black ribbons. A good walk is up to the waterfalls, starting from **El Calvario**. Follow the stations of the cross by the cemetery, off Calle Julio Zuazo Cuenca, which leads steeply uphill from the plaza. Facing the chapel at El Calvario, with your back to the town, look for the path on your left. This leads to the falls which are the town's water supply (Toma de Agua) and, beyond, to two more falls. **Cerro Uchumachi**, the mountain behind El Calvario, can be climbed following the same stations of the cross, but then look for the faded red and white antenna behind the chapel. From there it's about two hours' steep walk to the top (take water). A third walk goes to the pools in the **Río Vagante**, 7 km off the road to Coripata; it takes about three hours. The **tourist information** is at the Prefectura ① *Monse y Julio Zuazo Cuenca, corner of the main plaza*. There have been several incidents of young women being raped or attacked in this area; do not hike alone.

Caranavi → *Phone code: 02. Altitude: 600 m.*

From the junction at Puente Yolosita the paved road follows the river 11 km to Santa Bárbara, then becomes gravel for 65 km to Caranavi, an uninspiring town 156 km from La Paz. From here the road continues towards the settled area of the Alto Beni, at times following a picturesque gorge. Market days are Friday and Saturday. There is a range of hotels and *alojamientos* and buses from La Paz (Villa Fátima) to Rurrenabaque pass through. Beyond Caranavi, 70 km, is **Guanay** at the junction of the Tipuani and Mapiri rivers (basic lodging). From here there may be river transport to Rurrenabaque.

Chulumani and Sud-Yungas → *Phone code: 02. Altitude: 1750 m.*

The road from Unduavi to Chulumani goes through **Puente Villa**, where a branch runs north to Coroico through Coripata. The capital of Sud Yungas is **Chulumani** is a small town with beautiful views, 124 km from La Paz. There are many birds in the area and good hiking. The 24 August **fiesta** lasts 10 days and there is a lively market every weekend. **Tourist office** ① *in the main plaza, open irregular hours, mostly weekends*. There is no ATM in Chulumani, bring cash. **Irupana** (altitude 1900 m), 31 km east of Chulmani (mini-bus or shared taxi US$2), is a friendly little place with a lovely location, delightful climate, more good walking and birdwatching, and a couple of very nice places to stay. The 500-ha **Apa Apa Reserve** ① *5 km from Chulumani on the road to Irupana (see Where to stay, page 54)*, is the one of the last areas of original Yungas forest with lots of birds, other wildlife, hiking trails and pleasant accommodation.

The Yungas listings

For hotel and restaurant price codes and other relevant information, see pages 9-10.

⬤ Where to stay

Coroico *p52*

Hotel rooms are hard to find at holiday weekends and prices are higher.
$$$$ Río Selva Resort, in Río Huarinilla, off the paved road from La Paz, T289 5571. A self-contained resort, full board, cabins and rooms, restauran, several pools, water slide, sports fields, multi-day packages.
$$ El Viejo Molino, T279 7329, www.hotel viejomolino.com. 2 km on road to Caranavi, Upmarket hotel and spa with pool, gym, jacuzzi, games room, restaurant, etc.
$$ Gloria, C Kennedy 1, T289 5554, www.hotelgloria.com.bo. Traditional resort hotel, full board, pool, restaurant with set lunches and à la carte, internet, free transport from plaza.
$$-$ Bella Vista, C Héroes del Chaco 7 (2 blocks from main plaza), T213 6059. Beautiful rooms and views, includes breakfast, cheaper without bath, Wi-Fi, 2 racquetball courts, terrace, bike hire, restaurant, pool.
$$-$ Esmeralda, on the edge of town, 10 mins uphill from plaza (see website for transport), T213 6027, www.hotelesmeralda. com. Bolivian-German owned, most rooms include breakfast, cheaper in dorms, hot showers, satellite TV and DVD, English spoken, arranges hikes and local tours by open-sided truck, credit cards accepted, book exchange, good buffet restaurant, sauna, garden, pool, Wi-Fi, welding facilities

for overland drivers, van service to La Paz (US$50 for up to 11 passengers), book ahead. Very helpful.

$$-$ Hostal Kory, at top of steps leading down from the plaza, T7156 4050. Includes breakfast, cheaper without bath, electric showers, restaurant, huge pool, terrace, good value, helpful.

$ Don Quijote, 500 m out of town, on road to Coripata, T213 6007. Economical, with breakfast, electric shower, pool, quiet, nice views.

$ El Cafetal, Miranda, 10-min walk from town, T7193 3979. Economical, cheaper with shared bath, very nice, restaurant with excellent French/Indian/ vegetarian cuisine, French-run.

$ Los Silbos, Iturralde 4043, T7350 0081. Cheap simple rooms with shared bath, electric showers, good value.

$ Matsu, 1 km from town (call for free pick-up, taxi US$2), T7069 2219. Economical, includes breakfast, restaurant, pool, views, quiet, helpful.

$ Residencial de la Torre, Julio Zuazo Cuenca, ½ block from plaza. Welcoming place with courtyard, cheap sparse rooms, no alcoholic drinks allowed.

$ Sol y Luna, 15-20 mins beyond **Hotel Esmeralda**, La Paz contact: Maison de la Bolivie, 6 de Agosto 2464, Ed Jardines, T244 0588, www.solyluna-bolivia.com. 7 *cabañas*, bath and kitchen, splendid views, 2 apartments for 4 people, 2 rooms with bath, 7 rooms for 1-4 people with shared bath, restaurant (vegetarian specialities), camping US$3 pp (not suitable for cars), garden, pool, shiatsu massage (US$15-20), very good value, Sigrid (owner) speaks English, French, German, Spanish.

Chulumani and Sud-Yungas *p53*

Chulumani suffers from water shortages, check if your hotel has a reserve tank.

$ Apa Apa, 5 km from town on road to Irupana, then walk 20 min uphill from turnoff, or taxi from Chulumani US$3.50, T7254 7770, La Paz T213 9640, apapayungas@hotmail.com. A lovely old hacienda with simple rooms, private bath, hot water, includes breakfast, other delicious meals available, home-made ice-cream, pool, large campsite with bathrooms and grills, tours to Apa Apa Reserve, family run by Ramiro and Tildy Portugal, English spoken, very friendly.

$ Country House, 400 m out of town on road to cemetery, T7528 2212, La Paz T274 5584. With electric shower, lovely tranquil setting, pool and gardens, library, breakfast and other home-cooked meals available, family run. Enthusiastic owner Xavier Sarabia offers hiking tours, English spoken.

$ Hostal Familiar Dion, Alianza, ½ block below plaza, T289 6034. Includes breakfast, cheaper without bath, electric shower, very clean and well maintained, restaurant, attentive.

$ Huayrani, Junín y Cornejo, uphill from centre near bus stops, T213 6351. Includes breakfast, electric shower, nice views, pool, parking.

Irupana

$ Bougainville Hotel, near the centre of town, T213 6155. Includes good breakfast, pool, very clean modern rooms, electric shower, pizzería, family run, good value.

$ Nirvana Inn, uphill at the edge of town past the football field, T213 6154. Includes breakfast, other meals on request, comfortable cabins on beautiful grounds with great views, pool, parking, flower and orchid gardens lovingly tended by the owners.

🍴 Restaurants

Coroico *p52*

$$ Bamboos, Iturralde y Ortiz. Good Mexican food and pleasant atmosphere, live music some nights with cover charge. Happy hour 1800-1900.

$$-$ Back-stube, Pasaje Adalid Linares, 10 m from the main square. Mon 0830-1200, Wed-Fri 0830-1430, 1830-2200, Sat-

Sun 0830-2200. National and international food, vegetarian options, à la carte only, breakfasts, pastries, top quality, terrace with panoramic views, nice atmosphere, **$$-$ Carla's Garden Pub**, Pasaje Adalid Linares, 50 m from the main plaza. Open lunch until late. Sandwiches, snacks, pasta and international food, BBQ for groups of 5 or more. Lots of music, live music on weekends. Garden, hammocks, games, Wi-Fi, nice atmosphere.
$ Pizzería Italia, 2 with same name on the plaza. Daily 1000-2300. Pizza, pasta, snacks.

Chulumani and Sud-Yungas *p53*
$ La Cabaña Yungeña, C Sucre 2 blocks below plaza, Tue-Sun, simple set lunch and dinner.
    Couple of other places around plaza, all closed Mon. Basic eateries up the hill by bus stops.

⚙ What to do

Coroico *p52*
Cycling
CXC, Pacheco 79. Good bikes, US$20 for 6 hrs including packed lunch, a bit disorganized but good fun and helpful, English and German spoken.

Horse riding
El Relincho, Don Reynaldo, T7191 3675, 100 m past **Hotel Esmeralda** (enquire here), US$25 for 4 hrs with lunch.

⊖ Transport

Coroico *p52*
Bus From La Paz all companies are on C Yanacachi y Av Las Américas, beside the former YPFB station in Villa Fátima: buses and minibuses leave throughout the day US$4.25, 2½ hrs on the paved road. **Turbus Totaí**, T221 6592, is reported reliable and there are several others. Services return to La Paz from

the small terminal down the hill in Coroico, across from the fooball field. All are heavily booked at weekends and on holidays.
    Pick-ups from the small mirador at Pacheco y Sagárnaga go to **Puente Yolosita**, 15 mins, US$0.70. Here you can try to catch a bus to **Rurrenabaque**, but there's more chance of getting a seat in **Caranavi**, where La Paz-Rurre buses pass through in the evening, often full. Caranavi-Rurre 12 hrs, US$6-7, **Flota Yungueña**, at 1800-1900, **Turbus Totaí** 2100-2200, and others. Alternatively, take a shared taxi from the market area in Caranavi to **Guanay**, US$3.50, 2 hrs, where you can look for a boat (no public services) to Rurre. Ask for Gregorio Polo, T7300 8067, who has a canoe for the trip, US$300-400. A 3-day tour will cost US$500, with meals and camping. Some Rurre operators (see page 107), run tours upriver to Guanay and may have empty space for the way back, but it can be a long wait. See also **Andean Epics** of Sorata (page 50) and **Deep Rainforest**, La Paz (page 35). For Guanay to **Sorata** via **Mapiri** and **Santa Rosa**, see page 51.

Chulumani and Sud-Yungas *p53*
Bus From **La Paz**, several companies from Villa Fátima, leave when full, US$3.60, 4 hrs: eg **San Cristóbal**, C San Borja 408 y 15 de Abril, T221 0607. In Chulumani most buses leave from the top of the hill by the petrol station; minibuses and taxis to local villages from plaza.

ⓘ Directory

Coroico *p52*
Language classes Siria León Domínguez, T7195 5431. US$5 per hr, also rents rooms and makes silver jewellery, excellent English. **Medical services** Hospital is the best in the Yungas.

Southwest Bolivia

The mining town of Oruro, with one of South America's greatest folkloric traditions, shimmering salt flats, coloured lakes and surrealistic rock formations combine to make this one of the most fascinating regions of Bolivia. Add some of the country's most celebrated festivals and the last hide-out of Butch Cassidy and the Sundance Kid and you have the elements for some great and varied adventures. The journey across the altiplano from Uyuni to San Pedro de Atacama is a popular route to Chile and there are other routes south to Argentina.

Oruro → *Phone code: 02. Population: 236,110. Altitude: 3725 m.*

The mining town of Oruro is the gateway to the altiplano of southwest Bolivia. It's a somewhat drab, functional place, which explodes into life once a year with its famous carnival, symbolized by La Diablada. To the west is the national park encompassing Bolivia's highest peak: Sajama. The **tourist office** ① *Bolívar y Montes 6072, Plaza 10 de Febrero, T525 0144. Mon-Fri 0800-1200, 1430-1830*, is helpful and informative. The Prefectura and the Policía de Turismo jointly run information booths in front of the Terminal de Buses ① *T528 7774, Mon-Fri 0800-1200, 1430-1830, Sat 0830-1200*; and opposite the railway station ① *T525 7881, same hours.*

Although Oruro became famous as a mining town, there are no longer any working mines of importance. It is, however, a railway terminus and the commercial centre for the mining communities of the altiplano, as well as hosting the country's best-known carnival (see La Diablada, page 58). The Plaza 10 de Febrero and surroundings are well maintained and several buildings in the centre hint at the city's former importance. The **Museo Simón Patiño** ① *Soria Galvarro 5755, Mon-Fri 0830-1130, 1430-1800, Sat 0900-1500, US$1*, was built as a mansion by the tin baron Simón Patiño, it is now run by the Universidad Técnica de Oruro and contains European furniture and temporary exhibitions. There is a view from the Cerro Corazón de Jesús, near the church of the Virgen del Socavón, five blocks west of Plaza 10 de Febrero at the end of Calle Mier.

The **Museos Sacro y Minero** ① *inside the Church of the Virgen del Socavón, entry via the church daily 0900-1145, 1500-1730, US$1.50, guided tours every 45 mins*, contain religious art, clothing and jewellery and, after passing through old mining tunnels and displays of mining techniques, a representation of El Tío (the god of the underworld). **Museo Antropológico** ① *south of centre on Av España y Urquidi, T526 0020, Mon-Fri 0900-1200, 1400-1800, Sat-Sun 1000-1200, 1500-1800, US$0.75, good guides, getting there: take micro A heading south or any trufi going south*. It has a unique collection of stone llama heads as well as impressive carnival masks.

The **Museo Mineralógico y Geológico** ① *part of the University, Mon-Fri 0800-1200, 1430-1700, US$0.70, getting there: take micro A south to the Ciudad Universitaria*, has mineral specimens and fossils. **Casa Arte Taller Cardozo Velásquez** ① *Junín 738 y Arica, east of the* *centre, T527 5245, Mon-Sat 1000-1200, 1500-1800, US$1.* Contemporary Bolivian painting and sculpture is displayed in the Cardozo Velásquez home, a family of artists.

There are thermal baths outside town at Capachos (reported rundown) and **Obrajes** ⓘ *23 km from Oruro, minibuses leave from Caro y Av 6 de Agosto, US$1, 45 min; baths open 0700-1800, US$1.50, Oruro office: Murgía 1815 y Camacho, T525 0646.*

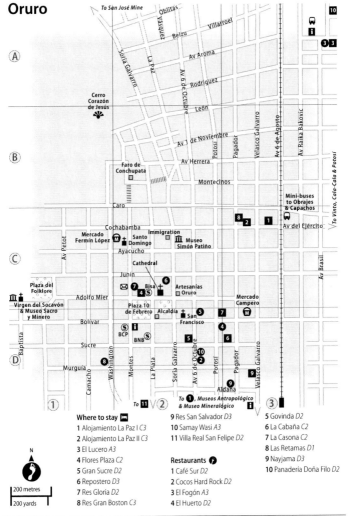

Oruro

Where to stay 🛏
1 Alojamiento La Paz I *C3*
2 Alojamiento La Paz II *C3*
3 El Lucero *A3*
4 Flores Plaza *C2*
5 Gran Sucre *D2*
6 Repostero *D3*
7 Res Gloria *D2*
8 Res Gran Boston *C3*
9 Res San Salvador *D3*
10 Samay Wasi *A3*
11 Villa Real San Felipe *D2*

Restaurants 🍴
1 Café Sur *D2*
2 Cocos Hard Rock *D2*
3 El Fogón *A3*
4 El Huerto *D2*
5 Govinda *D2*
6 La Cabaña *C2*
7 La Casona *C2*
8 Las Retamas *D1*
9 Nayjama *D3*
10 Panadería Doña Filo *D2*

N
200 metres
200 yards

La Diablada

Starting on the **Saturday before Ash Wednesday**, Los Carnavales de Oruro include the famous **Diablada** ceremony in homage to the miraculous Virgen del Socavón, patroness of miners, and in gratitude to Pachamama, the Earth Mother. The **Diablada** was traditionally performed by indigenous miners, but several other guilds have taken up the custom. The Carnival is especially notable for its fantastically elaborate and imaginative costumes.

The **Sábado de Peregrinación** starts its 5 km route through the town at 0700, finishing at the Sanctuary of the Virgen del Socavón, and continues into the early hours of Sunday. There the dancers invoke blessings and ask for pardon.

At dawn on Sunday, **El Alba** is a competition of all participating musicians at Plaza del Folklore near the Santuario, an amazing battle of the bands. The **Gran Corso** or **La Entrada** starts at 0800 on the Sunday, a more informal parade (many leave their masks off) along the same route.

Monday is **El Día del Diablo y del Moreno** in which the Diablos and Morenos, with their bands, bid farewell to the Virgin. Arches decorated with colourful woven cloths and silverware are set up on the road leading to the Santuario, where a mass is held. In the morning, at Avenida Cívica, the Diablada companies participate in a play of the Seven Deadly Sins. This is followed by a play about the meeting of the Inca Atahualpa with Pizarro, performed by the Fraternidad Hijos del Sol. At night, each company has a private party.

On Tuesday, **Martes de Chall'a**, families get together, with ch'alla rituals to invoke ancestors, unite with Pachamama and bless personal possessions. Throughout Carnaval everyone throws water and sprays foam at everyone else (plastic tunics are sold for US$0.20 by street vendors).

The Friday before carnival, traditional

Parque Nacional Sajama

A one-day drive to the west of Oruro is the **Parque Nacional Sajama** ① *park headquarters in Sajama village, T02-513 5526 (in La Paz SERNAP T02-242 6303), US$3.50 payable to community of Sajama*, established in 1939 and covering 100,230 ha. The park contains the world's highest forest, consisting mainly of the rare queñual tree (Polylepis tarapacana) which grows up to an altitude of 5500 m. The scenery is wonderful with views of several volcanoes, including Sajama – Bolivia's highest peak at 6542 m – Parinacota and Pomerape (jointly called Payachatas). The road is paved and leads across the border into the Parque Nacional Lauca in Chile. You can trek in the park, with or without porters and mules, but once you move away from the Río Sajama or its major tributaries, lack of water is a problem. There is basic accommodation in Sajama village (see below) as well as a more comfortable and expensive option at Tomarapi on the north side of the mountain; see page 61.

Sajama village → *Population: 500. Altitude: 4200 m.*

In Sajama village, visitors are billeted in basic family-run *alojamientos* on a rotating basis. All are basic to very basic, especially the sanitary facilities; no showers or electricity, solar power for lighting only. Alojamientos may provide limited food, so bring your own supplies. It can be very windy and cold at night; a good sleeping bag, gloves and hat are miners' ceremonies are held at mines, including the sacrifice of a llama. Visitors may only attend with advance permission.

Preparations for Carnival begin four months before the actual event, on the first Sunday of November, and rehearsals are held every Sunday until one week before Carnival, when a plain clothes rehearsal takes place, preceded by a mass for participants. In honour of its syncretism of ancestral Andean traditions and Catholic faith, the Oruro Carnaval has been included on UNESCO's Heritage of Humanity list.

Seating Stands are erected along the entire route and must be purchased from the entrepreneurs who put them up. Tickets are for Saturday and Sunday, there is no discount if you stay only one day. A prime location is around Plaza 10 de Febrero where the companies perform in front of the authorities, seats run US$35-55, some are sold at the more expensive hotels. Along Av 6 de Agosto seats cost US$20-25, good by the TV cameras, where performers try their best.

Where to stay During Carnival, accommodation costs two to three times more than normal and must be booked well in advance. Hotels charge for Friday, Saturday and Sunday nights. You can stay for only one night, but you'll be charged for three. Locals also offer places to stay in their homes, expect to pay at least US$10 per person per night.

Transport The maximum fare is posted at the terminal, but when demand is at its peak, bus prices from La Paz can triple. Buses get booked up quickly, starting Friday and they do not sell tickets in advance. There's usually no transport back to La Paz on Tuesday, so travel on Monday or Wednesday. Many agencies organize day trips from La Paz on Saturday, departing 0430, most will pick you up from your hotel. They return late, making for a tiring day. Trips cost US$45-60, and include breakfast, a snack and sometimes a seat for the parade.

essential. Crampons, ice axe and rope are needed for climbing the volcanoes and can be hired in the village. Local guides charge US$50-70 per day. Pack animals can be hired, US$8 per day including guide. Good bathing at the Manasaya thermal complex, 6 km northwest of village; jeeps can be rented to visit, US$8-16. Many villagers sell alpaca woolen items.

By road to Chile

The shortest and most widely used route from La Paz to Chile is the road to **Arica** via the border at Tambo Quemado (Bolivia) and **Chungará** (Chile). From La Paz take the highway south towards Oruro. Immediately before Patacamaya, turn right at green road sign to Puerto Japonés on the Río Desaguadero, then on to Tambo Quemado. Take extra petrol (none available after Chilean border until Arica), food and water. The journey is worthwhile for the breathtaking views.

Bolivian **customs and immigration** are at Tambo Quemado, where there are a couple of very basic places to stay and eat. Border control is open daily 0800-2000. Shops change bolivianos, pesos chilenos and dollars. From Tambo Quemado there is a stretch of about 7 km of 'no-man's land' before you reach the Chilean frontier at Chungará. Here the border crossing, which is set against the most spectacular scenic backdrop of Lago Chungará and Volcán Parinacota, is thorough but efficient; open 0800-2000. Expect a long wait behind lines of lorries. Drivers must fill in 'Relaciones de Pasajeros', US$0.25 from kiosk at border, giving details of driver, vehicle and passengers. Do not take any livestock, plants, fruit, vegetables, coca or dairy products into Chile.

An alternative crossing from Oruro: several bus companies travel southwest to Iquique, via the border posts of **Pisiga** (Bolivia) and **Colchane** (Chile). The road is paved from Oruro to Toledo (32 km) and from Opoquari to Huachachalla (about 30 km). The rest of the 240 km road in Bolivia is unpaved; on the Chilean side it's paved all the way to Iquique, 250 km. There is also service from Oruro to Arica via Patacamaya and Tambo Quemado.

South of Oruro

Machacamarca, about 30 minutes south of Oruro, has a good **railway museum** ⓘ *open Wed and Fri 0900-1200, 1500-1700*. Further south, the road runs between the flat plain of Lago Poopó and the Cordillera Azanaque, a very scenic ride. There are thermal baths at **Pazña**, 91 km from Oruro. About 65 km south is the **Santuario de Aves Lago Poopó** (a Ramsar site), an excellent bird reserve on the lake of the same name. The lake dries up completely in winter. The closest place to Oruro to see flamingos and other birds is **Lago Uru Uru** (the northern section of the Poopó lake system), go to Villa Challacollo on the road to Pisiga (minibuses 102, 10, 5 or blue micros) and walk from there. Birds start arriving with the first rains in October or November. Further along, at Km 10 is Chusakeri, where chullpas can be seen on the hillside.

Access to the lake is a little closer from **Huari**, 15 minutes south of Challapata along a paved road. Huari (124 km south of Oruro) is a pleasant little town with a large brewery; there is a small museum and Mirador Tatacuchunita, a lookout on nearby Cerro Sullka. Sunsets over the lake are superb. There are a couple of basic *alojamientos*, eg **25 de Mayo**, two blocks from the plaza towards Challapata, shared bath, cold water in morning only. It is about an 8 km walk from Huari to the lake, depending on the water level. Near the lake is the Uru-Muratos community of **Llapallapani** with circular adobe homes, those with straw roofs are known as *chillas* and those with conical adobe roofs are *putukus*. Cabins in putuku style form part of a community tourism programme. Boats can be hired when the water level is high, at other times Poopó is an unattainable mirage. There is good walking in the Cordillera Azanaque behind Huari; take food, water, warm clothing and all gear. **Challapata** (*fiesta* 15-17 July) has several places to stay, eg *Res Virgen del Carmen*, by main plaza, and a gas station.

Atlantis in the Andes Jim Allen's theory of Atlantis (www.atlantisbolivia.org) is well known around Oruro. **Pampa Aullagas**, the alleged Atlantis site, is 196 km from Oruro, southwest of Lago Poopó. Access is from the town of **Quillacas** along a road that branches west from the road to Uyuni just south of Huari, or from the west through Toledo and Andamarca. A visit here can be combined with visits to the Salar de Coipasa.

Southwest of Lago Poopó, off the Oruro-Pisiga-Iquique road (turn off at **Sabaya**), is the **Salar de Coipasa**, 225 km from Oruro. It is smaller and less visited than the Salar de Uyuni, and has a turquoise lake in the middle of the salt pan surrounded by mountains with gorgeous views and large cacti. Coipasa is northwest of the Salar de Uyuni and travel from one to the other is possible with a private vehicle along the impressive **Ruta Intersalar**. Along the way are tombs, terracing and ancient irrigation canals at the archaeological site of **Alcaya** ⓘ *US$1.25*, gradually being developed by the local community (near **Salinas de Garci Mendoza**, locally known as Salinas). At the edge of the Salar de Uyuni is **Coquesa** (lodging available), which has a mirador and tombs with mummies ⓘ *US$1.25 entry to each site*. Nearby are the towering volcanic cones of Cora Cora and Tunupa. Access to the north end of the Salar de Uyuni is at **Jirira**.

Note: Getting stranded out on the altiplano or, worse yet on the salar itself, is dangerous because of extreme temperatures and total lack of drinking water. It is best to visit this area with a tour operator that can take you, for example, from Oruro through the salares to Uyuni. Travellers with their own vehicles should only attempt this route following extensive local inquiry or after taking on a guide to avoid becoming lost or bogged. The edges of the salares are soft and only established entry points or ramps should be used to cross onto or off the salt.

Oruro listings

For hotel and restaurant price codes and other relevant information, see pages 9-10.

🛏 Where to stay

Oruro *p56, map p57*

$$ Flores Plaza, Adolfo Mier 735 at Plaza 10 de Febrero, T525 2561, www.floresplaza hotel.com. Includes breakfast, comfortable carpeted rooms, good central location.
$$ Gran Sucre, Sucre 510 esq 6 de Octubre, T527 6800, hotelsucreoruro@entelnet.bo. Refurbished old building (faded elegance), includes buffet breakfast, rooms and newer suites, heaters on request, internet in lobby, friendly helpful staff.
$$ Samay Wasi, Av Brasil 232 opposite the bus terminal, T527 6737, samaywasioruro@ hotmail.com. Includes breakfast, carpeted rooms, internet, discount for IYHF members.
$$ Villa Real San Felipe, San Felipe 678 y La Plata, south of the centre, T525 4993. Quaint hotel, nicely furnished but small rooms, heating, buffet breakfast, sauna and whirlpool, restaurant, tour operator.
$ Alojamiento La Paz, Cochabamba 180 y Galvarro, T527 4882; second location 1 block away at Cochabamba 266, T527 4987. Cheap, shared bath (hot shower US$0.75 extra), reasonably clean, basic.
$ El Lucero, 21 de Enero 106 y Brasil, opposite the terminal, T528 5884. Multi-storey hotel, reliable hot water, front rooms noisy, good value.
$ Repostero, Sucre 370 y Pagador, T525 8001. Includes breakfast, hot water, parking, restaurant serves set lunch. Renovated carpeted rooms are more expensive but better value than their old rooms.

$ Res Gloria, Potosí 6059, T527 6250. 19th-century building, private toilet, shared electric shower, cheaper with shared toilet, clean, basic.
$ Res Gran Boston, Pagador 1159 y Cochabamba, T527 4708. Refurbished house, economical rooms around a covered patio, cheaper with shared bath, good value.
$ Res San Salvador, V Galvarro 6325 near train station, T527 6771. Cheaper with shared bath, electric shower, basic.

Parque Nacional Sajama *p58*

$$ Tomarapi Ecolodge, north of Sajama in Tomarapi community, near Caripe, T02-241 4753, represented by Millenarian Tourism & Travel, Av Sánchez Lima 2193, La Paz, T02-241 4753, www.boliviamilenaria. com. Including full board (good food) and guiding service with climbing shelter at 4900 m, helpful staff, simple but comfortable, with hot water, heating.

South of Oruro *p60*

$ Alojamiento Paraíso, Sabaya. Take sleeping bag, shared bath, cold water, meals on request or take own food, sells petrol.
$ Doña Wadi, Salinas de Garci Mendoza, C Germán Busch, near main plaza, T513 8015. Shared bath, hot water, basic but clean, meals available.
$ Posada Doña Lupe, Jirira. Hot water, cheaper without bath, use of kitchen but bring your own food, no meals available, caters to tour groups, pleasant, comfortable.
$ Zuk'arani, on a hillside overlooking Salinas de Garci Mendoza and the Salar, T2513 7086, zukarani@hotmail.com. 2 cabins for 4, with bath, hot water, cheaper in rooms with shared bath, hot water, meals on request.

🍴 Restaurants

Oruro *p56, map p57*

$$ El Fogón, Brasil 5021. Regional dishes. Best of a poor lot by the bus terminal, overpriced.

$$ La Cabaña, Junín 609. Comfortable, smart, good international food, bar, Sun and Mon 1200-1530 only.

$$ Nayjama, Aldana 1880. Good regional specialties, very popular for lunch, huge portions.

$$-$ Las Retamas, Murguía 930 esq Washington. Mon-Sat 0930-2330, Sun 0930-1430. Excellent quality and value for set lunches (**$**), Bolivian and international dishes à la carte, very good pastries at **Kuchen Haus**, pleasant atmosphere, attentive service, a bit out of the way but well worth the trip. Recommended.

$ Cocos Hard Rock, 6 de Octubre y Sucre. Mon-Sat1200-1400, 1800-2400, Sun 1200-1400. Set meals, local and international dishes.

$ La Casona, Pres Montes 5970, opposite Post Office. Salteñas in them morning, closed midday, good *pizzería* at night.

$ Govinda, 6 de Octubre 6071. Excellent vegetarian, Mon-Sat 0900-2130.

$ El Huerto, Bolívar 359. Good, vegetarian options, open Sun.

Cafés

Café Sur, Arce 163, near train station. Live entertainment, seminars, films, Tue-Sat, good place to meet local students.

Panadería Doña Filo, 6 de Octubre esq Sucre. Excellent savoury snacks and sweets, closed Sun, takeaway only.

🍸 Bars and clubs

Oruro *p56, map p57*

Bravo, Montesinos y Pagador. Varied music, 2100-0300.

Imagine, 6 de Octubre y Junín. Latin and other music, 2200-0400.

🛍 Shopping

Oruro *p56, map p57*

Crafts On Av La Paz the blocks between León and Belzu are largely given over to workshops producing masks and costumes for Carnival. **Artesanías Oruro**, A Mier 599, esq S Galvarro. Lovely selection of regional handicrafts produced by 6 rural community cooperatives; nice sweaters, carpets, wall-hangings.

Markets Mercado Campero, V Galvarro esq Bolívar. Sells everything, also *brujería* section for magical concoctions. **Mercado Fermín López**, C Ayacucho y Montes. Food and hardware. C Bolívar is the main shopping street. **Global**, Junín y La Plata. Well stocked supermarket. **Irupana**, S Galvarra y A Mier. Natural food and snacks.

⛰ What to do

Oruro *p56, map p57*

Asociación de Guías Mineros, contact Gustavo Peña, T523 2446. Arranges visits to San José mine.

Freddy Barrón, T527 6776, lufba@hotmail. com. Custom-made tours and transport, speaks German and some English.

🚌 Transport

Oruro *p56, map p57*

Bus Bus terminal 10 blocks north of centre at Bakovic and Aroma, T525 3535, US$0.25 terminal use fee, luggage store, ATMs. Micro 2 to centre, or any saying 'Plaza 10 de Febrero'. To **Challapata** and **Huari**: several companies go about every hour, US$1, 1¾ hrs, and Huari, US$1.25, 2 hrs, last bus back leaves Huari about 1630. You can also take a bus to Challapata and a shared taxi from there to Huari, US$0.30. Daily services to: **La Paz** at least every hour 0400-2200, US$2-3.40, 4 hrs; also tourist van service with **Enjoy Bolivia**, see La Paz Tour operators, page 34. **Cochabamba**, US$3.35-4, 4 hrs, frequent with **Copacabana, Azul**

and Danubio. **Potosí**, US$2.70-4, 5 hrs, several daily, **Bustillo** and **San Miguel**. **Sucre** Bustillo, Trans Azul and San José, all around 2000, US$7, 9 hrs. **Tarija**, Belgrano and **Expreso Tarija** at 2030, US$9.30-14.50, 14hrs. **Uyuni**, several companies, all depart 1900-2100, US$4.35 regular, US$7.25 *semi-cama*, 7-8 hrs. **Todo Turismo**, offers a tourist bus departing from La Paz at 2100, arrange ahead for pick-up in Oruro at midnight, US$27. To **Tupiza**, via Potosí, **Boquerón** at 1230, **Illimani** at 1630 and 2000, US$9.75-12.40, 11-12 hrs, continuing to Villazón, US$10-13, 13-14 hrs. **Santa Cruz**, Bolívar at 2000, US$8.70, *bus cama* at 2130, US$14, 11 hrs. To **Pisiga** (Chilean border), **Trans Pisiga**, Av Dehene y España, T526 2241, at 2000 and 2030, or with Iquique bound buses, US$3.75, 4-5 hrs. **International buses** (US$2 to cross border): to **Iquique** via Pisiga, US$13-14, 8 hrs, buses leave around 1200 coming from Cochabamba; companies include Trans Luján, Trans Paraíso and Trans Copacabana. **Arica** via Patacamaya and Tambo Quemado, several companies daily around 1100-1300 and 2300, US$22 normal, US$26-29 *semi-cama*, US$33 *cama*, 8 hrs, some continue to Iquique, 12 hrs.

Train The station is at Av Velasco Galvarro y Aldana, T527 4605, ticket office Mon-Fri 0800-1200, 1430-1800, Sun 0830-1120, 1530-1800. Tickets for *ejecutivo* class are sold up to 2 weeks in advance, 1 week for *salón*. Tickets can also be purchased in La Paz, see page 38. Ferroviaria Andina (FCA, www.fca.com.bo), runs services from Oruro to **Uyuni**, **Tupiza**, and **Villazón** on the Argentine border: **Expreso del Sur** runs Tue and Fri at 1530, arriving in Uyuni at 2220, and **Wara Wara** on Sun and Wed at 1900, arriving in Uyuni at 0220.

Fares: Expreso del Sur to Uyuni: *Ejecutivo* US$16, *Salón* US$8; Tupiza, 12½ hrs: US$32, US$14.50 respectively: Villazón, 15½ hrs: US$38, US$17. Wara Wara del Sur to Uyuni: *Ejecutivo* US$14, *Salón* US$6.50; Tupiza, 13½-14 hrs: US$24.50, US$11 respectively; Villazón, 17½ hrs: US$29.50, US$13.50. For details of trains from Uyuni to **Villazón** and for trains from Uyuni to Oruro, see Uyuni Transport, page 69. For return times from Villazón, see page 74.

Parque Nacional Sajama *p58*
To get to the park, take a La Paz-Oruro bus and change at Patacamaya. Mini-vans from Patacamaya to Sajama Sun-Fri 1200, 3 hrs, US$2.50. Sajama to **Patacamaya** Mon-Fri 0600, some days via **Tambo Quemado**, confirm details and weekend schedule locally. From Tambo Quemado to Sajama about 1530 daily, 1 hr, US$0.65. Or take a La Paz-Arica bus, ask for Sajama, try to pay half the fare, but you may be charged full fare.

South of Oruro *p60*
To **Coipasa** ask if **Trans Pisiga**, address above, is running a fortnightly service. If not, you can take one of the buses for Iquique and get off at the turnoff, but it's difficult to hire a private vehicle for onward transportation in this sparsely populated area. Salinas de Garci Mendoza from **Oruro**, Trans Cabrera, C Tejerina y Caro, daily except Sat (Mon, Wed Fri, Sun 1900, Tue, Thu 0830, Sun also at 0730). Return to Oruro same days, US$3.40, 7 hrs.

ⓘ Directory

Oruro *p56, map p57*
Useful addresses Immigration, S Galvarro 5744 entre Ayacucho y Cochabamba, across from Museo Simón Patiño, T527 0239, Mon-Fri 0830-1230, 1430-1830.

Uyuni → *Phone code: 02. Population: 18,000. Altitude: 3670 m.*

Uyuni lies near the eastern edge of the Salar de Uyuni and is one of the jumping-off points for trips to the salt flats, volcanoes and lakes of southwest Bolivia. Still a commercial and communication centre, Uyuni was, for much of the 20th century, important as a major railway junction. Two monuments dominate Avenida Ferroviaria: one of a railway worker, erected after the 1952 Revolution, and the other commemorating those who died in the Chaco War. Most services are near the station. **Museo Arqueológico y Antropológico de los Andes Meridionales** ⓘ *Arce y Potosí, Mon-Fri 0800-1200, 1400-1800, US$0.35*, is small museum with local artefacts. The market is at Potosí y Bolívar. Fiesta 11 July. There is a Railway Cemetery of sorts outside town with engines from 1907 to the 1950s, now rusting hulks. **Pulacayo**, 25 km from Uyuni on the road to Potosí, is a town at the site of a 19th-century silver mine. The train cemetery here is more interesting and contains the first locomotive in Bolivia and the train robbed by Butch Cassidy and the Sundance Kid.

Tourist office Dirección de Turismo Uyuni ⓘ *at the clock tower, T693 2060, Mon-Sat 0800-1200, 1430-1830, Sun 0900-1200*. **Subprefectura de Potosí** ⓘ *Colón y Sucre, Mon-Fri 0800-1200, 1430-1830, Sat 0800-1200*, departmental information office, the place to file complaints in writing. There is only one ATM in Uyuni which does not always work, take cash.

Uyuni

Sleeping 🛏	7 Joya Andina	Eating 🍴
1 Avenida	8 Julia	1 Arco Iris
2 Dairson	9 Los Girasoles	2 Kactus
3 El Viajero	10 Mágia de Uyuni	3 La Loco
4 Hostal Marith	11 Tambo Aymara	
5 Hostelling International	12 Toñito &	
6 Jardines de Uyuni	Minuteman Pizza	

Salar de Uyuni

Crossing the Salar de Uyuni, the largest and highest salt lake in the world, is one of the great Bolivian trips. Driving across it is a fantastic experience, especially during June and July when the bright blue skies contrast with the blinding white salt crust. Farther south, and included on most tours of the region, is the **Reserva Eduardo Avaroa** (REA, see below) with the towering volcanoes, multi-coloured lakes with abundant birdlife, weird rock formations, thermal activity and endless puna that make up some of most fabulous landscapes in South America.

Trips to the Salar de Uyuni enter via the *terraplén* (ramp) at **Colchani (Museo de la Llama y de la Sal**; see also Where to stay, below) and include stops to see traditional salt mining techniques and the Ojos del Agua, where salt water bubbles to the surface of the slat flat, perhaps a call at a salt hotel (see Where to stay, below) and a visit to the **Isla Incahuasi** ① *entry US$1.40* (also known as Isla del Pescado because of its shape). This is a coral island, raised up from the ocean bed, covered in tall cactii. There is a walking trail with superb views, a café, basic lodging and toilets. If on an extended tour (see below), you may leave the Salar by another *terraplén*, eg Puerto Chuvica in the southwest. Some tours also include **Gruta de la Galáxia**, an interesting cave at the edge of the Salar.

The Salar de Uyuni contains the world's largest lithium deposits and the Bolivian government has announced plans to build large-scale extraction facilities. A pilot plant was operating in 2012 (away from usual tourist routes) and concern has been expressed about the impact of more extensive lithium mining.

San Cristóbal

The original village of **San Cristóbal**, southwest of Uyuni, was relocated in 2002 to make way for a huge open-pit mine, said to be one of the largest silver deposits in South America. The original church (1650) had been declared a national monument and was therefore rebuilt in its entirety. Ask at the Fundación San Cristóbal Office for the church to be opened as the interior artwork, restored by Italian techniques, is worth seeing. The fiesta is 27-28 July.

Reserva Nacional de Fauna Andina Eduardo Avaroa

① *SERNAP office at Colón y Avaroa, Uyuni, T693 2225, www.bolivia-rea.com, Mon-Fri 0830-1230, 1430-1800; entry to reserve US$22 (Bs150, not included in tour prices; pay in bolivianos). Park ranger/entry points are near Laguna Colorada, Lagunas Verde and Blanca, close to the Chilean border, and at Sol de Mañana, near Quetena Chico.*

In the far southwest of Bolivia, in the Lípez region, is the 714,745-ha **Reserva Nacional Eduardo Avaroa** (REA). There are two access routes from Uyuni (one via the Salar) and one from Tupiza. This is one of Bolivia's prime attractions and tour vehicles criss-cross the puna every day, many on the route from Uyuni to San Pedro de Atacama (Chile). Roads are still unmarked rugged tracks however, and may be impassable in the wet season. **Laguna Colorada** at 4278 m, 346 km southwest of Uyuni, is just one of the highlights of the reserve, its shores and shallows encrusted with borax and salt, an arctic white counterpoint to the flaming red, algae-coloured waters in which the rare James flamingos, along with the more common Chilean and Andean flamingos, breed and live. **Laguna Verde** (lifeless because it is laden with arsenic) and its neighbour **Laguna Blanca**, near the Chilean border, are at the foot of Volcán Licancábur, 5868 m. Between Lagunas Colorada and Verde there are thermal pools at Laguna Blanca (blissful water, a challenge to get out into the bitter wind – no facilities) and at Polques, on the shores of Río Amargo/Laguna Salada by the Salar de Chalviri. A *centro comunal* has been built at Polques (with dining room, changing room and toilets). All these places are on the 'classic' tour route, across the Salar de Uyuni to **San Juan**, which has a museum of local *chullpas*, and is where most tour companies stop: plenty of lodgings. Other tours stop at **Culpina K**. Then you go to the Salar de Chiguana, Mirador del Volcán de Ollagüe, Cinco Lagunas, a chain of small, flamingo-specked lagoons, the much-photographed Arbol de Piedra in the Siloli desert, then Laguna Colorada (spend the second night here: **Hospedaje Laguna Colorada**, the newer and better **$ Don Humberto** in Huayllajara, and **Campamento Ende**). From Colorada you go over the Cuesta del Pabellón, 4850 m, to the Sol de Mañana geysers (not to be confused with the Sol de Mañana entry point), the Desierto de Dalí, a pure sandy desert as much Daliesque for the spacing of the rocks, with snow-covered peaks behind, as for the shape of the rocks themselves, and Laguna Verde (4400 m).

Jurisdiction of the reserve belongs to the villages of **Quetena Chico** and Quetena Grande (the smaller of the two), to the east of Laguna Colorada. The villagers are entitled to run lodging in the reserve: Quetena Chico runs *hospedajes* at Laguna Colorada. Quetena Grande runs La Cabaña at Hito Cajónes (see below). In Quetena Chico is the reserve's visitors information centre, **Centro Ecológico Ch'aska** ① *daily 0730-1800*, informative displays about the region's geology, vulcanology, fauna, flora, natural and human history; a worthwhile stop. The village has two cheap *hospedajes* (**Piedra Preciosa** and **Hostal Quetena**, hot water extra), and places to eat.

Sadly, lakes in the reserve are gradually drying-up, most noticeably Laguna Verde. This has been attributed to global climate change but the real reason may be massive underground water consumption by mines in Bolivia as well as across the border in Chile and Argentina.

From Tupiza Tour operators in Tupiza run trips to the REA and Salar de Uyuni and go to places not included on tours from Uyuni. These include the beautiful **Lagunas Celeste** and **Negra** below Cerro Uturunco, which is near Quetena Chico; the **Valle de las Rocas**, 4260 m, between the villages of **Alota** and **Villa Mar** (a vast extension of rocks eroded into fantastic configurations, with polylepis trees in sheltered corners); and isolated communities in the puna. The high altitude scenery is out of this world. *Alojamientos* in the villages on the tour routes cannot be booked. You turn up and search for a room. All provide kitchen space for the tour's cook or independent traveller to prepare meals, take your own stove, though. See also **Tayka** in Uyuni, What to do, below. There is public transport from Uyuni into the region, but rarely more than one bus a week, with several hours rough travelling. If travelling independently, note that there are countless tracks and no signposts.

Crossing into Chile
There is a REA ranger station near Lagunas Blanca and Verde: if going from Bolivia, have your park entry receipt at hand, if crossing from Chile pay the entry fee here. Alongside is a *refugio*, La Cabaña; US$5 pp in comfortable but very cold dorms, solar-powered lighting, hot water seldom works, cooking facilities but bring your own food (in high season book in advance – tour agencies can do this by radio). There is good climbing and hiking in the area with outstanding views. You must register at the ranger station before heading out and they may insist that you take a guide (eg to climb Licancábur, US$30 for guide plus US$40 for transport). Mind the altitude, intense solar radiation and lack of drinking water.

From the ranger station it's 5 km to the border at Hito Cajones (on the Chilean side called Hito Cajón), 4500 m. Bolivian immigration open 0800-2100, charges US$2 in any currency. If you plan to cross to Chile here, you should first go to the immigration office in

Uyuni (see Directory, page 70). There are no services or facilities at the border. A further 6 km along a good dirt road into Chile is the intersection with the fully paved road from San Pedro de Atacama to Paso de Jama, the border between Chile and Argentina. From here it's 40 km (2000 m downhill) to San Pedro. Chilean customs and immigration are just outside San Pedro and can take 45 minutes at busy times. See Transport, page 69.

Uyuni listings

For hotel and restaurant price codes and other relevant information, see pages 9-10.

Where to stay

Uyuni *p64, map p64*
Many hotels fill early, reservations are advised in high season. Be conservative with water use, this is a very dry area, water is scarce and supplied at limited hours (better hotels have reserve tanks).
$$$ Jardines de Uyuni, Potosí 113, T693 2989, www.hotelesrusticosjardines.com. Includes breakfast, tasetefully decorated, comfortable, heating, open fire in the lounge, Wi-Fi, small pool, parking.
$$ Los Girasoles, Santa Cruz 155, T693 3323. Buffet breakfast, bright and warm (especially 2nd floor), comfortable, nice decor, heaters, cheaper in old section, internet extra.
$$ Mágia de Uyuni, Av Colón 432, T693 2541. Includes buffet breakfast, nice ample rooms and suites upstairs with heating, cheaper in older colder rooms downstairs (as for a heater), parking.
$$ Tambo Aymara, Camacho s/n y Colón, T693 2227, www.tamboaymara.com. Lovely colonial-style modern hotel, includes buffet breakfast, large comfortable rooms, heating, Belgian/Bolivian owned, operate their own tours.
$$-$ Toñito, Av Ferroviaria 48, T693 3186, www.bolivianexpeditions.com. Includes good breakfast, spacious rooms with good beds, solar-powered showers and heating in new wing, cheaper in old section with electric showers, parking, book exchange, tours.

$ Avenida, Av Ferroviaria 11, near train station, T693 2078. Simple but well maintained, economical, cheaper with shared bath, hot water (shared showers 0700-2100), long patio with laundry facilities, family run, helpful, good value, popular and often full.
$ Dairson, Av Ferroviaria next to train station, T693 3606. Functional carpeted rooms, cheaper with shared bath.
$ El Viajero, Cabrera 334 y 6 de Agosto, near bus terminals, T02-693 3549. Basic rooms, cheaper with shared bath, electric shower, parking.
$ Hostal Marith, Av Potosí 61, T693 2174. Basic, cheaper with shared bath and in dorm, electric showers from 0830, patio with laundry facilities, tours (have salt hotel at Atulcha near the Salar).
$ Hostelling International, Potosí y Sucre, T693 2228. Cheaper with shared bath, hot water, kitchen facilities, modern and popular but poor beds, discount for IYHF members.
$ Joya Andina, Cabrera 473 y Sucre, T693 2076, reservasjoyaandina@hotmail.com. Includes buffet, breakfast, small carpeted rooms, parking, a bit run-down.
$ Julia, Ferroviaria 314 y Arce, T693 2134, juliahotel5@hotmail.com. Includes breakfast, spacious rooms, cheaper with shared bath, electric showers, internet extra.

Salar de Uyuni *p65*
These *hoteles de sal* are generally visited on tours, seldom independently. See also Tayka in What to do, below.
$$$$-$$$ Luna Salada, 5 km north of Colchani near the edge of the salar, T7242 9716, La Paz T02-278 5438, www.lunasaladahotel.com.bo. Lovely salt hotel,

with breakfast, comfortable rooms, hot water, ample common areas with lovely views of the Salar, salt floors, skylights make it warm and cosy, reserve ahead.
$$$ Palacio de Sal, on the edge of the salar, near the ramp outside Colchani, www.palaciodesal.com.bo. Book through **Hidalgo Tours**, Potosí, T02-622 5186. Includes buffet breakfast, spacious, luxury salt hotel, decorated with large salt sculptures, heating, sauna, lookout on 2nd storey with views of the salar.
$ Alojamiento del Museo de Sal, on the road to the Salar from Colchani, by the *tranca*, T7272 0834. Simple cheap salt hotel, shared bath, kitchen facilities, dining area used by groups, has a small museum with salt sculptures, reserve ahead, good value.

San Cristóbal *p65*
$$ Hotel San Cristóbal, in centre, T7264 2117. Purpose-built and owned by the community. The bar is inside a huge oil drum, all metal furnishings. The rest is comfortable if simple, very hot water, good breakfast included, evening meal extra.

There are also a couple of inexpensive *alojamientos* in town.

🍴 Restaurants

Uyuni *p64, map p64*
Plaza Arce has various tourist restaurants serving mostly mediocre pizza.
$$-$ Kactus, Bolívar y Ferrovaria, daily 0830-2200. Set lunches and international food à la carte, also sells pastries and whole-wheat bread, slow service.
$$-$ La Loco, Av Potosí y Camacho, T693 3105. Mon-Sat 1600-0200 (food until about 2130), closed Jan-Feb. International food with a Bolivian and French touch, music and drinks till late, open fire, popular, reserve in Jul-Aug. Also run a small exclusive guest-house: **La Petite Porte**.
$ Arco Iris, Plaza Arce. Daily 1600-2230. Good Italian food, pizza, and atmosphere, occasional live music.

$ Extreme Fun Pub, Potosí 9. Restaurant/pub, pleasant atmosphere, good service, videos, friendly owner is very knowledgeable about Bolivia.
$ Minuteman, pizza restaurant attached to **Toñito Hotel** (see above), good pizzas and soups, also breakfast.

🎯 What to do

Uyuni *p64, map p64*
There are over 70 agencies in Uyuni offering salar tours and quality varies greatly. You generally get what you pay for but your experience may depend more on your particular driver, cook and companions than the agency that sells you the tour. Travel is in 4WD Landcruisers, cramped for those on the back seat, but the staggering scenery makes up for any discomfort. Always check the itinerary, the vehicle, the menu (especially vegetarians), what is included in the price and what is not. Trips are usually 3 to 4 days (3 is too short): Salar de Uyuni, Reserva Eduardo Avaroa, and back to Uyuni or on to San Pedro de Atacama (Chile); or Tupiza to Uyuni, San Pedro de Atacama or back to Tupiza. Prices range from US$50-350 pp plus park fee of Bs 150 (US$22) The cheapest tours are not recommended and usually involve crowding, insufficient staff and food, poor vehicles (fatal accidents have taken place) and accommodation. The best value is at the mid- to high-end, where you can assemble your own tour for a total of 4 to 5 passengers, with driver, cook, good equipment and services. Two factors often lead to misunderstandings between what is offered and what is actually delivered by the tour operator: 1) agencies pool clients when there are not enough passengers to fill a vehicle. 2) Agencies all over Bolivia sell Salar tours, but booking from far away may not give full information on the local operator. If the tour seriously fails to match the contract and the operator refuses any redress, complaints can be taken to the

Subprefectura de Potosí in Uyuni (see above) but don't expect a quick refund or apology. Try to speak to travellers who have just returned from a tour before booking your own, and ignore touts on the street and at the rail or bus stations.

Tour operators

Andes Travel Office (ATO), in Hotel Tambo Aymara (see above), T693 2227, tamboaymara@gmail.com. Upmarket private tours, Belgian-Bolivian owned, English and French spoken, reliable.
Andrea Tours, Arce y Potosí, T693 2638.
Coquesa Tours, Av Ferroviaria 326, T693 3565, coquesatours@hotmail.com.
Esmeralda, Av Ferroviaria y Arce, T693 2130, esmeraldaivan@hotmail.com. Economical end of market.
Fremen Creative Tours, Sucre 362, T693 3543, www.salar-amazon.com. Long-established company, partners in the Tayka chain of hotels, see below, tours in the region and throughout the country, with offices in La Paz, Cochabamba, Santa Cruz and Trinidad.
Oasis Odyssey, Av Ferroviaria, T693 3175, www.oasistours-bo.com. Also have office in Sucre.
Reli Tours, Av Arce 42, T693 3209.
Ripley Tours, in Hotel Palace, Plaza Arce y Av Ferroviaria, T693 3102. Owner speaks English.
Tayka, Sucre 7715 entre Uruguay y México, T693 2987, La Paz T7205 3438, www.taykahoteles.com.Tayka Hoteles Ecológicos Comunitarios, is a chain of 4 upmarket hotels in Salar de Uyuni-REA area, operating in conjunction with local communities. The hotels (one is built of salt) have comfortable rooms with bath, hot water, heating, restaurant, price in **$$$** range (discounts in low season), including breakfast.
Toñito Tours, Av Ferroviaria 152, T693 3186, www.bolivianexpeditions.com. Own hotel at Bella Vista on the edge of the Salar. Works mostly with organized groups, no walk-ins.

San Cristóbal *p65*
Llama Mama, T7240 0309. 60 km of exclusive bicycle trails descending 2-3 or 4 hrs, depending on skill, 3 grades, US$20 pp, all inclusive, taken up by car, with guide and communication.

⊖ Transport

Uyuni *p64, map p64*
Air To/from **La Paz**, **Amaszonas**, Potosí y Arce, T693 3333, 1 or 2 daily, US$143.
Bus Most offices are on Av Arce and Cabrera. To **La Paz**, US$17-12, 11 hrs, daily at 2000 (La Paz-Uyuni at 1900) with Panasur, www.uyunipanasur.com, and Trans Omar, www.transomar.com; or transfer in Oruro. Tourist buses with **Todo Turismo**, T693 3337, daily at 2000, US$33 (La Paz office, Plaza Antofagasta 504, Edif Paola, p1, opposite the bus terminal, T02-211 9418, daily to Uyuni at 2100), note this service does not run if the road is poor during the rainy season. **Oruro**, several companies 2000-2130, US$6, 7 hrs; **Todo Turismo** (see above), US$20. To **Potosí** several companies around1000 and 1900, US$5.50, 6 hrs, spectacular scenery. To **Sucre**, 6 de Octubre and **Emperador** at 1000, US$10, 9 hrs; or transfer in Potosí. To **Tupiza** US$7.50, 8 hrs, via **Atocha**, several companies daily at 0600 and 2030 (from Tupiza at 1000 and 1800), continuing to **Villazón** on the Argentine border, US$10, 11 hrs. For **Tarija** change in Potosí or Tupiza. Regional services to villages in **Nor- and Sud-López** operate about 3 times a week, confirm details locally. To **Pulacayo** take any bus for Potosí.
Road and train A road and railway line run south from Oruro, through Río Mulato, to Uyuni (323 km, each about 7 hrs). The road is sandy and, after rain, very bad, especially south of Río Mulato. The train journey is more comfortable. **Expreso del Sur** leaves for **Oruro** on Thu and Sun at 0005, arriving 0700. **Wara Wara del Sur** leaves on Tue and Fri at 0145, arriving 0910

(prices for both under Oruro, page 63). To Atocha, Tupiza and **Villazón Expreso del Sur** leaves Uyuni on Tue and Fri at 2240, arriving, respectively, at 0045, 0400 and 0705. **Wara Wara** leaves on Mon and Thu at 0250, arriving 0500, 0835 and 1205. The ticket office (T693 2320) opens Mon-Fri 0900-1200, 1430-1800, Sat-Sun 1000-1100, and 1 hr before the trains leave. It closes once tickets are sold – get there early or buy through a tour agent (more expensive). **Travelling to Chile** Chile is 1 hr ahead of Bolivia from mid-Oct to Mar. Do not attempt to take coca leaves across the border; it is an arrestable offence. Also Chile does not allow dairy produce, tea bags, fruit or vegetables to be brought in.

The easiest way is to go to San Pedro de Atacama as part of your tour to the Salar and REA (see above). **Colque Tours** runs 2 mini-buses daily from near the ranger station at Hito Cajones to San Pedro de Atacama, departing 1000 and 1700, US$6.50, 1 hr including stop at immigration. Another vehicle (*tránsito público*) also run from Hito Cajones to San Pedro de Atacama, most days at about 1000, US$6.50. At other times onward transport to San Pedro must be arranged by your agency, this can cost up to US$60 if it is not included in your tour. The ranger station may be able to assist in an emergency. The *tránsito público* leaves San Pedro for Hito Cajones at 0800 or 0830, but sometimes in the afternoon. It is usually booked through an agency in town. **Hostal Marith** (see Uyuni, Where to stay) runs a transport service from Uyuni to San Pedro de Atacama, US$30, confirm details in advance.

From Uyuni to **Avaroa** and on to **Calama**, Centenario, Cabrera y Arce, Sun, Mon, Wed, Thu at 0330, transfer at the border to **Frontera del Norte** (from Calama same days at 0600). To Avaroa, US$6, 4½ hrs; to Calama US$16, 14 hrs allowing 2 hrs at the border.

If driving your own vehicle, from **Colchani** it is about 60 km across to the southern shore of the **Salar**. Follow the tracks made by other vehicles in the dry season. The salt is soft and wet for about 2 km around the edges so only use established ramps. It is 20 km from the southern shore to Colcha K military checkpoint. From there, a poor gravel road leads 28 km to San Juan then the road enters the Salar de Chiguana, a mix of salt and mud which is often wet and soft with deep tracks which are easy to follow; 35 km away is Chiguana, another military post, then 45 km to the end of this Salar, a few kilometres before border at Ollagüe. This latter part is the most dangerous; very slippery with little traffic. Or take the route that tours use to Laguna Colorada and continue to Hito Cajones. **Toñito Tours** of Uyuni will let you follow one of their groups and even promise help in the event of a breakdown. There is no fuel between Uyuni and Calama (Chile) if going via Ollagüe, but expensive fuel is sold in San Pedro de Atacama. Keep to the road at all times; the road is impassable after rain, and there are still a few unmarked sections along the border that are mined!

❶ Directory

Uyuni *p64, map p64*
Useful addresses Immigration: Av Ferroviaria entre Arce y Sucre, T693 2062, Mon-Fri 0830-1230, 1430-1830, Sat-Sun 0900-1100, for visa extensions, also register here before travel to Chile.

Tupiza → *Phone code: 02. Population: 37,000. Altitude: 2975m.*

Set in a landscape of colourful, eroded mountains and stands of huge cactii (usually flowering December-February), Tupiza, 200 km south of Uyuni, is a pleasant town with a lower altitude and warmer climate, making it a good alternative for visits to the Reserva Eduardo Avaroa and the Salar. Several Tupiza operators offer Salar, REA and local tours. Beautiful sunsets over the fertile Tupiza valley can be seen from the foot of a statue of Christ on a hill behind the plaza.

There is good hiking around Tupiza but be prepared for sudden changes of climate including hailstorms, and note that dry gullies are prone to flash flooding. You can also take bike rides, horse and jeep tours in the surroundings. A worthwhile excursion is to **Quebrada Palala** with the nearby 'Stone Forest'. **Oploca** is a small town 17 km northwest of Tupiza with a lovely colonial church (ask around for the key) and a community tourism project. A hostel was under construction in 2011. There is public transport from Tupiza and the walk back along the Río Tupiza is very scenic; leave plenty of time, take water, sun protection, etc.

Tupiza is the base for **Butch Cassidy and the Sundance Kid tours**. The statue in the main plaza is to **Victor Carlos Aramayo** (1802-1882), of the 19th century mining dynasty. Butch and Sundance's last holdup was of an Aramayo company payroll at Huaca Huañusca

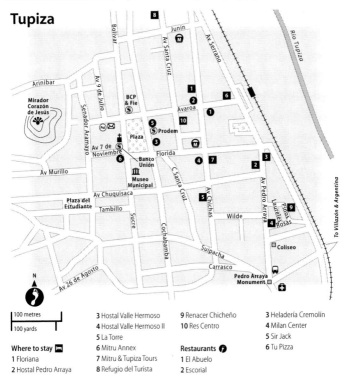

Tupiza

100 metres
100 yards

Where to stay 🛏
1 Floriana
2 Hostal Pedro Araya

3 Hostal Valle Hermoso
4 Hostal Valle Hermoso II
5 La Torre
6 Mitru Annex
7 Mitru & Tupiza Tours
8 Refugio del Turista

9 Renacer Chicheño
10 Res Centro

Restaurants 🍴
1 El Abuelo
2 Escorial

3 Heladería Cremolín
4 Milan Center
5 Sir Jack
6 Tu Pizza

on 4 November 1908. They are believed (by some, see *Digging Up Butch and Sundance*, by Anne Meadows, Bison Books, 2003) to have died soon afterwards at the hands of a police patrol in **San Vicente**, a tiny mining camp at 4500 m, but no grave in the San Vicente cemetery has yet to be positively identified as theirs. There is a small museum with local artifacts but no lodging or other services. Visits can be arranged by Tupiza agencies.

There is no ATM in Tupiuza, take cash; the nearest ATMs in Villazón and Uyuni.

South to Argentine border

Villazón The Argentine border is at Villazón *(Phone code: 02; Population: 39,900; Altitude: 3443 m)*, 81 km south of Tupiza. This is an important crossing but there is not much to see here. Many *casas de cambio* on Av República de Argentina, leading to the border, change US$, pesos and euros, all at poor rates. There are banks and an ATM in town. The border area must not be photographed.

Border with Argentina The Bolivian immigration office is on Avenida República de Argentina just before bridge, open daily 0600-2000, taxi from Villazón bus terminal US$0.50 pp. Queuing begins at 0500 and there may be long delays. Argentine immigration (open 0700-2400 Argentine time, see below) is on the other side of the bridge, 10 blocks from La Quiaca bus terminal, taxi US$1. Change all your bolivianos in Villazón as there is nowhere to do so in La Quiaca or beyond. Entering Bolivia, boys offer to wheel your bags uphill to the bus stations, US$1, but they will ask for more. The Argentine consulate is at Plaza 6 de Agosto 121, T597 2011, Monday-Friday 0800-1300. **Note** Argentine time is one hour later than Bolivia, two hours when Buenos Aires adopts daylight saving.

Tupiza listings

For hotel and restaurant price codes and other relevant information, see pages 9-10.

⊜ Where to stay

Tupiza *p71, map p71*
$$-$ Mitru, Av Chichas 187, T694 3001, www.hotelmitru.com. Pleasant ample grounds with pool, nice atmosphere, a variety of rooms and prices, cheaper in older section with private bath and even cheaper with shared bath. All include good buffet breakfast, reliable solar hot water, parking, luggage store, book exchange; surcharge on credit card payments and TCs. Very helpful and knowledgeable, popular, reserve ahead in high season. Warmly recommended.
$ Floriana, Av Chichas 146, T694 2597. Cheaper with shared bath, electric shower, patio, kitchen and washing facilities.
$ Hostal Pedro Arraya, Av P Arraya 494, T694 2734, hostalarraya@hotmail.com.

Convenient to bus and train stations, small rooms, cheaper with shared bath, hot water, breakfast available, laundry facilities, terrace, family run.
$ Hostal Valle Hermoso, Av Pedro Arraya 478, T694 2592, www.vallehermosotours. com. Breakfast available, cheaper with shared bath, cheaper in dorm. TV/breakfast room, book exchange, motorbike parking, 10% surcharge on credit cards, 20% on TCs. Second location, **Valle Hermoso II**, Av Pedro Arraya 585, T694 3441, near the bus station, 3 simple rooms with bath, several dorms with bunk beds, same prices as No 1, 10% discount for IYHF members in both locations.
$ La Torre, Av Chichas 220, T694 2633, www.latorretours-tupiza.com. Lovely refurbished house, newer rooms at back, comfortable, includes breakfast, cheaper with shared bath and no TV, great service, use of kitchen, good value. Recommended.

$ Mitru Annex, Avaroa 20, T694 3002, www.tupizatours.com. Nicely refurbished older hotel, buffet breakfast, cheaper with shared bath, good hot showers, use of pool and games room at Hotel Mitru.

$ Refugio del Turista, Av Santa Cruz 240, T694 3155, www.tupizatours.com. Refurbished home with garden, shared bath, reliable hot water, well-equipped kitchen, laundry facilities, parking and electric outlet for camper-vans, popular budget option, good value.

$ Renacer Chicheño, C Pinos 18, near bus station, T694 4683, mauroalemant@ hotmail.com. Cheap basic rooms with shared bath, electric shower, use of kitchen.

$ Res Centro, Av Santa Cruz 287, T694 2705. Nice patio, couple of rooms with private bath, most shared, basic but clean, hot water, parking, helpful owner, good value.

Villazón p72

$ Center, Plaza 6 de Agosto 121, T596 5472. Pleasant rooms, electric shower, restaurant, good value.

$ Grand Palace, 25 de Mayo 52 esquina Potosí, 1 block southwest of bus terminal, T596 5333. Older place but adequate, cheaper without bath, shower, no breakfast, helpful management.

$ Hostal Buena Vista, Av Antofogasta 508 y Santa Cruz, T596 3055. Good rooms, hot water, cheaper without bath, close to the train and bus stations, above reasonable restaurant.

$ Hostal Plaza, Plaza 6 de Agosto 138, T597 3535. Adequate rooms, cheaper without bath, electric shower, good restaurant, *La Perla*, underneath hotel, also internet below.

🍴 Restaurants

Tupiza p71, map p71

Several touristy pizza places on C Florida are mediocre to terrible, also watch your belongings here. The best options are just outside town (all **$$-$**), they serve grilled meat and good regional specialties like *picante de cabrito* (spicy goat) but open only Sat or Sun midday – go early. These include: **La Campiña**, in Tambillo Alto, 45 mins' walk north along the river; **La Chacra**, 2 km south on the road to Villazon; and La Estancia, 2 km north in Villa Remedios. There are food stalls upstairs in the market but mind the cleanliness.

$ El Abuelo, Avaroa y Chichas, open daily midday only. Outdoor seating, basic set lunch and grilled meat.

$ Escorial, Chichas esq Avaroa. Set lunch and à la carte in the evening. One of the few places serving decent food but poor service and higher prices for gringos.

$ Milan Center, Chichas y Florida. Pizzeria, reported clean and better than average.

$ Tu Pizza, Sucre y 7 de Noviembre, on Plaza, Mon-Sat 1830-2300. Cute name, variety of pizzas, slow service.

Heladería Cremolín, Cochabamba y Florida, on Plaza, ice cream, juices and fruit shakes.

Sir Jack, Cochabamba 407, on Plaza, daily 0800-1230, 1500-2130. Small place serving *salteñas* in the morning, pizza and snacks in the evening, also sells good whole-wheat bread.

Villazón p72

The restaurant at **Hotel Center** is reported good.

$ Los Alamos, La Paz e Independencia, 1 block from terminal. Serves breakfasts and lunches.

⚙ What to do

Tupiza p71, map p71

One-day jeep tours US$21-25 pp for group of 5; horse riding US$3.50-5 per hr; US$35 per day with food; 2-day San Vicente plus colonial town of Portugalete US$75 pp (plus lodging); Salar de Uyuni and REA, 4 days with Spanish speaking guide, about US$150 pp for a group of 5, plus Bs150 (US$22) park fee. Add US$5 per day for English speaking guide.

Tupiza Tours, in Hotel Mitru (see above), www.tupizatours.com. Highly experienced and well organized for Salar/REA tours. Also offer 1-day 'triathlon' of horse riding, biking and jeep, US$35 pp for group of 5; Butch Cassidy tours, and extensions to the Uyuni tour. Have offices in La Paz and Tarija, and offer tours in all regions of Bolivia. Highly recommended.

Valle Hermoso Tours, in Hostal Valle Hermoso 1 (see above), www.vallehermoso tours.com. Also recommended, offers similar tours, as do several other agencies and most Tupiza hotels.

⊖ Transport

Tupiza *p71, map p71*

Bus There is small, well-organized, bus terminal at the south end of Av Pedro Arraya. To **Villazón** several buses daily, USUS2.75, 2 hrs; also **ATL** mini-buses from opposite terminal, leave when full, US$4.To **Potosí**, several companies around 1000 and 2100, US$5, 8 hrs. To **Sucre**, Expreso Villazón at 1500, Trans Illimani at 2030 (more comfortable but known to speed), US$11, 12 hrs; or transfer in Potosí. To **Tarija**, several around 1930-2030, US$9, 8 hrs (change here for **Santa Cruz**). To **Uyuni**, several companies around 1000 and 1800, US$8, 8 hrs. To **Oruro**, Trans Illimani at 1300, 1800, US$15, 12 hrs; continuing to **Cochabamba**, US$19, 17 hrs. To **La Paz** several at 1200 and 1730-2030, US$19, 16-17 hrs. Agent for the Argentine company **Balut** at terminal sells tickets to Jujuy, Salta, Buenos Aires or Córdoba (local bus to the border at Villazón, then change to Balut), but beware overcharging or buy tickets directly from local companies once in Argentina.

Train Train station ticket office open Mon-Sat 0800-1100, 1530-1730, and early morning half an hour before trains arrive. To **Villazón**: Expreso del Sur Wed and Sat

0410; Wara Wara Mon and Thu at 0905. To **Atocha**, **Uyuni** and **Oruro**: Expreso del Sur Wed and Sat at 1825; Wara Wara Mon and Thu at 1905. Fares are given under Oruro, page 63.

Villazón *p72*

Bus Bus terminal is near plaza, 5 blocks from the border. Lots of company offices. Taxi to border, US$0.50 or hire porter, US$1, and walk. From **La Paz**, several companies, 18 hrs, US$16-28 (even though buses are called 'direct', you may have to change in Potosí), depart La Paz 1630, depart **Villazón** 0830-1000 and 1830-1900. To **Potosí** several between 0800-0900 and 1830-1900, US$9, 10 hrs. To **Tupiza**, several daily, US$2.75. To **Tarija**, US$5.50, 7 hrs. Tickets for buses in **Argentina** are sold in Villazón but beware of scams and overcharging. Buy only from company offices, never from sellers in the street. Safer still, cross to La Quiaca and buy onward tickets there.

Road The road north from Villazón north through Tupiza, Potosí and Sucre, to Cochabamba or Santa Cruz was being widened and paved in 2012. A mostly unpaved but scenic road goes to Tarija. The road linking Potosí with Villazón via Camargo is in poor condition and about 100 km longer than the better road via Tupiza.

Train Station about 1 km north of border on main road, T597 2565, taxi US$2.35. To **Tupiza**, **Atocha**, **Uyuni** and **Oruro**: Expreso del Sur Wed, Sat, 1530, Wara Wara del Sur Mon, Thu 1530. Ticket office open Mon, Thu 0800-1530, Tue, Fri 0800-1200, 1430-1800, Wed 0700-1530, Sat 0700-1000, 1200-1530.

❶ Directory

Tupiza *p71, map p71*

Useful addresses Public Hospital, on Suipacha opposite the bus terminal. IGM office, Bolívar y Avaroa, on Plaza, p 2.

Central and Southern Highlands

This region boasts two World Cultural Heritage sites, the mining city of Potosí, the source of great wealth for colonial Spain and of indescribable hardship for many Bolivians, and Sucre, the white city and Bolivia's official capital. In the south, Tarija is known for its fruit and wines and its traditions which set it apart from the rest of the country.

Potosí → *Phone code: 02. Population: 163,000. Altitude: 3977 m.*

Potosí is the highest city of its size in the world. It was founded by the Spaniards on 10 April 1545, after they had discovered indigenous mine workings at Cerro Rico (4824 m), which dominates the city. Immense amounts of silver were once extracted. In Spain 'es un Potosí' (it's a Potosí) is still used for anything superlatively rich.

By the early 17th century Potosí was the largest city in the Americas, but over the next two centuries, as its lodes began to deteriorate and silver was found elsewhere, Potosí became little more than a ghost town. It was the demand for tin – a metal the Spaniards ignored – that saved the city from absolute poverty in the early 20th century, until the price slumped because of over-supply. Mining continues in Cerro Rico (mainly tin, zinc, lead, antimony and wolfram) and the mountain is riddled with so many tunnels that it could collapse altogether.

Arriving in Potosí
Getting there The airport, possibly the world's highest, is 5 km out of town on the Sucre road. There are no scheduled flights. There is a modern bus terminal (Nueva Terminal), on Av de las Banderas at the north end of the city (taxi US$2; city buses F, I, 150, US$0.20). ▸▸ *See also Transport, page 80.*

Tourist office InfoTur Potosí ⓘ *C Ayacucho, behind the façade of Compañía de Jesús church, T623 1021, Mon-Fri 0830-1230, 1430-1800, Sat 0900-1200.* Also a kiosk on *Plaza 6 de Agosto,* staffed sporadically by tourist police; and information office at bus terminal, *Mon-Fri 0800-1200, 1430-1800.* Beware scams involving fake plainclothes policemen. The official police wear green uniforms and work in pairs. ▸▸ *See also Safety, pages 12 and 17.*

Places in Potosí
Large parts of Potosí are colonial, with twisting streets and an occasional great mansion with its coat of arms over the doorway. The city is a UNESCO World Heritage site. Some of the best buildings are grouped round the Plaza 10 de Noviembre. The old Cabildo and the Royal Treasury – Las Cajas Reales – are both here, converted to other uses. The massive Cathedral faces Plaza 10 de Noviembre.

The **Casa Nacional de Moneda**, or Mint, is nearby ⓘ *on C Ayacucho, T622 2777, Tue-Sat 0900-1230, 1430-1830, Sun 0900-1230, entry US$3, plus US$3 to take photos, US$6 for video, entry by regular, 2-hr guided tour only (in English or French if there are 10 or more people, at 0900, 1030, 1430 and 1630).* Founded in 1572, rebuilt 1759-1773, it is one of the chief monuments of civil building in Hispanic America. Thirty of its 160 rooms are a museum with sections on mineralogy, silverware and an art gallery in a splendid salon on the first floor. One section is dedicated to the works of the acclaimed 17th-18th century religious painter Melchor Pérez de Holguín. Elsewhere are coin dies and huge wooden presses which made the silver strips from which coins were cut. The smelting houses have carved altar pieces from Potosí's ruined churches. You can't fail to notice the huge, grinning mask of Bacchus

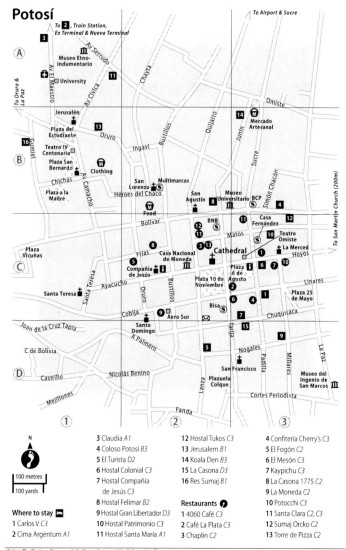

Potosí

Where to stay
1 Carlos V *C3*
2 Cima Argentum *A1*
3 Claudia *A1*
4 Coloso Potosí *B3*
5 El Turista *D2*
6 Hostal Colonial *C3*
7 Hostal Compañía de Jesús *C3*
8 Hostal Felimar *B2*
9 Hostal Gran Libertador *D3*
10 Hostal Patrimonio *C3*
11 Hostal Santa María *A1*
12 Hostal Tukos *C3*
13 Jerusalem *B1*
14 Koala Den *B3*
15 La Casona *D3*
16 Res Sumaj *B1*

Restaurants
1 4060 Café *C3*
2 Café La Plata *C3*
3 Chaplin *C2*
4 Confitería Cherry's *C3*
5 El Fogón *C2*
6 El Mesón *C3*
7 Kaypichu *C3*
8 La Casona 1775 *C2*
9 La Moneda *C2*
10 Potocchi *C3*
11 Santa Clara *C2, C3*
12 Sumaj Orcko *C2*
13 Torre de Pizza *C2*

over an archway between two principal courtyards. Erected in 1865, its smile is said to be ironic and aimed at the departing Spanish. Wear warm clothes; it's cold inside.

Potosí has many outstanding colonial churches. **Convento y Museo de Santa Teresa** ⓘ *Santa Teresa y Ayacucho, T622 3847, only by guided tour in Spanish, French or English, Mon, Wed, Sat at 0900, 1100, 1230, 1700; Tue and Sun 9000, 1100; US$3, US$1.50 to take photos, US$25(!) for video*, has an impressive amount of giltwork inside and an interesting collection of colonial and religious art. Among Potosí's baroque churches, typical of 18th-century Andean or 'mestizo' architecture, are the Jesuit **Compañía** church and bell-gable ⓘ *Ayacucho entre Bustillos y Oruro*, whose beautiful façade hides the modern tourist office building, and whose tower has a **mirador** ⓘ *0800-1200, 1400-1800, 30 mins later Sat-Sun, US$1.40*. **San Francisco** ⓘ *Tarija y Nogales, T622 2539, Mon-Fri 0900-1100, Sat 0900-1100, US$2.15*, with a fine organ, worthwhile for the views from the tower and roof, museum of ecclesiastical art, underground tunnel system. **San Lorenzo** (1728-1744) ⓘ *Héroes del Chaco y Bustillos, mass 0700-1000*, with a rich portal and fine views from the tower. **San Martín** ⓘ *on Hoyos, T622 3682, Mon-Fri 1000-1200, 1500-1830, Sat 1500-1800, free*, with an uninviting exterior, is beautiful inside, but is normally closed for fear of theft. Ask the German Redemptorist Fathers to show you around; their office is just to the left of the church. **La Merced** ⓘ *Hoyos y Millares, Mon-Fri 1100-1230, 1500-1800, Sat 1100-1230, US$1.40 for museo sacro and mirador, US$0.70 for mirador only (with café)*, views of Cerro Rico and the city are great. **Jerusalén** ⓘ *Av Cívica y Oruro, mass Mon-Fri 0800-1100, 1600-1800*. **San Agustín** ⓘ *Bolívar y Quijarro, open only for mass*, has crypts and catacombs (the whole city was interconnected by tunnels in colonial times).

Teatro Omiste (1753) *on Plaza 6 de Agosto*, has a fine façade. The **Museo Universitario** ⓘ *C Bolívar 54 y Sucre, T622 7310, Mon-Fri 0800-1200, 1400-1800, US$0.70*, displays archaeology, fossils, costumes, musical instruments and some good modern Bolivian painting. Guided tour to the *mirador* (tower) offers great views, US$0.70. **Museo del Ingenio de San Marcos** ⓘ *La Paz 1565 y Betanzos, T622 6717, 1000-1500, US$1.40; textiles museum and shop Mon-Sat 1430-2200; restaurant 1200-1500, 1900-2200*. This is a well-preserved example of the city's industrial past, with machinery used in grinding down the silver ore. It also has cultural activities and an exhibition of Calcha textiles. **Museo Etno-indumentario** ⓘ *Av Serrudo 152, T622 3258, Mon-Fri 0900-1200, 1500-1800, Sat 0900-1200, US$1.40, includes tour*. This fascinating museum displays in detail the dress, customs and histories of Potosí department's 16 provinces.

In Potosí, 2000 colonial buildings have been catalogued. Among the better preserved examples is the house of the Marqués de Otavi, now the BNB bank, on Junín between Matos and Bolívar. Next to Hostal Gran Libertador, Millares between Nogales and Chuquisaca, is a doorway with two rampant lions in low relief on the lintel. The Casa de las Tres Portadas (house of the three arches) is now Hostal Tukos, on Bolívar near La Paz.

Mine tours

For many, the main reason for being in Potosí is to visit the mines of Cerro Rico. The state mines were closed in the 1980s and are now worked as cooperatives by small groups of miners in medieval conditions. An estimated 14,000 miners work in 49 cooperatives, some 800 are children. *The Devil's Miner* is a recommended documentary film about child labour in the mines, shown regularly by Potosí agencies and Sucre cafés.

A tour to the mines and ore-processing plant involves meeting miners and seeing them at work first-hand. Mine entrances are above 4000 m and temperatures inside can reach 40ºC, with noxious dust and gasses. You should be acclimatized, fit and have no heart or breathing problems, such as asthma. The length and difficulty of tours varies, up to five hours; you can ask for a shorter, less gruelling, visit if you wish. Not all tours visit the processing plant.

Guided tours are conducted by former miners; by law all guides have to work with a tour agency and carry an ID card issued by the Prefectura. Essential equipment is provided: helmet, lamp and usually protective clothing but large size boots may not be available. Wear old clothes and take torch and a handkerchief or mask to filter the dusty air. The size of tour groups varies, some are as large as 20 people, which is excessive. The smaller the group the better. Tours cost about US$20 per person for two people, US$10 for four, and include transport. Many agencies say they give part of their proceeds to miners but such claims are difficult to verify. You can also contribute directly, for example by taking medicines to the health centre (*Posta Sanitaria*) on Cerro Rico. Saturday and Sunday are the quietest days (Sunday is the miners' day off). **Note** tourists are not allowed to buy dynamite to give to miners.

Museo Histórico Minero Diego Huallpa ① *by Mina Pailaviri on Cerro Rico, city buses P, Q, 70 and others, T623 1143, Mon-Sat 0900-1200, 1430-1800, Sun 0900-1500, US$10*, has exhibits of minerals and mining techniques, two-hour visits include mine tunnels with mannequins instead of real miners.

Tarapaya

A good place to freshen up after visiting the mines (or to spend a day relaxing) is Tarapaya, 21 km on the road to Oruro, where there are **thermal baths** ① *public pools US$0.60, private baths US$1.20 per hr, family baths US$2.80*, and cabins for rent. On the other side of the river from Tarapaya is a 60-m diameter crater lake, whose temperature is 30-34°C; take sun protection. Below the crater lake are boiling ponds, not fit for swimming. Camping by the lake is possible. **Balneario Miraflores** (25 km) ① *pools US$0.35, private baths US$2.80* has hotter water than Tarapaya, but is not as clean. Minibuses run to both balnearios from outside Chuquimia market on Avenida Universitaria, 0600-1800, US$0.55; taxi US$8.50. Last vehicle back to Potosí from Miraflores at 1800.

Potosí listings

For hotel and restaurant price codes and other relevant information, see pages 9-10.

● Where to stay

Potosí *p75, map p76*
Unless otherwise stated hotels have no heating.
$$$ Coloso Potosí, Bolívar 965, T622 2627, www.potosihotel.com. Comfortable modern rooms with frigo-bar, heating, bath tubs and nice views. Includes buffet breakfast, Wi-Fi, small indoor pool and sauna, parking.
$$$-$$ Hostal Patrimonio, Matos 62, T622 2659, www.hostalpatrimonio.com. Bright, warm, modern hotel. Includes buffet

breakfast, heating, conference facilities, Wi-Fi, frigo-bar and safe in each room, sauna and jacuzzi (suites each have their own).
$$ Cima Argentum, Av Villazón 239, T622 9538, www.hca-potosi.com. Includes breakfast, modern comfortable rooms and suites, warm and bright, Wi-Fi, heating, frigo-bar and safe in each room.
$$ Claudia, Av Maestro 322, T622 2242, www.hotelclaudia.com. Modern hotel, includes buffet breakfast, heating, Wi-Fi, helpful staff.
$$ El Turista, Lanza 19, T622 2492. Older place but well maintained, includes breakfast, heating, Wi-Fi, nice common areas, helpful staff, great view from top rooms.

$$ Hostal Colonial, Hoyos 8, T622 4809.
Older place but well maintained, includes
breakfast, Wi-Fi, carpeted rooms, heating,
bathtubs, frigo-bar.

$$ Hostal Gran Libertador, Millares 58,
T622 7877. Colonial-style hotel, Includes
good buffet breakfast, cafeteria,
comfortable rooms, central heating,
Wi-Fi, quiet, helpful, parking.

$$ Jerusalem, Oruro 143, T622 4633.
Includes breakfast, rooftop terrace, Wi-Fi
extra, ask for newer rooms, older ones small,
dark and overpriced, 10% IYHF discount.

$$-$ Hostal Tukos (Las Tres Portadas),
Bolívar 1092, T623 1025. Old colonial house
with spacious rooms, includes breakfast,
Wi-Fi, skylights, warm and nice.

$ Carlos V, Linares 42, T623 1010,
frontdesk@hostalcarlosv.com. With
breakfast, cheaper without bath, hot water,
Wi-Fi, kitchen facilities, luggage store.

$ Hostal Compañia de Jesús, Chuquisaca
445, T622 3173. Includes simple breakfast,
hot water, upstairs rooms are brighter,
helpful, popular, good value.

$ Hostal Felimar, Junín 14, T622 4357.
Includes breakfast (cheaper with shared
bath), electric showers, internet, 1 roof-top
suite, basement rooms have no exterior
windows but are warm and quiet.

$ Hostal Santa María, Av Serrudo 244,
T622 3255. With electric showers, old beds,
cafeteria, parking.

$ Koala Den, Junín 56, T622 6467,
papamilla@hotmail.com. Private rooms
with bath and breakfast (cheaper in dorm),
heating, Wi-Fi, TV and video, use of kitchen,
popular and often full.

$ La Casona, Chuquisaca 460, T623 0523,
www.hotelpotosi.com. cheaper with
shared bath and in dorm, courtyard,
kitchen facilities.

$ Res Sumaj, Gumiel 12, T622 2336,
hoteljer@ entelnet.bo. Cheap and basic,
small dark rooms with shared bath,
helpful, 10% IYHF discount.

🍴 Restaurants

Potosí *p75, map p76*
$$ 4060 Café, Hoyos y Sucre, open 1600-
late, food until 2300. Restaurant/bar serving
good meals, varied menu, large portions,
nice atmosphere, heating. Recommended.

$$ El Fogón, Frías 58 y Oruro, daily 1200-
2300. Good restaurant/grill and atmosphere.

$$ El Mesón, Tarija y Hoyos at Plaza 10
de Noviembre, T622 3087. Excellent food,
upmarket but good value.

$$-$ Kaypichu, Millares 16, Tue-Sun 0700-
1300, 1700-2300. Breakfast, vegetarian
options, *peña* in high season.

$$-$ La Casona 1775, Frías 41, Mon-Sat
1000-1230, 1815-2400. Good food (meat
fondue and trout recommended), nice
atmosphere and service.

$$-$ Potocchi, Millares 24, T622 2759,
open 0800-2230. International and local
dishes, can accommodate special diets
with advance notice, *peña* in high season.

$ La Moneda, Cobija entre Bustillos y
Oruro (may have moved, ask around),
daily 1200-1430, 1800-2300. Good quality
and value set lunch, less popular for
parrillada in the evening.

$ Sumaj Orcko, Quijarro 46, open 1000-
2200, closed Tue. Set lunch, large portions,
heating, could be cleaner.

$ Torre de Pizza, Matos 14, open 0700-
2200. Pizza, pasta, vegetarian options, also
breakfast, family run, attentive service.

Cafés
Café La Plata, Tarija y Linares at Plaza 10 de
Noviembre, Mon-Sat 1000-2200. Upmarket
place for coffee, sweets and drinks. Nice
atmosphere, English and French spoken.

Chaplin, Matos y Quijarro, Mon-Fri 0830-
1200. Breakfasts and excellent *tucumanas*
(fried empanadas).

Confitería Cherry's, Padilla 8, open
0800-2230. Small economical place,
good cakes, breakfast.

Santa Clara, Quijarro 32 y Matos, also
Sucre 33 y Bolívar and other locations,

Mon-Sat 0700-2300. Popular with locals for afternoon snacks.

✹ Festivals

Potosí *p75, map p76*

Fiesta de Manquiri: on 3 consecutive Sat at the end of **May**/ beginning of **Jun** llama sacrifices are made at the cooperative mines in honour of *Pachamama*. **Carnaval Minero**, 2 weeks before carnival in Oruro, includes Tata Ckascho, when miners dance down Cerro Rico and El Tío (the *Dios Minero*) is paraded. **San Bartolomé**, or **Chutillos**, is held from the middle of **Aug**, with the main event being processions of dancers on the weekend closest to the **24th-26th**; Sat features Potosino, and Sun national, groups. Costumes can be hired in *artesanía* market on C Sucre. Hotel and transport prices go up by 30% for the whole of that weekend. **10 Nov**, Fiesta Aniversiario de Potosí. Potosí is sometimes called the 'Ciudad de las Costumbres', especially at Corpus Cristi, Todos Santos and Carnaval, when special sweets are prepared, families go visiting friends, etc.

☉ Shopping

Potosí *p75, map p76*

Mercado Artesanal, at Sucre y Omiste, Mon-Sat 0830-1230, 1430-1830, sells handwoven cloth and regional handicrafts. Several craft shops on C Sucre between Omiste and Bustillos.
Mercado Central, Bustillos y Bolívar, sells mainly meat and some produce. There are several other markets around town.

♨ What to do

Potosí *p75, map p76*

All agencies offer mine tours (see page 77), trips to the Salar de Uyuni and REA (see page 65 for advice on booking a trip), as well as trekking at Kari-Kari lakes.
Andes Salt Expeditions, Plaza Alonso de Ibáñez 3, T622 5175, www.bolivia-travel.

com.bo. Owner Braulio Mamani speaks English. Also sells bus and flight tickets, and has an office in Uyuni.
Greengo Tours, Quijarro 42, T623 1362, www.greengotours.com.bo. English spoken, good reports.
Hidalgo Tours, Calle Bolívar esquina Junin, T622 9512, www.salardeuyuni.net. Upmarket and specialized services in Potosí and to Salar de Uyuni. Guide Efraín Huanca has been recommended for mine tours.
Koala Tours, Ayacucho 5, T622 2092. Owner Eduardo Garnica speaks English and French. Their mine tours are popular and have been recommended.
Silver Tours, Quijarro 12, T622 3600, www. silvertours.8m.com. Economical mine tours.
Sin Fronteras, Ayacucho 17 y Bustillos, T622 4058, frontpoi@entelnet.bo. Owner Juan Carlos Gonzales speaks English and French and is very helpful. Also hires camping gear.
Turismo Potosí, Lanza 12 y Chuquisaca, T622 8212. Guide and owner Santos Mamani has been recommended.

⊖ Transport

Potosí *p75, map p76*

Bus Large modern bus terminal (Nueva Terminal, use fee US$0.30) with ATMs, luggage store, information office, Tourist Police and food court. **Note** it is far from the centre and there are no city buses or taxis late at night; not safe to go out on the street, try to arrive by day or wait inside until morning. Daily services: **La Paz** several companies 1900-2230, US$7, 10 hrs by paved road; *bus cama* US$16 (departures from La Paz 1830-2030). To travel by day, go to **Oruro**, San Miguel and others, all day, US$4.50, 5 hrs. **Cochabamba** several companies 1830-2030, US$7.50, 10 hrs; San José at 0500 and 1530. **Sucre** frequent service 0630-1800, US$2.50, 3 hrs; also shared taxis from behind the old bus terminal, **Cielito Lindo**, T624 3381, 2½ hrs, US$6 pp, drop-off at your hotel. For **Santa Cruz** change in Sucre or Cochabamba.

SALT FLAT UYUNI

www.salardeuyuni.net

HOTELES
RÚSTICOS JARDINES

Palacio de Sal
HOTEL : SPA & GOLF COURSE
PRIMER HOTEL DE SAL EN EL MUNDO

El Jameson
RESTAURANT

Tupiza several companies around 0730 and 2000, US$5, 8 hrs; continuing to **Villazón**, US$9, 10 hrs. **Tarija** several companies 1800-1830, US$8.50, 11 hrs, spectacular journey. To go by day take a bus to **Camargo**, 6 hrs, US$6, then change. Buses to **Uyuni** leave from either side of the railway line at Av Toledo y Av Universitaria, 1000-1200 and 1800-2000, US$5, 5-6 hrs on a partly paved road, superb scenery; book in advance.

Train Station is at Av Sevilla y Villazón, T622 3101. A 25-passenger railcar to **Sucre** Tue, Thu, Sat 0800, 6 hrs, US$3.50; seldom-used service, confirm details in advance.

① Directory

Potosí *p75, map p76*
Airline offices Areo Sur, Cobija 25, T622 8988, nearest flights are from Sucre. **Useful addresses** Migración: Calama 188 entre Av Arce y Av Cívica, T622 5989. Mon-Fri 0830-1230, 1430-1830, beware unnecessary charges for extensions. **Police station:** on Plaza 10 de Noviembre. Emergency T110.

Sucre → *Phone code: 04. Population: 272,000. Altitude: 2,790 m.*

Founded in 1538 as La Plata, it became capital of the audiencia of Charcas in 1559. Its name was later changed to Chuquisaca before the present name was adopted in 1825 in honour of the second president of the new republic. Sucre is sometimes referred to as La Ciudad Blanca, owing to the tradition that all buildings in the centre are painted in their original colonial white. This works to beautiful effect and in 1991 UNESCO declared the city a World Heritage site. There are two universities, the older dating from 1624. From 1825 to 1899 Sucre was capital of Bolivia, but lost this role in all but name to La Paz after a civil war. *La capitalidad* remains an emotionally charged issue among *sucrenses*, who strive to see Sucre regain its status as true capital.

Arriving in Sucre
Getting there Juana Azurduy de Padilla airport is 5 km northwest of town (T645 4445); US$3.50. Bus terminal is on north outskirts of town, 3 km from centre on Ostria Gutiérrez, T644 1292; taxi US$1.15; Micro A or 3. Taxis cost US$0.60 per person within city limits.
➤ *See also Transport, page 88.*

Tourist office Dirección de Turismo de la Alcaldía ① *Argentina 65, p 2, Casa de la Cultura, T643 5240, www.sucreturistico.gob.bo, Mon-Fri 0800-1200, 1400-1800,* some English spoken; also have information kiosks at the airport, bus terminal, **Plazuela Libertad** ① *Destacamento 111 y Arenales* and La Recoleta ① *Polanco e Iturrichia.* **Tourist office** ① *Estudiantes 25, T644 7644, open Mon-Fri 0900-1200, 1500-1830,* staffed by university students (open only during term). **Safety** Caution is advised after 2200 and in market areas.

Places in Sucre centre
Plaza 25 de Mayo is large, spacious, full of trees and surrounded by elegant buildings. Among these are the **Casa de la Libertad** ① *T645 4200, www.casadelalibertad.org.bo, Tue-Sat 0900-1230, 1430-1800, US$2.15 with tour; US$5.80 video.* Formerly the Assembly Hall of the Jesuit University, where the country's Declaration of Independence was signed, this house contains a famous portrait of Simón Bolívar by the Peruvian artist Gil de Castro, admired for its likeness. Also on the Plaza are the beautiful 17th century **Cathedral** and **Museo Eclesiástico** ① *Ortiz 61, T645 2257, Mon-Fri 1000-1200, 1500-1700, US$1.45.* Worth

seeing are the famous jewel-encrusted Virgin of Guadalupe, 1601, and works by Viti, the first great painter of the New World, who studied under Raphael.

San Felipe Neri ① *entrance through school, Ortiz 165 y Azurduy, T645 4333, Mon-Sat 1400-1800, US$1.45 (extra charge for photos).* Visits include the neoclassical church with its

Sucre

Where to stay 🛏
1 Austria *B3*
2 Avenida *B1*
3 Casa de Huéspedes Finita *D3*
4 Casa Kolping *D3*
5 Cretassic Hostal *B1*
6 El Hostal de Su Merced *D2*
7 Grand *C2*
8 Hostal Charcas *C2*
9 Hostal Colón 220 *D1*
10 Hostal Cruz de Popayán *C1*
11 Hostal Los Pinos *D1*
12 Hostal Patrimonio *D2*
13 Hostal San Francisco *B2*
14 Hostal San Marcos *B2*
15 Hostal Santa Teresa de Jesús *D3*
16 Hostelling International Sucre *B3*
17 ICBA Wasi & Kultur-Café Berlin *D3*
18 Independencia *C2*
19 La Posada *D2*
20 Pachamama Hostal *A3*
21 Paola Hostal *D1*
22 Parador Santa María La Real *D2*
23 Real Audiencia *D3*
24 Res Bolivia *C2*
25 San Marino Royal *C2*
26 Villa Antigua *D3*
27 Villa de la Plata *B3*

Restaurants 🍴
1 Amsterdam *C3*
2 Bibliocafé *D2*
3 Café Florín *D2*
4 Café Mirador *D3*
5 Cumaná *D3*
6 El Germen *C3*
7 Flavour Sucre *D1*
8 Joy Ride Café, tour agency & shop *D2*
9 Las Delicias *C2*
10 La Taverne *C2*
11 La Vieja Bodega *D2*
12 Locot's Café Aventura *C3*
13 Los Balcones *C2*
14 Pizzería Napoli *D2*

courtyard, the crypt and the roof (note the penitents' benches), which offers fine views over the city. The monastery is used as a school. Diagonally opposite is the church of **La Merced** ⓘ *T645 1338*, which is notable for its gilded central and side altars. **San Miguel** ⓘ *Arenales 10, T645 1026, mass Mon-Sat 0800 and 1915, Sun 1100, no shorts, short skirts or short sleeves allowed*, completed in 1628, has been restored and is very beautiful with Moorish-style carved and painted ceilings, *alfarjes* (early 17th century), pure-white walls and gold and silver altar. In the Sacristy some early sculpture can be seen. Santa Mónica, Arenales y Junín, is perhaps one of the finest gems of Spanish architecture in the Americas, but has been converted into the theatre and hall for Colegio Sagrado Corazón. **San Francisco** (1581) ⓘ *Ravelo y Arce, mass daily 0700 and 1900, Sun also 1030 and 1700*, has altars coated in gold leaf and 17th century ceilings; one of its bells summoned the people of Sucre to struggle for independence. **San Lázaro** (1538) ⓘ *Calvo y Padilla, mass daily 0700, Sun also 1900*. This is regarded as the first cathedral of La Plata (Sucre). On the nave walls are six paintings attributed to Zurbarán; it has fine silverwork and alabaster in the Baptistery. San Miguel, San Francisco and San Lázaro are only open during mass. **Monasterio de Santa Clara** ⓘ *Calvo 212, mass daily 0730, museum open Mon-Fri 1400-1800, Sat 1400-1730, US$2, good guided tours in Spanish*, Displays paintings by Bitti, sculptures, books, vestments, some silver and musical instruments (including a 1664 organ). Small items made by the nuns on sale.

The excellent **Museo de Arte Indígena ASUR** (Museo Téxtil Etnográfico) ⓘ *opposite Casa Kolping in La Recoleta, T645 3841, www.asur.org.bo, Mon-Fri 0830-1200, 1430-1800, Sat from 0930, US$2.25, English and French-speaking guides*, displays regional textiles and traditional techniques, shop sells crafts. Near the main plaza is the **Museo Nacional de Etnografía y Folklore (MUSEF)** ⓘ *España 74 y San Alberto, T645 5293, Tue-Fri 0930-1230, 1430-1830, Sat 0930-1230, free*, with an impressive exhibit of masks. The **Museo Universitario Charcas** ⓘ *Bolívar 698, T645 3285, Mon-Fri 0830-1200, 1430-1800, Sat 0900-1200, 1500-1800, US$2.90, photos extra*, has anthropological, archaeological and folkloric exhibits, and colonial collections and presidential and modern-art galleries.

Four blocks northwest of Plaza 25 de Mayo is the **Corte Suprema de Justicia** ⓘ *Luis Paz Arce 352, Mon-Fri 1000-1200, 1500-1800, free*, the seat of Bolivia's national judiciary and what remains of the city's official status as capital of Bolivia. To enter you must be smartly dressed and leave your passport with the guard; guides can be found in the public relations office. The nearby **Parque Bolívar** contains a monument and a miniature of the Eiffel Tower and Arc de Triomphe in honour of one of Bolivia's richest 20th-century tin barons, Francisco Argandoña, who created much of Sucre's splendour. At the downhill-end of the park is Fuente del Bicentenario, where a sound and light show is displayed ⓘ *Thu-Sun 1900-2100*. The **obelisk** opposite the Teatro Gran Mariscal, in Plazuela Libertad, was erected with money raised by fining bakers who cheated on the size and weight of their bread. Also on this plaza is the Hospital Santa Bárbara (1574).

Around Sucre

Southeast of the city, at the top of Dalence is **La Recoleta**, a lookout with arches, offering good views over the city. Here, within the Franciscan convent of La Recoleta is the **Museo de la Recoleta** ⓘ *Plaza Pedro de Anzúrez, T645 1987, Mon-Sat 0900-1130, 1500-1800, US$1.45 for entrance to all collections, guided tours only*. It is notable for the beauty of its cloisters and gardens; the carved wooden choir stalls above the nave of the church are especially fine (see the martyrs transfixed by lances). In the grounds is the Cedro Milenario, a 1400-year-old cedar. Behind Recoleta monastery a road flanked by Stations of the Cross ascends an attractive hill, **Cerro Churuquella**, with large eucalyptus trees on its flank, to a statue of Christ at the top. In the **Cementerio General** are mausoleums of presidents and other famous people, boys give guided tours; take Calle Junín south to its end, 8 blocks from main plaza.

About 5 km south on the Potosí road is the **Castillo de la Glorieta** ① *Mon-Sat 0830-1200, 1300-1700, US$0.75, take Micro 4 marked Liceo Militar.* The former mansion of the Argandoña family, built in a mixture of contrasting European styles with painted ceilings, is in the military compound. Ask to see the paintings of the visit of the pope, in a locked room. Some 3 km north of Sucre is **Cal Orcko**, considered the world's largest paleontological site, where tracks from eight types of dinosaur have been identified (inside the Fancesa cement works, not open to the public). Nearby is **Parque Cretácico** ① *T645 7392, Mon-Thu 0900-1700, Fri-Sat 1000-2000, Sun 1000-1700, US$4.35, children US$0.75, crowded at weekends*, with fibreglass dinosaurs, recorded growls, a 30-minute guided tour and binoculars through which (for an extra US$0.30) you can look at the prints on Cal Orcko, 300 m away. The **Sauro Tours** bus leaves daily 0930, 1200, 1430 from corner of cathedral, US$1.75 return, or take Micro 4 from C Junín.

Tarabuco → *Altitude: 3295 m.*

Tarabuco, 64 km southeast of Sucre, is best known for its colourful indigenous market on Sunday, with local people in traditional dress. It starts around 0930-1000 and is very popular with tourists, but is still an enjoyable experience. Textiles are sold in a purpose-built market on Calle Murillo. Next to the market is a small museum, **Incapallay** ① *Murillo 25, T646 1936, www.incapallay.org, Sun 0930-1400*, run by a weavers' association. The *Pujllay* independence celebration on the third Sunday in March is very colourful and lively. No one sleeps during this fiesta but basic accommodation and meals are available. The market is not held at Carnival (when all Tarabuco is dancing in Sucre), Pujllay, Easter Sunday or All Saints' Day.

Sucre listings

For hotel and restaurant price codes and other relevant information, see pages 9-10.

⬤ Where to stay

Sucre *p82, map p83*

$$$ Parador Santa María La Real, Bolívar 625, T643 9630, www.parador.com.bo. Tastefully restored colonial house, includes buffet breakfast, bathtub, safety box, frigobar, heating, Wi-Fi.

$$$ Refugio Andino Bramadero, 30 km from the city towards Ravelo, details from Raul y Mabel Cagigao, Avaroa 472, T645 5592, bramader@yahoo.com, or Restaurant Salamandra (Avaroa 510, good food). Cabins or rooms, well-furnished, full board, drinks and transport included, excellent value, owner Raul can advise on hikes and astronomy, book in advance. Recommended.

$$$ Villa Antigua, Calvo 237, T644 3437, www.villaantiguahotel.com. Tastefully restored colonial house with garden, includes buffet breakfast, Wi-Fi, internet room, Gym, large rooftop terrace has great views, some suites with kitchenette, airport transfers.

$$ Casa Kolping, Pasaje Iturricha 265, La Recoleta, T642 3812, www.grupo-casas-kolping.net. Pleasant, lovely location with nice views, includes buffet breakfast, good **Munay Pata** restaurant (**$$-$**), Wi-Fi and internet lounge, wheelchair access, parking.

$$ El Hostal de Su Merced, Azurduy 16, T644 2706, www.desumerced.com. Beautifully restored colonial building, lots of character, owner and staff speak French and English, good breakfast buffet included, Wi-Fi, sun terrace, restaurant. Recommended.

$$ Hostal Patrimonio, Grau 154, T644 8101, www.hostalpatrimonio.com. Colonial style house with nice common areas, bright warm rooms, some with bathtub, includes breakfast, fridge, Wi-Fi, cafeteria, airport transfer.

$$ Hostal Santa Teresa de Jesús, San Alberto 431, T645 4189. Refurbished colonial house, includes breakfast, restaurant, comfortable, garage. Recommended.

$$-$ Hostelling International Sucre, G Loayza 119 y Ostria Gutiérrez, T644 0471, www.hostellingbolivia.org. Functional hostel 1½ blocks from bus terminal, cheaper without bath and in dorms, breakfast available, kitchen, garden, Wi-Fi, internet extra, parking, discount for HI members.

$$ Independencia, Calvo 31, T644 2256, www.independenciahotel.com. Historic colonial house, opulent salon, spiral stairs, lovely garden, comfortable, some rooms with bathtub, Wi-Fi, café, buffet breakfast included, attentive service.

$$ La Posada, Audiencia 92, T646 0101, www.hotellaposada.com.bo. Smart, colonial-style, includes buffet breakfast, Wi-Fi, good restaurant. Recommended.

$$ Paola Hostal, Colón 138, T645 4978, paolahostal@gmail.com. Comfortable hotel, a bit faded for the price, includes buffet breakfast, cafeteria, bathtub, Wi-Fi, airport transfer, helpful.

$$ Real Audiencia, Potosí 142, T642 5176, www.hotelrealaudiencia.net. Modern, large rooms, includes breakfast, Wi-Fi, restaurant, heated pool. Recommended.

$$ San Marino Royal, Arenales 13, T645 1646, www.sanmarinoroyalhotel.com.bo. Nicely converted colonial house, includes buffet breakfast, frigobar, cafeteria, Wi-Fi, cafeteria, **$$$** for suite with jacuzzi.

$$-$ ICBA Wasi, Avaroa 326, T645 2091, www.icba-sucre.edu.bo. Part of Insituto Cultural Boliviano-Alemán, imaginatively designed, Wi-Fi, spotless rooms with solar hot water, some with kitchenette. Includes breakfast. Recommended.

$ Austria, Av Ostria Gutiérrez 506, by bus station, T645 4202, www.hostalaustria.com. bo. Includes breakfast, hot showers, good beds and carpeted rooms, cafeteria, parking,

cheaper with shared bath and no breakfast, parking extra.

$ Avenida, Av H Siles 942, T645 1245. Shared bath, hot showers, breakfast US$1, use of kitchen, laundry, cheap and basic but adequate, helpful.

$ Casa de Huéspedes Finita, Padilla 233 (no sign), T645 3220, delfi_eguez@hotmail. com. Some rooms with bath, good breakfast included, hot water, heaters, tasty lunch available on request, garden, terrace, also apartments with fully equipped kitchens for longer stays. Good value and recommended for warm family atmosphere.

$ Cretassic Hostal, Av Hernando Siles 901 y Tarapacá, T645 6250, www.hostalcretassic. com. Includes breakfast, rooms with tile floors, Wi-Fi, front rooms noisy but otherwise good.

$ Forastero, Colón 331, T7181-3654, pichicamichel@hotmail.com. Rooms with shared bath, hot water, kitchen facilities, nice garden, friendly owner, English spoken.

$ Grand, Arce 61, T645 2461. Older hotel but well maintained, comfortable, ground floor at the back is noisy, some rooms dark, electric showers, good value lunch in **Arcos** restaurant, Wi-Fi in patio, motorcycle parking.

$ Hostal Charcas, Ravelo 62, T645 3972, hostalcharcas@yahoo.com. Cheaper without bath or TV, good value, huge breakfast extra, hot showers, at times runs bus to Tarabuco on Sun.

$ Hostal Colón 220, Colón 220, T645 5823, colon220@bolivia.com. Very nice guest house, cheaper with shared bath, laundry, helpful owner speaks English and German and has tourist information, coffee room.

$ Hostal Cruz de Popayán, Loa 881 y Colón, T644 0889, www.hotelsucre.com. Colonial house with 3 courtyards, rooms are simple to basic, cheaper without bath and in dorm, breakfast included, Wi-Fi in lobby, internet extra, book exchange, arrange transport and language classes. A bit faded, grubby and overpriced; mixed reports.

$ Hostal los Pinos, Colón 502, T645 5639. Comfortable, hot showers, garden, quiet, peaceful, includes breakfast, kitchen, parking.

$ Hostal San Francisco, Av Arce 191 y Camargo, T645 2117. Colonial building, electric showers, breakfast available, quiet, patio, good value.

$ Hostal San Marcos, Arce 233, T646 2087. Cheaper without bath, more for apartment with kitchenette, patio, use of kitchen, quiet. A bit run-down but good value.

$ Pachamama Hostal, Arce 450, T645 3673, hostal_pachamama@hotmail.com. Simple rooms with bath, electric shower, kitchen facilities, pleasant patio, parking, good value.

$ Res Bolivia, San Alberto 42, T645 4346. Includes good breakfast, cheaper without bath or breakfast, spacious rooms, some old beds, electric showers, Wi-Fi in patio, clothes washing not allowed, helpful.

$ Villa de la Plata, Arce 369, T645 6849, villadelaplata888@gmail.com. Good value apartments with kitchenette, discounts for long stays, popular.

🍴 Restaurants

Sucre *p82, map p83*
Sausages and chocolates are among the locally produced specialties. Many visitors to Sucre develop stomach problems, be extra careful with raw vegetables and fruits here.

$$ Cumaná, Plaza Cumaná, east of the centre. Good *churrasquería* (grill).

$$ El Huerto, Ladislao Cabrera 86, San Matías, T645 1538. International food with salad bar, good *almuerzo*, in a beautiful garden, daily 1130-1600 and Thu-Sun 1830-2100. Take a taxi there at night.

$$ La Taverne of the **Alliance Française**, Arce 35. Mon-Sat 1200-1500, 1800-2230, Sun 1900-2200, lovely terrace seating, weekly lunch specials, international food, also regular cultural events.

$$-$ El Germen, San Alberto 231. Mon-Sat 0800-2200. Mostly vegetarian, set lunches, excellent breakfast, German pastries, book exchange, German magazines. Recommended.

$$-$ Los Balcones, Plaza 25 de Mayo 33, upstairs. Good food, popular with locals, set

lunch with salad bar, open 1200-2400, views over plaza.

$ Pizzería Nápoli, Argentina 85, daily 1800-2330. Good wood-oven pizzas and pasta.

Cafés

Amsterdam, Bolivar 426, Mon-Fri from 1200, Sun from 1530. Drinks, snacks and meals, book exchange, Wi-Fi, live music Wed-Thu. Dutch run, works witha programme for migrant children from the countryside.

Bibliocafé, N Ortiz 38, near plaza. Good pasta and light meals, *almuerzo* 1200-1500, 1800-0200, Sun 1900-2400, music and drinks, Wi-Fi.

Café Florín, Bolívar 567, daily 0730-0200, weekends to 0300. Breakfast, sandwiches, snacks and international meals (**$$**), large portions, micro brews. Sunny patio, Wi-Fi, tour bookings, cosy atmosphere. Dutch run, popular.

Café Mirador, Pasaje Iturricha 297, La Recoleta. Very good garden café, fine views, good juices, snacks and music, popular, open 0930-2000.

Flavour Sucre, Bustillos 117, Mon-Fri 1000-1930, Sat 1000-1630. Good pastries, coffee, chesses and other imported products, Dutch-run.

Joy Ride Café, N Ortiz 16, www.joyridebol. com, daily 0730-2300. Great international food and drink, music, Wi-Fi, very popular, upstairs lounge shows films, also cultural events.

Kultur-Café Berlin, Avaroa 326, same building as *Instituto Cultural Boliviano Alemán*, Mon-Sat 0830-2300. Good breakfasts, German newspapers, cultural events every other Fri.

Las Delicias, Estudiantes 50, Mon-Sat 1600-2000. Great cakes and snacks, popular.

La Vieja Bodega, N Ortiz 38. Good value pasta, pizza and *pique macho*.

Locot's Café Aventura, Bolívar 465, Mon-Sat 0800-0000, Sun 1100-2300. Bar serving international and Mexican food (poor set lunch), live music and theatre, Wi-Fi, also offer adventure tours.

🍷 Bars and clubs

Sucre *p82, map p83*
Mitos, Pje Tarabuco y Junín. Disco, popular
with travellers, Thu-Sat 2200-0300.
Stigma, Bolívar y Camargo. Varied music,
young crowd.
Tabaco's, Eduardo Berdecio, east of
centre. Varied music, popular with
university students.

❋ Festivals

Sucre *p82, map p83*
24-26 May: Independence celebrations,
most services, museums and restaurants
closed on 25. **8 Sep**: Virgen de Guadalupe,
2-day fiesta. **21 Sep**: Día del Estudiante,
music around main plaza. **Oct/Nov**: Festival
Internacional de la Cultura, 2nd week,
shared with Potosí.

⟳ Shopping

Sucre *p82, map p83*
Handicrafts ASUR, opposite Casa
Kolping in La Recoleta. Weavings from
around Tarabuco and from the Jalq'a.
Weavings are more expensive, but of higher
quality than elsewhere. **Artesanías Calcha**,
Arce 103, opposite San Francisco church.
Recommended, knowledgeable proprietor.
Several others nearby. **Bolsa Boliviana**,
Calvo 64, non-profit with many nice items,
especially bags. **Casa de Turismo**, Bustillos
131, several craft shops and tour operators
under one roof. **Incapallay**, Audiencia 97
y Bolívar, T646 1936, www.incapallay.org.
Fair trade shop selling textiles by Tarabuco
and Jalq'a weavers; also in Tarabuco and
La Paz. Artisans sell their wares at the **La
Recoleta** lookout. **Chocolates Para Tí**,
Arenales 7, Audiencia 68, at the airport and
bus terminal. One of the best chocolate
shops in Sucre. **Taboada**, Arce y Arenales,
at airport and bus terminal, www.taboada.
com.bo. Also very good.

Markets The central market is colourful
with some stalls selling *artesanía*, but
beware of theft and crafty vendors.

⊘ What to do

Sucre *p82, map p83*
Bolivia Specialist, N Ortiz 30, T643 7389,
www.boliviaspecialist.com. Dutchman Dirk
Dekker's agency for local hikes, horse riding
and 4WD trips, all sorts of tours throughout
Bolivia and Peru, bus and plane tickets,
loads of information and connections.
Candelaria Tours, JJ Pérez 303-305 y
Colón, T646 0289, catur@entelnet.bo.
Hikes around Sucre, tours to weaving
communities, English spoken.
Joy Ride Tourism, N Ortiz 2, at corner of
Plaza, T645 7603, www.joyridebol.com.
Mountain- and motor-biking, hiking,
climbing, horse riding, paragliding, tours
to Potosí and Salar de Uyuni.
L y D, final Panamá 127 y Comarapa, Barrio
Petrolero, T642 0752, turismo_lyd@hotmail.
com. Lucho and Dely Loredo and son Carlos
(who speaks English) offer custom-made
tours using private or public transport, to
regional communities and attractions, and
further afield. Recommended.
Locot's Adventure, Bolívar 465, at the
bar, T691 5958. Offers many types of
adventure sports: mountain biking,
hiking, riding, paragliding.
Oasis Tours, Arce 95, of 2, T643 2438,
www.oasistours-bo.com. City walking tour,
indigenous communities, Chataquila, Inca
Trail. Also sell bus tickets and have their
own office in Uyuni for Salar trips. Very
helpful owner.
Seatur, Plaza 25 de Mayo 24, T646 2425.
Local tours, hiking trips, English, German,
French spoken.

⊖ Transport

Sucre *p82, map p83*
Air Aero Sur (Arenales 31, T646 2141) flies
to **La Paz** and **Santa Cruz**. BoA (Calvo 94,

T691 2325) 3 per week to Cochabamba. **TAM** (Arenales 217, T646 0944) daily to **La Paz**, **Santa Cruz** and **Cochabamba**, 5 weekly to **Tarija** and 2 weekly to **Yacuiba**. **Aerocon** (at airport, T645 0007) flies to **Trinidad**. Airport tax US$1.60. Micros 1, D and F go from entrance to Av Hernando Siles, a couple of blocks from main plaza, US$0.20, 25 mins. Taxi US$3.50.

Bus Daily to/from **La Paz** several companies at 1700-2000, 12 hrs, regular US$7-10, *semi-cama* US$12-13, *cama* US$18-20. To **Cochabamba**: several companies daily at 1830-1930, 9 hrs via Aiquile; at 2100 via Oruro, 12 hrs, US$6-7.50. To **Potosí**: frequent departures between 0630 and 1800, US$2.15-2.50, 3 hrs. Shared taxis with pick up service: **Cielito Lindo**, at Casa de Turismo, Bustillos 131, T643 2309, **Cielito Express**, T643 1000 and **Expreso Dinos**, T643 7444, both outside the bus terminal, 2½ hrs, US$6 pp. To **Oruro**: 2000-2200, 4 companies via Potosí, 8 hrs, US$7-8.70. To **Tarija**: 4 companies, at 1500-1600, 14 hrs, US$9-14 via Potosí. To **Uyuni**: direct at 0830, **6 de Octubre**, 9 hrs, **Emperador** 0700, 1230, with change and 2-hr wait in Potosí, US$7.25-10. Or catch a bus to Potosí and change; try to book the connecting bus in advance. To **Villazón** via Potosí and Tupiza: at 1330, 1730, **6 de Octubre**, 12 hrs, US$11.60; to **Tupiza**, 9 hrs, US$9.50. To **Santa Cruz**: many companies 1600-1730, 15 hrs, US$10-12; *semi cama* US$15.

To Tarabuco Mini-vans leave when full from C Túpac Yupanqui (Parada de Tarabuco), daily starting 0630, US$1, 1¼ hrs on a good paved road. To get to the Parada take a micro "C" or "7" from the Mercado Central. Also buses to Tarabuco from Av de las Américas y Jaime Mendoza, same fare and times. Tourist bus from the Cathedral on Sun at 0830, US$5 round-trip, reserve at Oasis Tours (address above); also **Real Audiencia**, depart San Alberto 181 y España, T644 3119, at 0830, return 1330; you must use the same bus you went on. Shared taxi with **Cielito Lindo** (see

transport to Potosí above), Sun at 0900, US$5 return.

Car hire Imbex, Serrano 165, T646 1222, www.imbex.com. Recommended.

Road 164 km from **Potosí** (fully paved), 366 km to **Cochabamba** (paved 100 km to Puente Arce; under construction in 2012 from there to Aiquile; 50 km, dirt and poor from Aiquile to Epizana, then paved).

Train To **Potosí**, 20-passenger railcar at 0800, Mon, Wed, Fri, US$3.60, 6 hrs. Station at El Tejar, 1 km south on Potosí road, take Micro 4, T644 0751.

ⓘ Directory

Sucre *p82, map p83*

Cultural centres The Instituto Cultural Boliviano-Alemán (ICBA, Goethe Institute), Avaroa 326, T645 2091, www.icba-sucre. edu.bo. Has a lending library with Spanish and German books and newspapers (0930-1230, 1500-2100), runs Spanish, German, Portuguese and Quechua courses, shows films, runs cultural events and has the Kulturcafé Berlín (see above). Spanish lessons cost from US$7.50 for 45 mins for 1 person, with reductions the more students there are in the class. **Centro Cultural Masis**, Bolívar 561, T645 3403, www.losmasis. com. Teaches local youth traditional music and culture. Stages musical events (daily practice 1900-2000, visitors welcome, contributions appreciated) and exhibitions; items for sale. **Alianza Francesa**, Aniceto Arce 35, T645 3599. Offers Spanish and French classes and stage cultural events. **Centro Boliviano Americano**, Calvo 301, T644 1608. Library open Mon-Fri 0900-1200, 1500-2000 (good for reference works). Recommended for language courses. The **Casa de la Cultura**, Argentina 65, presents art exhibitions, concerts, folk dancing etc. **Language schools** Academia Latinoamericana de Español, Dalence 109, T646 0537, www.latinoschool. com. Professional, good extracurricular activities, US$90 for 20 hrs per week

(US$120 for private teacher – higher prices if you book by phone or email). **Bolivian Spanish School**, C Kilómetro 7 250, T644 3841, www.bolivianspanishschool.com. Near Parque Bolívar, pleasant school, good value, excellent teachers. **Fox Academy**, San Alberto 30, T644 0688. Spanish and Quechua classes, US$5 per hr, non-profit, proceeds go to teaching English to children, volunteering arranged. **Casa Andina de Lenguas**, Loa 779, T645 1687. US$6 per hr. **Sucre Spanish School**, Calvo 350, T643 6727, www.sucrespanishschool.com, US$6 per hr, salsa and cooking classes, friendly and flexible. Several cultural centres also offer language classes. **Medical services** Hospital Santa Bárbara, Ayacucho y R Moreno, Plazuela Libertad, T646 0133, public hospital. Hospital Cristo de las Américas, Av Japón s/n, T644 3269, private hospital. **Useful addresses** Immigration: Bustillos 284 entre La Paz y Azurduy, T645 3647, Mon-Fri 0830-1230, 1430-1830. Police radio patrol: T110.

Tarija → Phone code: 04. Population: 194,000. Altitude: 1840 m.

Tarija has a delightful climate and streets and plazas planted with flowering trees. Formerly known for its fruit, wines and traditions which set it apart from the rest of the country, it has experienced an economic boom and rapid growth since 2005 due to natural gas development in the department. It retains much of its bucolic charm for the time being, but traffic noise and fumes are becoming annoying in the city centre. The best time to visit is from January to April, when the fruit is in season. The indígena strain is less evident here than elsewhere in Bolivia, but Tarija has its own strong cultural heritage. Founded 4 July 1574 in the rich valley of the Río Guadalquivir, the city declared itself independent of Spain in 1807, and for a short time existed as an independent republic before joining Bolivia. In Plaza Luis de Fuentes there is a statue to the city's founder, Capitán Luis de Fuentes Vargas. The **Secretaría de Turismo y Cultura** ① *Ingavi esquina Gral Trigo, T663 1000, Mon-Fri 0800-1200, 1500-1900*, is helpful, city and departmental map. **Dirección Municipal de Turismo** ① *Bolívar y Sucre, Mercado Central, T663 3581, Mon-Fri 0800-1200, 1430-1830*, helpful, city map, Some English spoken; also have a booth at the Terminal de Buses ① *T666 7701, 0700-1100, 1430-2200*. In the wine producing area of **Valle de la Concepción**, **Información Turística** ① *Plaza Principal, T667 2854, Mon-Sat 0800-1600*, offer maps and pamphlets. Note that blocks west of C Colón have a small O before number (oeste), and all blocks east have an E (este); blocks are numbered from Colón outwards. All streets north of Av Las Américas are preceded by N.

Places in Tarija The oldest and most interesting church in the city is the **Basílica de San Francisco** ① *corner of La Madrid y Daniel Campos, 0700-1000, 1800-2000, Sun 0630-1200, 1800-2000*. It is beautifully painted inside, with praying angels depicted on the ceiling and the four evangelists at the four corners below the dome. The library is divided into old and new sections, the old containing some 15,000 volumes, the new a further 5000. To see the library, go to the door at Ingavi O-0137. Behind the church is the **Museo Fray Francisco Miguel de Mari** ① *Colón y La Madrid, T664 4909, 1000-1100, 1600-1700, US$2.85*, with colonial and contemporary art collections, colonial books, the oldest of which is a 1501 *Iliad*, 19th-century photograph albums and other items. Tarija's **Museo de Arqueología y Paleontología** ① *Trigo y Lema, Mon-Fri 0800-1200, 1500-1800, Sat 0900-1200, 1500-1800, US$0.45*, contains a palaeontological collection (dinosaur bones, fossils, remains of several Andean elephants), as well as smaller mineralogical, ethnographic and anthropological collections. **Casa Dorada** ① *Trigo e Ingavi (entrance on Ingavi), guided tours every 30 mins Mon-Fri, US$0.70*. Begun in 1886 and also known as the Maison d'Or, it is now part of Casa de la Cultura. It belonged to importer/exporter Moisés Narvajas and his wife Esperanza Morales and was beautifully restored inside and out in 2009.

The outskirts of the city can be a good place to look for **dinosaur fossils**. Should you find anything, leave it in situ and report it to the university. About 15 km north of the centre is the charming village of **San Lorenzo**. Just off the plaza is the **Museo Méndez** ① *0900-1230, 1500-1830, minimum US$0.30 entry*, the house of the independence hero Eustaquio Méndez, 'El Moto'. The small museum exhibits his weapons, his bed, his 'testimonio'. At lunchtime on Sunday, many courtyards serve cheap meals. Minibuses from Domingo Paz y J M Saracho, every five minutes, US$0.30. The road to San Lorenzo passes **Tomatitas** (5 km) a popular picnic and river bathing area. Other good day trips include the waterfalls at **Coimata** (take micro or taxi from Tomatitas); hiking up the valley at **Rincon de la Victoria** (also via Tomatitas); or hiking the spectacular 1-2 day Camino del Inca from Tajzara in **Reserva de Sama** to Pinos Sud, from where public transport can take you back to the city. For information about the latter contact **SERNAP** (Av Jaime Paz 1171, T665 0605) or the NGO **Prometa** (Alejando del Carpio 659, T664 1880, www.prometa.org.bo).

Tarija produces the best **wine and singani** (brandy) in Bolivia and winemaking is a proud local tradition. To visit a *bodega* (winery, see below) contact their shop in town beforehand to make arrangements or take a tour (see What to do, page 93) which provides transport and allows you to visit several different bodegas on the same day. **Campos de Solana** ① *15 de Abril E-0259 entre Suipacha y Méndez, T664 5498*. Increasingly recognized for their selection of fine wines (the Malbec is highly regarded), as well as the popular Casa Real brand of singani. Their bodega is in El Portillo, 6 km on road to Bermejo. Casa Vieja ① *15 de Abril 540, T667 2349*. A traditional *bodega artesanal*, small-scale winery, located in Valle de la Concepción, 25 km from Tarija. Interesting and recommended. El Potro ① *C José María Villena, San Gerónimo near the airport, T7298 8832, daily 1000-1900*. Guided tours and wine-tasting. **Kohlberg** ① *15 de Abril E-0275, T666 6366*. Largest and most industrialized of the wineries. **La Concepción** ① *Colón y La Madrid, T665 1514*. Wines (try their Cabernet Suavignon) and Rugero singani, bodega in Valle de Concepción. Wine shops (*vinotecas*) include: **Las Duelas Calamuchita** ① *opposite the sports field in village of Calamuchita, T666 8943, daily 0900-1700*. Small winery, *vinos artesanales*, wine-tasting and regional preserves. **La Vinoteca** ① *Ingavi O-0731 y Gral Trigo, Mon-Sat 0900-1900*. For wine, cheese and ham.

To Argentina → *Bolivia is 1-2 hrs behind Argentina, depending on the time of year.*

The road to Villazón (see page 72) is the shortest route to Argentina; 189 km, but a tiring eight hours in all, mostly unpaved and scenic. The alternative route via Bermejo is the most easily reached from Tarija; 210 km all paved, the views are also spectacular (sit on right). **Bermejo** (Population: 13,000, Altitude: 415 m) is well supplied with places to sleep and eat, there are many *casas de cambio*, and this border area is considered safer than Yacuiba (see below). Note there are thorough customs searches here and it's very hot. Expect to spend up to four hours at customs and immigration. An international bridge crosses the river from Bermejo to Aguas Blancas, Argentina. A third option, from Tarija to the Yacuiba/Pocitos border (see page 125), is 290 km. This is the busiest of the border crossings, open 24 hours, and reported less than safe due to drug smuggling.

Tarija listings

For hotel and restaurant price codes and other
relevant information, see pages 9-10.

🛏 Where to stay

Tarija *p90*
Some hotels may offer low-season
discounts, May-Aug.
\$\$\$\$-\$\$\$ Los Parrales Resort, Urb
Carmen de Aranjuez Km 3.5, T664 8444 (ask
for Lic Miguel Piaggio), www.losparrales
hotel.com. Large luxury hotel offering fine
views over the city and surrounding hills.
Includes buffet breakfast, pool, spa, gym,
Wi-Fi in communal areas. Non-guests can
pay to use the pool and other facilities.
\$\$\$ Los Ceibos, Av Las Américas y La
Madrid, T663 4430, www.hotellosceibos.
com. Includes buffet breakfast, large rooms
with frigobar, restaurant/bar, pool, parking,
Wi-Fi in communal areas, mixed reports.
\$\$ Gran Hostal Baldiviezo, La Madrid
O-0443, T663 7711. Includes breakfast,
well-maintained, cheaper with shared bath,
good beds and facilities, central location.
\$\$ Hostal Carmen, Ingavi O-0784, T664
3372, vtb.hostalcarmen@gmail.com.
Older place but well maintained, includes
excellent buffet breakfast, hot water,
Wi-Fi, heating, airport transfers available.
Often full, advance booking advised, very
friendly and helpful, good value, long-stay
discounts. Recommended.
\$\$ Hostal Loma de San Juan, Bolívar s/n
(opposite Capilla Loma de San Juan), T663
6101. Includes breakfast, pool and garden,
Wi-Fi, comfortable rooms.
\$\$ La Pasarela, 10 km north of Tarija near
the village of Coimata, T666 1333, www.
lapasarelahotel.com. Belgian-owned
hotel with good restaurant/bar, includes
breakfast, country views, tranquil, family
atmosphere, living room, jacuzzi, swimming
pool, internet, mountain bikes, laundry and
camping. Larger apartments available for
families and groups.

\$\$ Luz Palace, Sucre 921 y Domingo Paz,
T663 5700, luzpalac@cosett.com.bo.
Includes breakfast, comfortable rooms,
some with frigobar.
\$ Alojamiento Familiar, Rana S 0231
y Navajas, T664 0832. Shared bath, hot
shower, cheap, clean, helpful, close to bus
terminal, traffic noise.
\$ Hostería España, Alejandro Corrado
O-0546, T664 1790. Hot showers, cheaper
with shared bath, cheap simple rooms,
some are dark and dingy.
\$ Miraflores, Sucre 920, T664 3355.
Includes breakfast, hot water, cheaper
rooms with shared bath are simple, popular
place but indifferent service.
\$ Res Rosario, Ingavi O-0777, T664 2942.
Simple rooms, cheaper with shared bath,
hot water, good budget option, family
atmosphere, friendly and helpful.
\$ Zeballos, Sucre 0966, T664 2068. Ageing
hotel, some rooms small, cheaper with
shared bath, includes breakfast, quiet, safe,
central, staff could be friendlier.

🍴 Restaurants

Tarija *p90*
Many restaurants (and much else in town)
close between 1400 and 1600.
\$\$\$-\$\$ Mediterráneo, 15 de Abril y Colón,
Plaza Sucre, T666 6083, daily 1230-1500,
1900-2400. International menu, good trout,
elegant, upscale for Tarija.
\$\$ Don Pepe Rodizio, D Campos N-0138,
near Av Las Américas. Stylish restaurant
serving tasty daily set lunch, all-you-can-eat
rodizio on wekkends for US\$10.
\$\$ El Fogón del Gringo, La Madrid O-1053,
Plaza Uriondo, Mon-Sat 1900-2300, on
Fri-Sun also 1200-1430. Upmarket *parillada*
includes excellent salad bar.
\$\$ La Taberna Gattopardo, on main
plaza, 0800-2100 daily. Pizza, *parillada* with
Argentine beef, local wines, deserts, snacks,
excellent salads, popular meeting place, Wi-Fi.

$ Miiga Comida Coreana, Cochabamba 813 y Ballivian, open every night except Tue. Sushi with salmon and a small but tasty range of Korean dishes

$ El Molino, Ingavi O-550 entre Sarancho y Campero, midday only. Tasty and healthy vegetarian set lunch.

$ El Patio, Sucre N-0458, Mon-Sat. Good set lunch with small salad bar, pleasant seating in patio, also great *tucumanas al horno*.

Cabaña Tentaguazú, Av Heroés del Chaco y Monseñor Font, Barrio Juan XXIII. *Peña/* restaurant serving good local fish and recommended for live folk music on Fri from 2200.

DeliGelato, Colón N-0421, Plaza Sucre, daily until 2130. Good ice cream.

Nougat Café-Bar, Gral. Trigo corner 15 de Abril, daily 0800-2400. Nicely decorated. European-style café. Breakfast, à la carte dishes, snacks and sweets, Wi-Fi.

Pastelería Jenny, 15 de Abril 0215. Good coffee and cakes.

⊛ Festivals

Tarija *p90*

The city is famous for its colourful niño (child) processions on **15 Apr**, Día de Tarija. In the 3-day San Roque festival from the **1st Sun in Sep** the richly dressed saint's statue is paraded through the streets; wearing lively colours, cloth turbans and cloth veils, the men dance before it and women throw flowers from the balconies. Dogs are decorated with ribbons for the day. In **Oct**, Exposur is held, approximately 20 km northwest of city; admission free; local and regional crafts, cuisine, and dances; much commercial activity as well. On **2nd Sun in Oct** the flower festival commemorates the **Virgen del Rosario** (celebrations in the surrounding towns are recommended, eg San Lorenzo and Padcaya). Another flower festival takes place in San Lorenzo in **Easter** week. Also in **Oct**, on 2 weekends mid-month, there is a **beer festival** on Av las Américas. La Virgen de Chaguaya, **15 Aug**, people walk from Tarija to Santuario Chaguaya, south of El Valle, 60 km south of the city. For less devoted souls, Línea P *trufi* from Plaza Sucre, Tarija, to Padcaya, US$1; bus to Chaguaya and Padcaya from terminal daily, 0700, returns 1700, US$1.35.

◔ What to do

Tarija *p90*

Educación y Futuro, at the Ecosol shop, Virgino Lema y Suipacha, Plazuela Sucre, T666 4973, www.educacionyfuturo.com. An NGO offering homestays with rural families, cheese making and guided trekking.

Internacional Tarija, Sucre 721, T664 4446. Flights and tours, helpful.

Mara Tours, Gral Trigo N-739, T664 3490. Helpful.

Sur Bike, Ballivián 601 e Ingavi, T7619 4200. Cycling trips in the countryside outside Tarija US$27-41, for a day trip including snack. Bike rentals US$16.50 per day.

Tupiza Tours, Avaroa 450, entre Isaac Attie y Delgadillo, T7022 5715, www.tupizatours. com. Tarija contact of the Tupiza agency.

VTB, at Hostal Carmen (see Where to stay above). All tours include a free city tour; 4-6 hr trips including bodegas, US$23 pp; comprehensive 10 hr "Tarija and surroundings in 1 Day", US$35; can also try your hand at excavation with palaeontology specialist! Good vehicles, recommended.

Viva Tours, Bolivar 251, Edificio Ex-Hansa, of 6. Vineyard tours US$30 with lunch.

◔ Transport

Tarija *p90*

Air Aero Sur (15 de Abril entre Daniel Campos y Colón, T663 0894) flies daily either to **La Paz**, or **Cochabamba**. BoA (General Trigo 327, T611 1389) flies Mon-Sat to **Cochabamba**, Sun to **La Paz**. TAM (La Madrid O-0470 entre Trigo y Campero, T662 2734), to either **La Paz, Sucre, Santa Cruz** or **Yacuiba**, depending on day of week. Aerocon (Ballivián 525, T665 8634) flies to **Santa Cruz**. Shared taxi from airport to centre, US$0.75 pp, or *micro* A from Mercado Central which drops you 1 block away. Some hotels have free transport to town, you may have to call them. Airport information T664 3135.

Bus The bus station is southeast of centre on Av Las Américas (30-min walk from centre), T666 6701. Note that the **Copa Moya** bus company has a poor safety record. To **La Paz** several buses at 0700-0800 and 1700 (935 km) 17 hrs, US$14, via Potosí and **Oruro** (US$12.50); check which company operates the best buses. To **Potosí**, several additional departures 1630-1800, 10 hrs, US$10. To **Sucre** at 1630 and 1800, US$12.50. To **Tupiza**, Diamante, 1930, and Juárez, 2030, US$9.50, 10 hrs. To **Santa Cruz** via Villamontes, several companies at 1830, US$14, 17 hrs. To get to Villamontes in daylight, take a La Guadalupana or La Entreriana bus from Parada del Chaco (east end of Av Las Américas) to **Entre Ríos**, US$3, 3½ hrs, some continue to Villamontes (spectacular route), mostly in daylight.

To Argentina: to **Villazón**, several companies daily, 1930-2030, 8 hrs, US$5.50, unpaved road. To **Salta**, Dragón Rojo (Chifa), Sucre N-0235, T666 5014, runs private vans departing daily at 0700, US$27, 8-9 hrs. To **Bermejo**, shared taxis leave when full from opposite the bus station, US$5.50, 3 hrs; bus US$3, 4 hrs. Buses to **Yacuiba** US$7, 9 hrs, most depart in the evening.

❶ Directory

Tarija p90
Useful addresses Immigration, Ingavi O-0789, T664 3450, Mon-Fri 0830-1230, 1430-1830. Visa renewals in 48 hrs.

Cochabamba and around → *Phone code: 04. Population: 604,000. Altitude: 2570 m.*

Set in a bowl of rolling hills at a comfortable altitude, Cochabamba enjoys a wonderfully warm, dry and sunny climate. Its parks and plazas are a riot of colour, from the striking purple of the bougainvillaea to the subtler tones of jasmin, magnolia and jacaranda. Bolivia's fourth largest city was founded in 1574 and in colonial times it was the 'breadbasket' of Bolivia, providing food for the great mining community of Potosí. Today it is an important commercial centre. Many visitors particularly enjoy La Cancha market, one of the largest in Bolivia, as well as Cochabamba's very good dining and nightlife.

Fertile foothills surrounding the city still provide much of the country's grain, fruit and coca. Markets, colonial towns and archaeological sites are all close by too. Further afield, the dinosaur tracks and great scenery at Torotoro National Park are worth the exhausting trip. The paved lowland route to Santa Cruz de la Sierra has much more transport than the rough old road over the mountains via Comarapa and Samaipata. Both offer access to Carrasco and Amboro national parks. There is an animal refuge by Villa Tunari, along the lowland road.

Arriving in Cochabamba

Getting there and around The city is served by paved roads from La Paz and Santa Cruz. Neither airport, nor bus station are far from the centre. Buses and taxis serve both. The city is divided into four quadrants based on the intersection of Avenida Las Heroínas running west to east, and Avenida Ayacucho running north to south. In all longitudinal streets north of Heroínas the letter N precedes the four numbers. South of Heroínas the numbers are preceded by S. In all transversal streets west of Ayacucho the letter O (Oeste) precedes the numbers and all streets running east are preceded by E (Este). The first two numbers refer to the block, 01 being closest to Ayacucho or Heroínas; the last two refer to the building's number. ▸▸ *See also Transport, page 102.*

Cochabamba

N

100 metres
100 yards

Where to stay 🛏
1 Americana *D2*
2 Aranjuez *A3*
3 Gran Hotel Cochabamba *A3*
4 Hostal Buenos Aires *A2*
5 Hostal Elisa *D1*
6 Hostal Florida *C2*
7 Hostal Maya *B1*
8 Hostal Ñawpa House & Restaurant Gopal *B2*
9 Hostal Versalles *D1*
10 Hostería Jardín *B1s*
11 Monserrat *A2*
12 Regina *A2*
13 Res Familiar *C2*
14 Res Familiar Annex *B2*
15 Res Jordán *C3*
16 Res Jordán Annex *C2*

Restaurants 🍴
1 Brazilian Coffee *A2*
2 Bufalo *A3*
3 Café París *B2*
4 Casablanca *A2*
5 Churrasquería Tunari *A3*
6 Doña Alcira *A3*
7 Dumbo *A2, B2*
8 Eli's Pizza *B2*
9 Ganesha *A2*
10 La Cantonata *A2*
11 La Estancia *A3*
12 Lai-Lai *A3*
13 Los Castores *A2*
14 Paprika *A3*
15 Sole Mio *A3*
16 Suiza *A2*

Bars & clubs 🍸
17 Cocafé *A2*
18 Green Pepper *A3*
19 La Muela del Diablo *A3*
20 La Tirana *A2*
21 Na Cunna *A3*

Tourist information Dirección de Turismo de la Alcaldía ① *Plaza Colón 448, T425 8030, ext 4419, Mon-Fri 0800-1200, 1430-1830*, is the best option. Other offices at the bus station, Pasaje Catedral, and Jorge Wilstermann airport (0700-1100, 1500-2200). The **departmental tourist office** is at ① *Colombia E-0340, entre 25 de Mayo y España, T422 1793, Mon-Fri 0800-1200, 1430-1830*. **Tourist police** ① *Plaza 14 de Septiembre, north side, T450 3880*. The unofficial web resource for the city: www.bolivia-online.net.

Safety Both Cochabamba city and department have public safety issues. Do not venture into any of the hills around town on foot (including San Pedro with the Cristo de la Concordia, San Sebastián and La Coronilla), take only radio taxis at night, and mind your belongings in markets, on public transport, and other crowded places. In the main towns in the coca growing region of Chapare tourists are reasonably safe, but off the beaten track remains hazardous for outsiders. ▶▶ *See also Safety, page 12.*

Places in Cochabamba

At the heart of the old city is the arcaded **Plaza 14 de Septiembre** with the **Cathedral** ① *Mon-Fri 0800-1200, 1700-1900, Sat-Sun 0800-1200*, dating from 1571, but much added-to. Nearby are several colonial churches: **Santo Domingo**, Santiváñez y Ayacucho, begun in 1778 and still unfinished; **San Francisco**, 25 de Mayo y Bolívar, 1581, but heavily modernized in 1926; the **Convent and Museum of Santa Teresa** ① *Baptista y Ecuador, T422 1252, Mon-Fri 0830-1200, 1430-1800, Sat 1430-1700, US$3, camera US$ 3.50 extra, guides included*, original construction 1760-90, with a beautiful interior; and **La Compañía**, Baptista y Achá, whose whitewashed interior is completely devoid of the usual riot of late Baroque decoration.

Museo Arqueológico ① *Aguirre y Jordán, T425 0010, Mon-Fri 0800-1800, Sat 0830-1200, US$3, free student guide in Spanish (English Mon-Fri 1300-1600)*. Part of the Universidad de San Simón, one of the most complete museums in Bolivia, displaying artefacts including Amerindian hieroglyphic scripts and pre-Inca textiles, through to the colonial era. **Casona Santiváñez** ① *Santiváñez O-0156, Mon-Fri 0800-1200, 1430-1800, free*, has a nice colonial patio, and exhibition of paintings and historic photographs.

From Plaza Colón, at the north end of the old town, the wide **Avenida Ballivián** (known as **El Prado**) runs northwest to the wealthy modern residential areas. To the north of Plaza Colón lies the Patiño family's **Palacio Portales** ① *Av Potosí 1450, T448 6414, guided tours in Spanish Tue-Fri 1530, 1630, 1730, in English 1600, 1700, 1800, Sat in Spanish at 0930, 1000, 1100, English 1100, 1130, Sun Spanish 1100, English 1030, 1130, US$1.50. The gardens are open Tue-Fri 1500-1830, Sat-Sun 0930-1130*. Built in French renaissance style, furnished from Europe and set in 10 ha of gardens inspired by Versailles, the Patiño mansion was finished in 1927 but never occupied. It is now the *Centro Cultural Simón I Patiño*, with an excellent art gallery in the basement. Take micro G from Avenida San Martín.

To the south of the old town lie the bus and train stations and one of the best markets in Bolivia. The huge and fascinating **La Cancha market** ① *between Esteban Arze, Punata, República and Pulacayo*, is open all week but best on Wednesday and Saturday when it is packed with campesinos and trading spills over into surrounding streets. These are tourist items and souvenirs for sale as well as a vast array of foodstuffs and local goods.

Around Cochabamba

Parque Nacional Tunari, 329,183 ha, is just outside the city. Despite this proximity, it remains a beautiful unspoilt natural area and a good place for acclimatization to altitude. There are llamas and alpacas above 4000 m and even the occasional condor. The highest point in the park, Cerro Tunari (5035 m), offers magnificent views. **Note** armed attacks of visitors have taken place along the marked trail from the park entrance in the north of the city. Safer alternatives include the park entrance reached from Quillacollo via the thermal springs of **Liriuni**, with pool and private tubs, worth a visit. There are no signs along this route however, so it may be best to hire a 4WD and a guide. Or you can access the south side of Cerro Tunari from above Hacienda Pairumani (see below) or from Refugio Tunari Mountain Lodge, which arranges tours with pack animals (see page 99).

Quillacollo, 13 km west of the city, has a Sunday market geared entirely to local produce and a famous festival (see page 102 and box, page 98). Take any micro or trufi marked "Quillacollo" along Av Heroinas. Eight km beyond Quillacollo is a turn-off to the beautiful **Hacienda Pairumani** ⓘ *T426 0083 to check if it is open, Mon-Fri 1500-1600, Sat 0900-1130*, centre of the Patiño agricultural foundation, also known as **Villa Albina**, built in 1925-1932, furnished from Europe and inhabited by Patiño's wife, Albina. Take Trufi 211 from Plaza Bolívar in Quillacollo, or directly from Avenida Aroma in Cochabamba. Some 27 km west of Cochabamba are **Inka-Rakay** ruins, with fine views of the Cochabamba valley and the mountains around the ruins. A day trip to the ruins can end at the plaza in nearby Sipe Sipe or one of its local restaurants with a bowl of *guarapo* (wine-based drink) and a plate of *charque* (sun tried beef), served with potatoes, eggs and corn; best at weekends. Or take trufi "Sipe Sipe" from Plaza Bolivar in Quillacollo and get off at the church on the main square, then ask for the way up to the ruins.

Tarata, 33 km southeast of Cochabamba, is a colonial town with a traditional arcaded plaza on which stand the cathedral (daily 0800-1300) and the Casa Consistorial. In the plaza, the clock tower ⓘ *Mon-Fri 0800-1200, 1330-1700, Sat-Sun 0800-1200* houses a German timepiece with chimes. Inside the **Franciscan Convent** overlooking the town ⓘ *Mon-Sat 0930-1130, 1430-1800, US$0.30, guided visits from Casa de Cultura y Turismo, main square, T457 8727*, are the remains of the martyr, San Severino, patron saint of the town, more commonly known as the 'Saint of Rain'; festival, on the last Sunday of November, attracts thousands of people. Large procession on 3 May, day of La Santa Cruz, with fireworks and brass band. Market days Thursday and Sunday (bus US$0.65, one hour, last return 1900). For fine alpaca products, visit Doña Prima Fernández Prado ⓘ *Arce E-0115, opposite the convent*, who sells sweaters, bags and textiles from two rooms off a beautiful colonial patio. The local sausages are nationally famous.

A good way to visit villages around Cochabamba is by **ferrobus**, a bus running on train tracks. It leaves the station in the middle of La Cancha market, on Tuesday, Thursday and Saturday at 0800; returning Wednesday, Friday and Sunday at 0800. The 10 to 12-hour journey goes through more than 17 tunnels and over many bridges, passing through Tarata, Cliza and Mizque to Aiquile, which has basic lodging and where you can catch a bus back to Cochabamba, or on to Sucre or Santa Cruz. Train tickets are sold at the **Estacion Central** ⓘ *C Tarata 442, Plaza San Antonio, T455 6208, Mon-Fri 0800-1200, 1430-1800, Sat 0800-1200, US$3 to Aiquile.*

Parque Nacional Torotoro
ⓘ *Entry US$4.50, payable at the Oficina de Turismo, Calle Cochabamba, Main Plaza, T02-613 8932, 04-413 5736.* In the department of Potosí, but best reached from Cochabamba (150 km), is **Torotoro**, a small village, set amid beautiful rocky landscape in the centre of the Parque Nacional Torotoro, covering an area of 16,570 ha and declared a National Park in 1989. Attractions include caves, a canyon, waterfalls, pictographs, ruins, fossilized dinosaur tracks and rock paintings, some of which can be seen by the Río Toro Toro just outside the

Fiesta de la Virgen de Urkupiña, Quillacollo

The festival is 14-15 August with much dancing and religious ceremony. Plenty of transport from Cochabamba, hotels all full. Be there before 0900 to be sure of a seat, as you are not allowed to stand in the street. The first day is the most colourful with all the groups in costumes and masks, parading and dancing in the streets till late at night. Many groups have left by the second day and dancing stops earlier. The third day is dedicated to the pilgrimage. Full details at www.urcupina.com. (Many buses, micros and *trufis* from Heroínas y Ayacucho, 20 minutes, US$0.30.)

village. **Umajalanta cave**, which has many stalactites and a lake with blind fish, is about 8 km northwest of Torotoro, with an hour's caving (take a head torch if possible). **El Vergel** waterfalls are fantastic and the walk along the river bed is great fun if you like rock-hopping and skipping over pools. Fossils can be seen at Siete Vueltas, 5 km from the village.

Tours or day trips can be organized by the **Asociación de Guías** ① *Main Plaza across from the Oficina de Turismo*. Every visitor gets a map and a personal guide; Mario Jaldín, T7141 2381, is excellent. Tours are also offered by **Bolivia-Online Tours** (www.bolivia-online.net) and other Cochabamba agencies.

Cochabamba to Santa Cruz

The lowland road from Cochabamba through Villa Tunari to Santa Cruz is fully paved but prone to landslides after heavy rain. **Villa Tunari** is a relaxing place and holds an annual Fish Fair the first weekend of August, with music, dancing and food. **Parque Ecoturístico Machía**, just outside town, is managed by **Inti Wara Yassi** ① *T04-413 6572, www.intiwarayassi.org, entrance US$0.90, US$2 for camera, US$3.60 for video, donations welcome, open daily 0900-1700*. This 36-ha park includes a well-signposted 3-km interpretive trail, which explains the park's ecology and other good trails through semi-tropical forest. There are panoramic lookouts and picturesque waterfalls as well as a wide variety of wildlife. The park is run by an animal rescue organization, which attempts to rehabilitate captive animals and return them to the wild. They also operate two other parks, one about half way between Santa Cruz and Trinidad and another near Rurrenabaque. Volunteer opportunities with on-site accommodation are available.

Parque Nacional Carrasco South of Villa Tunari, this park covers 622,600 ha between 300 and 4500 m. It has 11 ecological life zones, superb birdwatching and many rivers, waterfalls, canyons and pools. Access is from Villa Tunari, Totora and Monte Punku – Sehuencas. From the park entrance closest to Villa Tunari, a cable car takes you across the river for a 2½-hour walking circuit to the Cavernas de Repechón (Oil-bird caves). Guides may be hired from the Kawsay Wasi community ① *T7939 0894, www.tusoco.com*.

The highland road to Santa Cruz The 500 km highland road from Cochabamba to Santa Cruz is very scenic. Some sections are unpaved and the newer lowland route is preferred by most transport. Between Monte Punku (Km 119) and Epizana is the turnoff to Pocona and the ruins of Incallajta. To reach the ruins follow the road for 13 km as far as the village of Collpa, then take the left fork for a further 10 km. The Inca ruins of **Inkallajta** (1463-1472, rebuilt 1525), on a flat spur of land at the mouth of a steep valley, are extensive and the main building of the fortress is said to have been the largest roofed Inca building. There are several good camping sites near the river, but no facilities or services. The mountain road continues to **Epizana**, junction for the road to Sucre (being paved in 2012) via the beautiful colonial village of **Totora** and the more modern town of **Aiquile**. Past Epizana the road from Cochabamba goes on to **Pojo**, Comarapa and Samaipata (see page 121).

Cochabamba and around listings

For hotel and restaurant price codes and other relevant information, see pages 9–10.

⊖ Where to stay

Cochabamba *p94, map p95*
Places to stay south of Av Aroma and near the bus station are unsafe at all times.

\$\$\$ Aranjuez, Av Buenos Aires E-0563, T428 0076, www.aranjuezhotel.com. The most beautiful of the luxury hotels with a nice garden and lots of style, 4-star, small, good restaurant, jazz in the bar Fri-Sat night, small pool open to public (US\$1). Recommended.

\$\$\$ Gran Hotel Cochabamba, Plaza de la Recoleta E-0415, T448 9520, www.granhotelcochabamba.com. One of the best hotels in Cochabamba, pool, tennis courts, business centre, Wi-Fi, airport transfers, parking.

\$\$ Americana, Esteban Arce S-788, T425 0552, www.americanahotel.com.bo. Fan, lift, laundry, parking, **Rodizio** grill next door, good service.

\$\$ Monserrat, España 0342, T452 1011, http://hotelmonserrat.com. In the bohemian zone with bars and restaurants, internet, cable TV Cable, sauna, cafetería, buffet breakfast.

\$ Hostal Buenos Aires, 25 de Mayo N-0329, T425 4005. Cheaper without bath, pleasant, clean communal baths, breakfast US\$1.35.

\$ Hostal Elisa, Agustín López S-0834, T425 4404. Cheaper with shared bath, good showers, hot water, good breakfast US\$2.25, modern, garden, 2 blocks from bus station, laundry service, very popular with travellers, quiet, helpful owner, but small single rooms and area is unsafe.

\$ Hostal Florida, 25 de Mayo S-0583, T425 7911. Cheaper with shared bath, hot water, noisy, popular, safe deposit box, breakfast.

\$ Hostal Maya, Colombia 710 y Suipacha, T425 9701. Includes breakfast, private bath, hot water, Wi-Fi, centrally located.

\$ Hostal Ñawpa House, España 250, T452 7723. Simple rooms with electric shower, large courtyard, laundry facilities, Wi-Fi, book exchange.

\$ Hostal Versalles, Av Ayacucho S-714, T422 1096, www.hostalversalles.com. HI affiliate, 3 categories of room: carpeted, with bath and TV, cheaper without carpet, cheaper with shared bath, breakfast extra, 1½ long blocks from the bus terminal.

\$ Hostería Jardín, Hamiraya N-0248, T424 7844. Cheaper with shared bath, garden, secure car and motorcycle parking, breakfast available, basic but in a nice area.

\$ Regina, Reza 0359, T425 7382. Spacious, efficient, with breakfast, restaurant.

\$ Res Familiar, Sucre E-0554, T422 7988. Very pleasant, economical, secure, cheaper without bath, good showers, sunny courtyard. Its annex at 25 de Mayo N-0234 (entre Colombia y Ecuador), T422 7986, is also pleasant, with a big courtyard, shared bath, hot water, comfortable.

\$ Res Jordán, C Antesana S-0671, T422 9294. Youth hostel, *ABAJ* affiliate, modern, basic, with cable TV and small pool. Annex at 25 de Mayo S-0651, T422 5010.

Around Cochabamba *p96*
\$\$ El Poncho Eco Center, Marquina, Quillacollo, T439 2283, T7648 6666, www.elponcho.org. Ecological cabins, restaurant and pool. Offers volunteer options and permaculture courses.

\$\$ Refugio Tunari, Pairumani, at the foot of the Cerro Tunari, T7213 0003, www.refugiotunari.com, scheduled to open 2012. Arranges private transport (25 mins) from Plaza Bolívar in Quillacollo. Mountain lodge with 5 comfortable rooms with private bath, restaurant, bar, living room with fireplace, sauna and large terrace. Organizes guided 2-day walking tours with tent to the Laguna Cajón (4100 m), Cerro Tunari and other peaks in Parque Tunari. Walking trails start right from the Refugio.

Parque Nactional Torotoro *p97*
$$ Hostal Asteria, in the centre of the village, T6707 3401, La Paz office T02-211 6552. Colonial-style hotel, includes breakfast, restaurant serving all meals, living room with books and DVDs, beautiful patio, parking.
$$ Villa Etelvina, 15-min walk from plaza, T7073 7807, www.villaetelvina.com. Includes breakfast, bugalow for 4 with private bath, cheaper in rooms with shared bath.
$ El Molino, 1.5 km from the village, T7647 5999, Cochabamba office T04-402 6172, www.elmolinotorotoro.com. Beautiful Spanish-style country house surrounded by mountains and a river, includes breakfast, comfortable rooms with private bath, nice common areas, fireplace, bar, pool table.
$ Hostal Las Hermanas, on main road from Cochabamba, 1 block before plaza on the left, T7221 1257, likee_daz@hotmail.com. Basic rooms, cheaper with shared bath, Doña Lily serves delicious food and is very attentive.
$ Tata Santiago, on the plaza, T7379 9506. Cheaper with shared bath.

Cochabamba to Santa Cruz: Villa Tunari *p98*
$$ Los Tucanes, outside town past second bridge on road to Santa Cruz, T413 6506, www.lostucaneshotel.com. Cabins around a nice tropical garden, pool, restaurant.
$$ Victoria Resort, on the road to Santa Cruz, 4 km before Villa Tunari on the right, T413 6538, www.victoria-resort.com. Modern, cabaña style, 500 m from the main road in the middle of the forest, quiet, large pool, a/c, breakfast buffet.
$ El Puente Jungle Lodge, Av de la Integración, 3 km from town, T458 0085 (or

book in advance through **Fremen Tours**, see below). With breakfast and bath, cabins from 2 people to family-size, pool, the hotel has a zip-line, stream and natural pools.
$ Hostal Mirador, on road to Santa Cruz, before first bridge, T7795 5766, boborgne36@yahoo.fr. With bath, small pool and tower with views of river San Mateo.
$ La Querencia, Beni 700, T488 0944. With shared bath, economical, pleasant terrace on river front, avoid noisy rooms at front, good cheap food, clothes-washing facilities.
$ Res América, Santa Cruz y Av Hans Grether, T7170 7096. Excellent budget place owned by Sra Edilia, spacious rooms and shared bathrooms which are spotless.

The mountain road to Santa Cruz *p98*
$ Casa de Huespedes Villa Eva, Totora on main road, T7437 1530. Country house with large living room, fully equipped kitchen, comfortable rooms with private bath.

❼ Restaurants

Cochabamba *p94, map p95*
The restaurant and nightlife district is on España, Ecuador, Mayor Rocha and Av Ballivian (El Prado), and north of the Río Rocha on the Pasaje Boulevard de la Recoleta and Av Pando. Those on very tight budgets can find an edible lunch at the **Mercado 25 de Mayo** at 25 de Mayo entre Sucre y Jordán.
$$ Bufalo, Torres Sofer, p 2, Av Oquendo N-0654, T425 1597. Brazilian *rodizio* grill, all-you-can-eat buffet for US$10, great service. Recommended.
$$ Churrasquería Tunari, Pasaje Boulevard de la Recoleta, T448 8153. The most delicious meat you can find in Cochabamba.
$$ La Cantonata, España y Mayor Rocha, T425 9222. Good Italian restaurant.
$$ La Estancia, Pasaje Boulevard de la Recoleta 786, T424 9262. Best steak in town, salads and international food.
$$ Lai-Lai, Boulevard de la Recoleta 722, T428 0998. Excellent Chinese with take-away service.

$$ Sole Mio, Av América 826 y Pando, T428 3379. A smart Neapolitan pizza restaurant, delicious, also good for desserts. Attentive service.

$$ Suiza, Av Ballivián 820, T425 7102. International cuisine, good value.

$$-$ Ganesha, Mayor Rocha E-0375. Good filling vegetarian food, buffet lunch and breakfast, mostly soy-protein based dishes, closed Sun.

$$-$ Paprika, Chuquisaca 688 y Antezana, www.paprika.com.bo. Opens in the evening, nice atmosphere, international food, good cocktails and desserts.

$ Eli's Pizza, 25 de Mayo N-0254 y Colombia. Son of the famous La Paz branch, great pizzas, also home delivery.

$ Gopal, C España 250, inside Hostal Ñawpa House, Mon-Sat 1200-1500. Bolivian Hare-Krishna, vegetarian single-serve buffet lunch.

Cafés

Brazilian Coffee, Av Ballivián 537 just off Plaza Colón. Upmarket, tables on pavement, open 24 hrs.

Café París, Bolívar, corner of Plaza 14 de Septiembre. Serves good coffee and crêpes.

Casablanca, 25 de Mayo entre Venezuela y Ecuador. Attractive, buzzing, good food and a wide selection of coffee, popular for wine and cocktails in the evening.

Doña Alcira, Plazuela La Recoleta. Serves traditional *empanaditas* and *helados de canela* (cinnamon ice cream).

Dumbo, Av Heroínas 0440. Good ice cream parlour, popular eating and meeting spot, also does cheap meals.

Los Castores, Ballivián y Oruro. Popular, good for *salteñas*.

Parque Nacional Torotoro *p97*
Pensión La Huella and food market 2 blocks above the main plaza.

Cochabamba to Santa Cruz: Villa Tunari *p98*

The more expensive eating places are on the riverside of the road to Santa Cruz. The more popular food stalls, 1 block from the bus terminal, serve fish and have a cheap daily menu. Upstairs at the market (breakfast and lunch) is a very cheap option.

🍸 Bars and clubs

Cochabamba *p94, map p95*

Cocafé, Mayor Rocha entre 25 de Mayo y España. Caring, family atmosphere, good place for foreigners to meet. Street musicians always pass by to show off their skills.

Green Pepper, Av América casi Villarroel. Thu-Sat nights, popular dancing spot with locals and foreigners, all kinds of music.

La Muela del Diablo, Potosí 1392 y Portales, next to Palicio de Portales. Bolivian rock music, theatre groups, German beer.

La Tirana, Lanza y Av Ramón Rivero. Popular bar and club for a beer or to dance to mixed Latin and rock music, in a 2-storey house with different spaces up and downstairs.

Na Cunna, Av Salamanca 577, T452 1982. Irish pub/restaurant, opens in the evenings, Fri live music. They serve Guinness.

🎭 Entertainment

Cochabamba *p94, map p95*

Theatre mARTadero, Av 27 de Agosto entre Ollantay y Ladislao Cabrera, T458 8778, www.martadero.org. Cultural and artistic centre for local and international artists, exhibitions, and events, in a refurbished slaughterhouse. Daily 1500-1800. Micros/trufis P, Q, and 212 to Plaza de los Arrieros. **Teatro Achá**, España 280 y Plaza 14 de Septiembre, T425 8054. The city's oldest cultural centre, with monthly presentations. **Teatro Hecho a Mano**, Venezuela 0655 entre Lanza y Antezana, T452 9790. Theatre school.

✳ Festivals

Cochabamba *p94, map p95*

Carnival is celebrated 15 days before **Lent**. Rival groups (*comparsas*) compete in music, dancing, and fancy dress, culminating in El Corso on the last Sat of the Carnival. **Mascaritas** balls also take place in the carnival season, when the young women wear long hooded satin masks. **14 Sep**: Día de Cochabamba.

___

Around Cochabamba *p96*
Fiesta de la Virgen de Urkupiña (www. urcupina.com), in Quillacollo, 14-15 Aug. Plenty of transport from Cochabamba, hotels all full. Be there before 0900 to be sure of a seat, as you are not allowed to stand in the street. The 1st day is the most colourful with all the groups in costumes and masks, parading and dancing in the streets till late at night. Many groups have left by the 2nd day and dancing stops earlier. The 3rd day is dedicated to the pilgrimage.

Shopping

___

Cochabamba *p94, map p95*
Bookshops Los Amigos del Libro, España S-153, www.librosbolivia.com. **The Spitting Llama**, España 615 entre Plazuela Barba de Padilla y El Prado, T489 4540, www.thespittingllama.com (see under La Paz, page 32). **IGM**, 16 de Julio S-237, T425 5503, Mon-Thu 0800-1200, 1430-1800, Fri 0800-1200, sells topographic maps of Cochabamba department.
Handicrafts Artesanos Andinos, Pasaje Catedral, T450 8367. An artisans' association selling textiles. **Fotrama**, Bolívar 0349, entre San Martín y 25 de Mayo, www.fotrama. com. High-quality alpaca clothing.

What to do

___

Cochabamba *p94, map p95*
Adventure sports
Cochabamba is growing in popularity for parapenting, with several outfits offering tamdem jumps and courses more cheaply than other places, starting at US$30-35 and US$200-250 respectively.

AndesXtremo, La Paz 138 entre Ayacucho y Junín, T452 3392, www.andesxtremo. com. Adventure sports company offering parapenting, climbing, rafting, trekking and bungee-jumps, good value, professional staff. Recommended.
Bolivia Cultura, C España N-301, esquina Ecuador, T452 7272, www.boliviacultura. com. Offers the most complete service for tours to Torotoro. They run year-round tours for 3 and 4 days to all the major sites and can arrange longer trips, hikes and camping. They also have reliable information on road conditions and hotels.
Bolivia-Online Tours, T7213 0003, www. bolivia-online.net. Specializes in community-based tourism and nature sports: hiking, rafting, paragliding, biking. Also cultural tours throughout Bolivia. German run, English and Spanish also spoken.
D'Orbigny Travel, Pasaje de la Promotora 344 entre España y Heroínas, T451 1367. Run by an enthusiastic Bolivian couple, excursions in Cochabamba department and throughout Bolivia. Recommended.
Fremen Tours, Av Heroínas 301 y España, T458 0085, www.salar-amazon.com. Offers tours throughout the country, including their own facilities at Villa Tunari and on the *Reina de Enín* riverboat.

Transport

___

Cochabamba *p94, map p95*
Air Jorge Wilstermann airport, T412 0400. Airport bus is Micro B from Plaza 14 de Septiembre, US$0.40; taxis from airport to centre US$4. Reconfirm all flights (and obtain reconfirmation number), and arrive early for international flights. Cochabamba is an air transport hub with several daily flights to/from **La Paz** (35 mins) and **Santa Cruz** (40 mins) with **Aero Sur** (Av Villarroel 105 y Av Oblitos, T440 0909, and San Martín O-150, T451 1727), **Boliviana de Aviacion**, Jordán 202 y Nataniel Aguirre, T901-105010, and **TAM** (Av América Oeste casi George Washington, Ed Torres América, T441 1545).

Aerocon (Anieto Padilla 755, T448 9210) and **TAM** have flights to **Trinidad**, with connections to other northern cities.
Bus *Micros* and *colectivos*, US$0.20; *trufis*, US$0.30. Anything marked 'San Antonio' goes to the market. *Trufis* C and 10 go from bus terminal to the city centre. The main bus terminal is on Av Aroma y Ayacucho, 600-700 m south of Plaza 14 de Septiembre (T155). To **Santa Cruz**, almost hourly 0600-2130, 12 hrs, US$7.50; Trans Copacabana semi cama, 2130, US$10; **Bolívar** buscama, US$15; all via the paved lowland road through Villa Tunari. See page 98. To **Mairana, Samaipata** and **Santa Cruz**, along the old mountain road via Epizana and Comarapa, a beautiful ride, **Trans Carrasco**, 6 de Agosto y República, T456-9348, daily at 0730 to Santa Cruz (14 hrs), 1200 to Mairana (11 hrs), US$6. To/from **La Paz** almost hourly 0530-2300, 7 hrs, US$6 (**Trans Copacabana** semi cama, 2230, US$8.50, **Bolívar** buscama, 2230, 2300, US$12.50). To **Oruro**, 0600-1730 (Sun last bus at 2100), 4 hrs, US$3.35-4. To **Potosí**, departures at 2000 (US$7), 2100 (semi cama, US$11) with **Bolívar** and Trans Copacabana, 10 hrs. Daily to **Sucre**, 8 hrs, several companies (**Bolívar** and Trans Copacabana at 1930, 2000 US$7, 2030 semi cama, US$8.50). To **Sucre** by day; go to Aiquile by bus (several from Av 6 de Agosto entre Av República y Av Barrientos, none before 1200) or **ferrobus** (see page 97), then a bus at 0200-0300 passing en route to Sucre, or Fri and Sun, 2000. Local buses leave from Av Barrientos y Av 6 de Agosto, near La Coronilla for **Tarata**, **Punata** and **Cliza**. From Av 6 de Agosto y Av República to **Totora**. Av Oquendo y 9 de Abril (be careful in this area), to **Villa Tunari**, US$4.50, 4-5 hrs, several daily; **Puerto Villarroel**, US$7.75, 6 hrs (from 0800 when full, daily). **Taxi** About US$0.75 from anywhere to the Plaza, more expensive to cross the river; double after dark.

Parque Nacional Torotoro *p97*
Bus From the end of Av República, Wed, Fri, Sat, Sun at 1800; Thu, Sun at 0600; return to Cochabamba Mon, Tue, Fri, Sat at 0600; Thu, Sun at 1500; Fri at 1800; US$3, about 6 hrs on a cobbled road.

Cochabamba to Santa Cruz: Inkallajta *p98*
Take a trufi from 0500 onwards from 6 de Agosto y Manuripi (Av República) in Cochabamba (ask for the "Parada Pocona"). For 3 people the trufi will drop you off at the entrance to the Inca ruins (US$3 pp). Arrange with the driver to pick you up at a specific time to return to Cochabamba. If alone, ask to get off after arriving in Collpa at a big green sign, where the road to the ruins turns off to the right. Walk along the cobbled road for approximately 10 km to the ruins. Trufis return from Pocona to Cochabamba when full till 1600. Taxis from Pocona charge around US$14 one way to the ruins.

⚙ Directory

Cochabamba *p94, map p95*
Language classes Bolivia Sostenible, Julio Arauco Prado 230, Zona Las Cuadras, T423 3786, www.boliviasostenible.org. Offers home stays and paid placements for volunteers. Centro de Idiomas Kori Simi, Lanza 727, entre La Paz y Chuquisaca, T425 7248, www.korisimi.com. Spanish and Quechua school run by staff from Switzerland, Germany and Bolivia, also offers activity programme, homestays and volunteer placements. Runawasi, Maurice Lefebvre 0470, Villa Juan XXIII, Av Blanco Galindo Km 4.5, T424 8923, www.runawasi. org. Spanish, Quechua and Aymara, also has accommodation. Volunteer Bolivia, Ecuador E-0342, T452 6028, www. volunteerbolivia.org. Bolivian/US-run organization which offers language classes, homestays and a recommended volunteer programme. There are many qualified language teachers in the city.

Northern Lowlands

Bolivia's Northern lowlands account for about 70% of national territory. Flat savannahs and dense tropical jungle stretch northwards from the great cordilleras, sparsely populated and, until recently, rarely visited by tourists. Improved roads and frequent flights, particularly to Rurrenabaque and Trinidad, are opening up the area and wildlife and rainforest expeditions are becoming increasingly popular. Most people head to Rurrenabaque. If seeking hard travel off the beaten track, try Cobija, Riberalta or Guayaramerín, all near the border with Brazil. Beni department has 53% of the country's birds and 50% of its mammals, but destruction of forest and habitat by loggers and colonists is proceeding at an alarming rate.

Madidi and Rurrenabaque

Caranavi to San Borja

From Caranavi, a road runs north to Sapecho, where a bridge crosses the Río Beni. Beyond Sapecho (7 km from the bridge), the road passes through Palos Blancos (several cheap lodgings). The road between Sapecho and Yucumo, three hours from Sapecho *tránsito*, is a good all-weather gravel surface. There are basic *hospedajes* and restaurants in **Yucumo** where a road branches northwest, fording rivers several times on its way to Rurrenabaque. Taking the eastern branch from Yucumo it is 50 km (1-2 hours) to **San Borja**, a small, relatively wealthy cattle-raising centre with simple hotels and restaurants clustered near the plaza. From San Borja the road goes east to Trinidad via **San Ignacio de Moxos** (see page 111). The road passes through part of the Pilón Lajas Reserve (see below).

Parque Nacional Madidi

ⓘ *Headquarters in San Buenaventura, about 4 blocks upriver from the plaza, T03-892 2540. US$13.50 entry is collected near the dock in San Buenaventura. Insect repellent and sun protection are essential.*

Parque Nacional Madidi is quite possibly the most bio-diverse of all protected areas on the planet. It is the variety of habitats, from the freezing Andean peaks of the Cordillera Apolobamba in the southwest (reaching nearly 6000 m), through cloud, elfin and dry forest to steaming tropical jungle and pampas (neo-tropical savannah) in the north and east, that account for the array of flora and fauna within the park's boundaries. In an area roughly the size of Wales or El Salvador (1,895,750 ha) are an estimated 900 bird species, 10 species of primate, five species of cat (with healthy populations of jaguar and puma), giant anteaters and many reptiles. Madidi is at the centre of a bi-national system of parks that spans the Bolivia-Peru border. The Heath river on the park's northwestern border forms the two countries' frontier and links with the Tambopata National Reserve in Peru. To the southwest the Area Protegida Apolobamba protects extensive mountain ecosystems. It is easiest to visit the lowland areas of Madidi through Rurrenabaque.

Pilón Lajas Biosphere Reserve and Indigenous Territory
ⓘ *HQ at Campero y Germón Busch, Rurrenabaque, T892 2246, crtmpilonlajas@yahoo.com. No entrance fee at the time of updating, but one is planned.*

Beyond the Beni River in the southeast runs the Pilón Lajas Biosphere Reserve and Indigenous Territory, home to the Tsimane and Mosetene peoples. Together with Madidi, it constitutes approximately 60,000 sq km, one of the largest systems of protected land in the neotropics. Unfortunately, much of this land is under pressure from logging interests, especially along the western border of the reserve. Set up under the auspices of UNESCO, Pilón Lajas has one of the continent's most intact Amazonian rainforest ecosystems, as well as an incredible array of tropical forest animal life. NGOs have been working with the people of La Unión, Playa Ancha, Nuevos Horizontes and El Cebú to develop sustainable forestry, fish farming, cattle ranching and *artesanía*.

Rurrenabaque → *Phone code: 03. Population: 17,900. Altitude: 200 m.*
The charming, picturesque jungle town of Rurre (as the locals call it), on the Río Beni, is the main jumping off point for tours in the Bolivian Amazon and pampas, from 2-4 day trips through to full expeditions. Across the river is the smaller town of San Buenaventura (canoe US$0.15). Despite its growth as a trading, transport and ecotourism centre, Rurre is a pleasant town to walk around, although the climate is usually humid. Market day is Sunday. **Dirección Regional de Turismo** ⓘ *Avaroa y Vaca Díez, Mon-Fri 0800-1200, 1400-1800, Sat 0900-1100,* has general information and a bulletin board for posting comments on tours; read this before booking a tour and write your own feedback. Bicycles rented at US$2 per hour. There are no ATMs in Rurrenabaque (one is planned for 2012), bring cash.

Forty minutes upstream from Rurre is **San Miguel del Bala**, in a beautiful setting, 3 km from the entrance to Madidi. This community lodge gives a good taste of the jungle, offers day trips, well-laid out trails and has en suite cabins where you can stay, bar and a pool fed by a waterfall. It is owned and operated by the indigenous Tacana community. Community tourism is also being developed at **Santa Rosa de Yacuma**, 100 km northeast of Rurre, for information contact **FAN** (page 6).

Madidi and Rurrenabaque listings

For hotel and restaurant price codes and other relevant information, see pages 9-10.

ⓢ Where to stay

Madidi *p104*
Chalalán Ecolodge is 5 hrs up-river from Rurrenabaque, at San José de Uchupiamonas, in Madidi National Park. La Paz office: Sagárnaga 189, Edif Shopping Doryan, of 22, T02-231 1451; in Rurrenabaque, C Comercio entre Campero y Vaca Díez, T892 2419, www.chalalan.com. This is Bolivia's top ecotourism project, founded by the local Quechua-Tacana community, Conservation International and the Interamerican Development Bank, and now has a well-deserved international reputation. Accommodation is in thatched cabins, and activities include fantastic wildlife-spotting and birdwatching, guided and self-guided trails, river and lake activities, and relaxing in pristine jungle surroundings. 3 day/2 night packages cost US$350 pp (US$320 with shared bath), plus transport to Rurre and national park fees.

San Miguel del Bala, 40-min boat trip up river from Rurre (office at C Comercio entre Vaca Díez y Santa Cruz), T892 2394, www.sanmigueldelbala.com. Seven cabins in a delightful setting, good bathrooms, nice public areas, good restaurant, attentive staff,

3 days/2 nights cost US$225 pp. Advance booking required. Highly recommended.

Pilón Lajas *p105*

Mapajo, Mapajo Ecoturismo Indígena, Santa Cruz entre Avaroa y Comercio, Rurrenabaque, T892 2317. A community-run ecolodge 3 hrs by boat from Rurrenebaque has 6 *cabañas* without electricity (take a torch), shared cold showers and a dining room serving traditional meals. 3 days/2 nights cost US$225 pp. You can visit the local community, walk in the forest, go birdwatching, etc. Take insect repellent, wear long trousers and strong footwear.

Rurrenabaque *p105*

In high season hotels fill up very quickly.

$$ El Ambaibo, Santa Cruz entre Bolívar y Busch, T892 2107, hotel_ambaibo@hotmail.com. Includes breakfast and airport transfer, large pool (US$3 for non-guests), Wi-Fi, parking, a step up from the average in Rurre.

$$ Safari, Comercio on the outskirts down-river (can be a hot walk), T892 2410. A peaceful spot with beautiful garden and comfortable rooms, pool, terrace and a good restaurant. Recommended.

$ Asaí, Vaca Díez y Busch, T7355 8946. Electric showers, cheap, quiet, laundry area, courtyard and hammocks, luggage store, breakfast extra.

$ Beni, Comercio y Arce, along the river, T892 2408. Best rooms have a/c and TV, hot showers, cheaper with fan (cheaper without bath), kitchen facilities. Spacious, good service.

$ El Curichal, Comercio 1490, T892 2647. Nice courtyard, hammocks, laundry and small kitchen facilities, helpful staff, will change cash and TCs. Good economy option, popular with backpackers.

$ Hostal El Balsero, Comercio y Pando, T892 2042. Very cheap without bath, electric shower, fan, bare but clean rooms, functional.

$ Hostal Pahuichi, Comercio y Vaca Díez, T892 2558. Some big rooms with electric shower, fan, rooftop views, cheap and good.

$ Mirador del Lobo, upstream end of Comercio, contact through El Lobo in La Paz, T02-245 1640. Cheap rooms in large breezy building overlooking the river, some rooms with electric shower.

$ Oriental, on plaza, T892 2401. Hot showers, fan, small breakfast included, quiet, hammocks in peaceful garden, family-run. A good option.

$ Res Jislene, C Comercio entre La Paz y Beni, T892 2526. Erlan Caldera and family are very hospitable, hot water, fan, hammock area, cheap basic rooms, good breakfast if booked in advance, information, helpful.

$ Rurrenabaque, Vaca Díez y Bolívar, T892 2481, hotelrurrenabaque@hotmail.com. Cheap, safe, hot water, laundry facilities, adequate.

$ Santa Ana, Avaroa entre Vaca Díez y Campero, T892 2399. Cheap basic rooms, laundry, luggage store, pleasant hammock area in garden.

🍴 Restaurants

Rurrenabaque *p105*

$$ Camila's, Avaroa y Campero, daily 0800-0130. International food, *parrillada* on Sun, drinks.pool tables, fast service.

$$ Casa del Campo, Vaca Díez y Avaroa, daily 0700-2100. Good sandwices, juices, fresh organic food, great salad selection, breakfast, delicious desserts, garden, friendly staff but very slow service.

$$ Juliano's, Santa Cruz entre Bolívar y Avaroa, daily 1200-1430, 1800-late. French and Italian food, good presentation and service. Recommended.

$$-$ El Tacuaral, Avaroa y Santa Cruz, daily 0630-2200. International and Bolivian food, breakfasts and burgers.

$$-$ Luna Café, Comercio entre Santa Cruz y Vaca Diez, open 0800-2200. International meals, pizza, snacks and drinks.

$$-$ Pizzería Italia & Monkey's Bar,
Avaroa entre Santa Cruz y Vaca Díez, open
0900-0100. Big pizzas, imaginative pastas,
lively crowd, big screen TV, pool tables.
$ La Cabaña, Santa Cruz, by the river,
Mon-Sat 0800-2200, Sun 0800-1600. Wide
selection of international and Bolivian food.
$ La Perla de Rurre, Bolívar y Vaca Díez,
open 0730-2100. Set lunch and à la carte.

Cafés

French Bakery, Vaca Díez entre Avaroa y
Bolívar, Mon-Sat 0600-1200. Run by Thierry.
Delicious croissants and *pain au chocolat*,
get there early.
Moskkito Bar, Vaca Díez y Avaroa. Cool
bar for tall jungle tales. Burgers, pizzas,
rock music and pool tables.
Pachamama, south end of Avaroa, open 1200-
2230. English/Israeli café/bar, snacks, films
(US$3), board games and a book exchange.
Ron, an American expat, drives round town
in a kit car offering banana bread, cinnamon
rolls, granola bars and his views on the sad
state of the world. Catch him while they're
hot, at the corner of Santa Cruz and Avaroa.

⊙ What to do

Rurrenabaque *p105*

There are 2 types of tours, jungle or pampas.
Both cost about US$65-$80 pp plus
US$13.50 park fee for a typical 3-day tour.
Prices and quality both vary but booking
in Rurre is usually cheaper than in La Paz.
Jungle tours normally involve travelling by
boat on the Río Beni. Lodging is either in
purpose-built camps on higher-end tours,
or tents at the budget end. Tours are long
enough for most people to get a sense of
life in the jungle. In the rainy season the
jungle is very hot and humid with many
more biting insects and far fewer animals
to be seen. In the more open terrain of the
Pampas you will see a lot more wildlife.
Pampas tours involve 4-hr jeep ride to the
Río Yacuma at either end, and a series of
boat trips. You may have to wade through

knee-deep water; wear appropriate shoes.
You might see howler, squirrel and capuchin
monkeys, caiman, capybara, pink dolphins,
possibly anacondas and a huge variety of
birds. One-day trips are not recommended
as they spend most of the time travelling,
unless going to San Miguel del Bala.

Rurrenabaque has thrived on its steadily
increasing number of visitors but also
suffered the consequences of haphazard
growth in tourism. Not all of the many
tour operators here are reputable nor do
all tourists in Rurre behave responsibly.
Many agencies offer ecologically unsound
practices such as fishing, feeding monkeys,
catching caiman or handling anaconda.
Before signing up for a tour, check the
bulletin board at the Dirección Municipal
de Turismo and try to talk to other travellers
who have just come back. Post your own
comments after you return. Go with an
established company as competition has
been forcing down prices and, consequently,
the quality of tours. Some operators pool
customers, so you may not go with the
company you booked with. There are many
more agencies in town than those listed
below. Shop around and choose carefully.

Tour operators

Aguilar Tours, Av Avaroa, T892 2478,
www.aguilar.lobopages.com. Jungle
and pampas tours.
Bala Tours, Av Santa Cruz y Comercio, T3892
2527, www.balatours.com. Arranges Pampas
and jungle tours, with their own lodge in
each (with bath and solar power). English-
speaking guides. Combined trips to Pampas
and jungle arranged. Recommended.
Donato Tours, Avaroa entre Pando y Arce,
T892 2571, donatotours@hotmail.com.
Regular tours plus the opportunity to stay in
a community in Pilón Lajas for 1 to 20 days.
Lipiko Tours, Av Santa Cruz s/n,
between Bolívar and Avaroa, T892
2221, www.travel-bolivia.co.uk.
Madidi Travel, Comercio y Vaca Díez,
T892 2153, in La Paz, Linares 968, T02-231

8313, www.madidi-travel.com. Specializes in tours to the private Serere Sanctuary in the Madidi Mosaic (details on website), minimum 3 days/2 nights, good guiding. **Mashaquipe Tours**, Avaroa y Arce, www.mashaquipe.com. Run by an organization of indigenous families with a lodge in Madidi National Park.

✈ Transport

Caranavi to San Borja p104
Bus See page 55 for buses in Caranavi. **Yucumo** is on the La Paz-Caranavi-Rurrenabaque and San Borja bus routes. Rurrenabaque-La Paz bus passes through about 1800. If travelling to Rurrenabaque by bus take extra food in case there is a delay (anything from road blocks to flat tyres to high river levels). **Flota Yungueña** daily except Thu at 1300 from San Borja to **La Paz**, 19 hrs via Caranavi. Also San Borja to **Rurrenabaque**, **Santa Rosa**, **Riberalta**, **Guayaramerín** about 3 times a week. Minibuses and *camionetas* normally run daily between San Borja and **Trinidad** throughout the year, US$15, about 7 hrs including 20 mins crossing of Río Mamoré on ferry barge (up to 14 hrs in wet season). Gasoline available at Yolosa, Caranavi, Yucumo, San Borja and San Ignacio.

Rurrenabaque p105
Air Several daily flights to/from **La Paz** with **Amaszonas**, Comercio entre Santa Cruz y Vaca Diez, T892 2472, US$95; and 3 a week with **TAM**, Santa Cruz y Avaroa, T892 2398, US$68. Amaszonas also flies to **Trinidad** and **Santa Cruz**. Book flights as early as possible and buy onward ticket on arrival. Check flight times in advance; they change frequently. Delays and cancellations are common. Airport taxes US$2. Airlines provide transport to/from town, US$1.
Bus To/from **La Paz** via Caranavi with Flota Yungueña, Totaí and Vaca Díez; 18-20 hrs, US$8.50, daily at 1030 and Sat-Mon also at 1900. Some continue to **Riberalta** (US$17, 13 hrs from Rurre), **Guayaramerín** (US$18, 15 hrs) or **Cobija** (US$32, 30 hrs). Rurrenebaque-**Riberalta** may take 6 days or more in the wet season. Take lots of food, torch and be prepared to work. To **Trinidad**, with Trans Guaya (buses) or Trans Rurrenabaque (minibuses) daily, Flota Yungueña Mon, Wed, via **Yucumo** and **San Borja**, US$18, check that the road is open.

① Directory

Rurrenabaque p105
Immigration Arce entre Bolívar y Busch, T892 2241, Mon-Fri 0830-1230, 1430-1830, same-day extensions.

Riberalta to Brazil

Riberalta → *Phone code: 03. Population: 60,000. Altitude: 175 m.*
This town, at the confluence of the Madre de Dios and Beni rivers, is off the beaten track and a centre for brazil nut production. It's very laid back, but take great care if your bus drops you in the middle of the night and everything is closed. Change cash in shops and on street.

Guayaramerín and border with Brazil → *Phone code: 03.*
Guayaramerín is a cheerful, prosperous little town on the bank of the Río Mamoré, opposite the Brazilian town of Guajará-Mirim. It has an important *Zona Libre*. Passage between the two towns is unrestricted; boat trip US$1.65 (more at night).

Bolivian immigration Avenida Costanera near port; open 0800-1100, 1400-1800. Passports must be stamped here when leaving, or entering Bolivia. On entering Bolivia, passports must also be stamped at the Bolivian consulate in Guajará-Mirim. The Brazilian consulate is on 24 de Septiembre, Guayaramerín, T855 3766, open 0900-1300, 1400-1700; visas for entering Brazil are given here. To enter Brazil you must have a yellow fever certificate, or be inoculated at the health ministry (free). Exchange cash at the dock on the Bolivian side where rates are written up on blackboards (no traveller's cheques), although there is an ATM at the Banco do Brasil in Guajará-Mirim; no facilities for cash.

Cobija → *Phone code: 03. Population: 30,000.*
The capital of the lowland Department of Pando lies on the Río Acre which forms the frontier with Brazil. A new, single-tower suspension bridge has been built across the river to Brasiléia. As a duty-free zone, shops in centre have a huge selection of imported consumer goods at bargain prices. Brazilians and Peruvians flock here to stock up. As this is a this border area, watch out for scams and cons. **Bolivian immigration** ① *Av Internacional 567, T842 2081, open daily 0900-1800.* **Brazilian consulate** ① *Av René Barrientos s/n, T842 2110, vcbrasco@entelnet.bo, Mon-Fri 0830-1230.* There are *casas de cambio* on Av Internacional and Av Cornejo. Most shops will accept dollars or reais, and exchange money.

Riberalta to Brazil listings

For hotel and restaurant price codes and other relevant information, see pages 9-10.

🛏 Where to stay

Riberalta *p108*
Ask for a fan and check the water supply.
$$ Colonial, Plácido Méndez 1, T852 3018. Charming colonial casona, large, well-furnished rooms, no singles, nice gardens and courtyard, comfortable, good beds, helpful owners.
$ Lazo, NG Salvatierra. With a/c, cheaper with fan, comfortable, laundry facilities, good value.
$ Res El Pauro, Salvatierra 157, T852 2452. Cheap and basic, shared baths, good café.
$ Res Los Reyes, near airport, T852 2628. With fan, cheap, safe, pleasant but noisy disco nearby on Sat and Sun.

Guayaramerín *p108*
$$ San Carlos, 6 de Agosto, 4 blocks from port, T855 3555. With a/c, hot showers, changes dollars cash, TCs and reais, swimming pool, reasonable restaurant.
$ Santa Ana 25 de Mayo, close to airport, T855 3900. With bath, fan, cheap and recommended.

Cobija *p109*
$$ Diana, Av 9 de Febrero 123, T842 3653. A/c, TV, safe, buffet breakfast, internet and pool.
$$ Nanijos, Av 9 de Febrero 147, T842 2230. Includes breakfast, a/c, TV, *comedor* does good lunch, internet, helpful.
$$ Triller, Av Internacional 640, T842 2024. With a/c (cheaper with fan) and bath, restaurant.
$ Avenida, 9 de Febrero y Tarija, T842 2108. With breakfast, a/c, fan and bath.

🍴 Restaurants

Riberalta *p108*
$ Club Social Progreso, on plaza. Good value *almuerzo*, excellent fish.
$ Tropical, Oruro y Juan Alberdi, near the airport. Nice atmosphere, good typical food.

Guayaramerín *p108*
$$ Los Cocos, at entrance to town. *Parrilla* and à la carte.
There are several places on the plaza:
$ Gipssy, good *almuerzo*; **$ Los Bibosis**, popular; **Made in Brazil**, good coffee.
$ Only, 25 de Mayo y Beni, good *almuerzo*, plus Chinese.

Cobija p109

$$-$ Las Palmas, Av Chelio Luna Pizarro y G Fernández. Tue-Sun lunch and dinner, à la carte meals, karaoke at night.

$$-$ Paladar Brasilero, 16 de Julio y Santa Cruz. Brazilian buffet, pay by weight.

La Esquina de la Abuela, Fernández Molina y Sucre. Varied menu, good food, not cheap. *Salteñas* sold in morning.

⚙ What to do

Riberalta p108

Riberalta Tours, Av Sucre 646, T852 3475, www.riberaltatours.com. Multi-day river and jungle tours, airline tickets, very helpful.

Cobija p109

Turismo Verde and **Yaminagua Tours**, Plaza del Deportista 50, T842 3456. Biking, rafting, tours to the jungle and native communities.

⊖ Transport

Riberalta p108

Air Flights to **Trinidad** and **Cobija** with Aerocon (at airport, T852 4679). TAM (Av Suárez Chuquisaca, T852 3924) to **Trinidad, Santa Cruz, Cochabamba** and **La Paz**. Expect cancellations in the wet season.

Bus Roads to all destinations are appalling, even worse in the wet season. Several companies (including **Yungueña**) to **La Paz**, via **Rurrenabaque** and **Caranavi** daily, 35 hrs to 3 days or more, US$27. To **Trinidad** via Rurrenabaque and San Borja, 25-35 hrs. To **Guayaramerín** 7 daily, US$5, 2 hrs. To **Cobija** several companies, none with daily service, 10-11 hrs.

River Cargo boats carry passengers along the **Río Madre de Dios**, but they are infrequent. There are no boats to Rurrenabaque.

Guayaramerín p108

Air Daily flights to **Trinidad**, with onward connections, with **Aerocon** (25 de Mayo y Beni, T855 5025). **TAM** has same services as for Riberalta.

Bus Buses leave from General Federico Román. Same long-haul services as Riberalta, above. To **Riberalta** 2 hrs, US$5, daily 0700-1730.

River Check the notice of vessels leaving port on the Port Captain's board, prominently displayed near the immigration post on the riverbank. Boats sailing up the Mamoré to **Trinidad** are not always willing to take passengers.

Cobija p109

Air Daily flights to **Riberalta** and **Trinidad**, with onward connections, with **Aerocon**, Leoncio Justiniano 43, T842 4575. **Aero Sur**, Cornejo 123, T842 3598, flies 3 times a week to **La Paz** and **Santa Cruz**. TAM (Av 9 de Febrero 49, T842 2267), to **La Paz** or **Trinidad** on alternating days.

Bus Flota Yungueña and Flota Cobija to **La Paz** via Riberalta and Rurrenabaque, 2-3 days or more, US$30-40. To **Riberalta** with several bus companies, depart from 2 de Febrero, most on Wed, Fri, Sun at 0600; good all-weather surface; 2 river crossings on pontoon rafts, takes 10-11 hrs.

Taxi US$0.60 in centre, but more expensive beyond, charging according to time and distance, expensive over the international bridge to Brasiléia. Besides taxis there are motorbike taxis (US$0.60). **Brasiléia** can also be reached by **canoe**, US$0.35. The bridge can be crossed on foot as well, although one should be dressed neatly in any case when approaching Brazilian customs. Entry/exit stamps (free) are necessary and yellow fever vaccination certificate also (in theory), when crossing into Brazil. From Brasiléia **Real Norte**, has buses to **Rio Branco**, US$7.60, and **Assis Brasil**, US$4, and Taxis Brasileiros run to Rio Branco, US$10.

Cochabamba to Trinidad

Villa Tunari to the Lowlands

Another route into Beni Department is via the lowland road between Cochabamba and Santa Cruz. At Ivirgazama, east of Villa Tunari, the road passes the turn-off to **Puerto Villarroel**, 27 km further north, from where cargo boats ply irregularly to Trinidad in about four to 10 days. You can get information from the Capitanía del Puerto notice board, or ask at docks. There are only a few basic places to sleep in Villarroel and very few stores.

Trinidad → *Phone code: 03. Population: 96,400. Altitude: 327 m.*

The hot and humid capital of the lowland Beni Department is a dusty city in the dry season, with many streets unpaved. Primarily a service centre for the surrounding ranches and communities, most travellers find themselves in the area for boats up and down the Río Mamoré. There are two ports, Almacén and Varador, check which one your boat is docking at. Puerto Varador is 13 km from town on the Río Mamoré on the road between Trinidad and San Borja; cross the river over the main bridge by the market, walk down to the service station by the police checkpoint and take a truck, US$1.70. Almacén is 8 km from the city. The main mode of transport in Trinidad is the motorbike (even for taxis, US$0.40 in city); rental on plaza from US$2 per hour, US$8 per half day. Transport can be arranged from the airport. **Tourist office** ⓘ *in the Prefectura building at Joaquín de Sierra y La Paz, ground floor, T462 4831, zwww.trinidad.gob.bo; also at Centro de Informacion Turistica, 6 de Agosto, next to Hotel Campanario.*

About 5 km from town is the Laguna Suárez, with plenty of wildlife; swimming is safe where the locals swim, near the café with the jetty (elsewhere there are stingrays and alligators). Motorbike taxi from Trinidad, US$1.30.

San Ignacio de Moxos → *Electricity is supplied in town from 1200-2400.*

San Ignacio de Moxos, 90 km west of Trinidad, is known as the folklore capital of the Beni Department. It's a quiet town with a mainly indigenous population; 60% are *Macheteros*, who speak their own language. San Ignacio still maintains the traditions of the Jesuit missions with big *fiestas*, especially during Holy Week and the **Fiesta del Santo Patrono de Moxos**, the largest festival in the lowlands, at the end of July.

Magdalena and Bella Vista

Magdalena, northeast of Trinidad, stands on the banks of the Río Itonama. There is an abundance of wildlife and birds in the surrounding area. The city's main festival, Santa María Magdalena, is on 22 July attracting many visitors from all over. There is a Prodem office (N García entre 6 de Agosto y 18 de Noviembre, changes US$ cash). East of Magdalena, **Bella Vista** on the Río Blanco is considered by many to be one of the prettiest spots in northeast Bolivia. Lovely white sandbanks line the Río San Martín, 10 minutes' paddling by canoe from the boat moorings below town (boatmen will take you, returning later by arrangement; also accessible by motorcycle). Check that the sand is not covered by water after heavy rain. Other activities are swimming in the Río San Martín, canoeing, good country for cycling. Three well-stocked shops on plaza, but none sells mosquito repellent or spray/coils (bring your own, especially at the beginning of the wet season). There is no bank or phone office.

Cochabamba to Trinidad listings

For hotel and restaurant price codes and other relevant information, see pages 9-10.

Where to stay

Trinidad *p111*

$$ Campanario, 6 de Agosto 80, T462 4733. Includes breakfast, rooms with a/c and frigobar, meeting room, restaurant, bar, pool, Wi-Fi.

$$ Jacaranda Suites, La Paz entre Pedro de la Rocha y 18 de Noviembre, T462 2400, Includes breakfast, a/c, restaurant, pool, meeting rooms, internet.

$ Copacabana, Tomás Villavicencio, 3 blocks from plaza, T462 2811. Good value, some beds uncomfortable, cheaper with shared bath, helpful staff.

$ Monteverde, 6 de Agosto 76, T462 2750. With a/c (cheaper with fan), frigobar, includes breakfast, owner speaks English. Recommended.

$ Res 18 de Noviembre, Av 6 de Agosto 135, T462 1272. With bath, cheaper without, clean and welcoming, laundry facilities.

San Ignacio de Moxos *p111*

There are some cheap *alojamientos* on and around the main plaza.

Magdalena *p111*

$$ Internacional, near airport, T03-886 2210, http://magdalena-d.hwz-inc.com (in German). With breakfast, pools and gardens, beautiful setting. Also some cheap and basic hotels.

Bella Vista *p111*

$$$ Cabañas el Tucunare, T03-465 4858, www.amazon-tours.com. Cabins on the shore of the Río San Martín, includes breakfast. **$$$$** with full board and guided boat and horse-riding tours. French-run.

Restaurants

Trinidad *p111*

$$ Club Social 18 de Noviembre, N Suárez y Vaca Díez on plaza. Good lunch for US$1.35, lively, popular with locals.

$$ El Tábano, Villavicencio entre Mamore y Néstor Suárez. Good fish and local fare, relaxed atmosphere.

$$ La Estancia, Barrio Pompeya, on Ibare entre Muibe y Velarde. Excellent steaks.

$$ Pescadería El Moro, Bolívar 707 y 25 de Diciembre. Excellent fish. Also several good fish restaurants in Barrio Pompeya, south of plaza across river.

$ La Casona, Plaza Ballivián. Good pizzas and set lunch, closed Tue.

Heladería Oriental, on plaza. Good coffee, ice cream, cakes, popular with locals.

What to do

Trinidad *p111*

Most agents offer excursions to local *estancias* and jungle tours. Most *estancias* can also be reached independently in 1 hr by hiring a motorbike.

Fremen, Cipriano Berace 332, T462 2276, www.amazoncruiser.com. Operate the *Reina de Enin* riverboat, US$358 pp for 3 day/2 night cruise including guided visits to local communities, jungle walks, horseback riding and fishing.

La Ruta del Bufeo, T462 7739, www.laruta delbufeo.blogspot.com. Spezializes in river tours for seeing dolphins.

Moxos, 6 de Agosto 114, T462 1141. Multi-day river and jungle tours with camping. Recommended.

Paraiso Travel, 6 de Agosto 138, T462 0692. Offers excursions to Laguna Suárez, Rio Mamoré, camping and birdwatching tours.

⊖ Transport

Villa Tunari to the Lowlands: Puerto Villarroel *p111*

From Cochabamba you can get a bus to **Puerto Villarroel** (see Cochabamba Transport, Bus), **Puerto San Francisco**, or **Todos Santos** on the Río Chapare.

Trinidad *p111*

Air Daily flights with **Aerocon** (6 de Agosto y 18 de Noviembre, T462 4442) and **TAM** (Bolívar 42, T462 2363) to La Paz, Santa Cruz, Cochabamba, Cobija, Riberalta and Guayaramerín (Aerocon also to Sucre); 1-2 weekly to Magdalena (Bella Vista).**Amaszonas** (18 de Noviembre 267, T462 2426) Mon, Wed, Fri to **Rurrenabaque**. Airport, T462 0678. Mototaxi to airport US$1.20.

Bus Bus station is on Rómulo Mendoza, between Beni and Pinto, 9 blocks east of main plaza. Motorbike taxis will take people with backpacks from bus station to centre for US$0.45. To **Santa Cruz** (10 hrs on a paved road, US$8-18) and **Cochabamba** (US$12-17, 20 hrs), with **Copacabana**, **Mopar** and **Bolívar** mostly overnight (*bus cama* available). To **Rurrenabaque**, US$18, 12-20 hrs. Enquire locally what services are running to San Borja and **La Paz**. Similarly to **Riberalta** and **Guayaramerín**.

River Cargo boats down the Río Mamoré to **Guayaramerín** take passengers, 3-4 days, assuming no breakdowns, best organized from Puerto Varador (speak to the Port Captain). **Argos** is recommended as friendly, US$22 pp, take water, fresh fruit, toilet paper and ear-plugs; only for the hardy traveller.

San Ignacio de Moxos *p111*

Bus The Trinidad to San Borja bus stops at the **Donchanta** restaurant for lunch, otherwise difficult to find transport to San Borja. Minibus to Trinidad daily at 0730 from plaza, also *camionetas*, check road conditions and times beforehand.

Magdalena *p111*

Air SAPSA flies twice a week from Santa Cruz via Trinidad. **ITNAMA** offers air taxi service.

Road An unpaved road goes to Trinidad via San Ramón (pick-up US$10.50, 9 hrs), passable only in the dry season; also nightly buses from Trinidad. San Ramón to Magdalena takes 6 hrs on motorbike taxi, US$16.

Bella Vista *p111*

Bus There are daily buses from **Magdalena** (except in the rainy season), 2½ hrs, US$2.

Santa Cruz and Eastern Lowlands

In contrast to the highlands of the Andes and the gorges of the Yungas, eastern Bolivia is made up of vast plains stretching to the Chaco of Paraguay and the Pantanal wetlands of Brazil. Agriculture is well-developed and other natural resources are fully exploited, bringing a measure of prosperity to the region. There are a number of national parks with great biodiversity, such as Amboró and Noel Kempff Mercado. Historical interest lies in the pre-Inca ceremonial site at Samaipata, the beautiful Jesuit Missions of Chiquitos and, of much more recent date, the trails and villages where Che Guevara made his final attempt to bring revolution to Bolivia.

Santa Cruz → *Phone code: 03. Population: 1,566,000. Altitude: 416 m.*

A little over 50 years ago, what is now Bolivia's largest city was a remote backwater, but rail and road links ended its isolation. The exploitation of oil and gas in the Departments of Santa Cruz and Tarija, and a burgeoning agribusiness sector, helped fuel rapid development. Since the election of Evo Morales in 2006 however, *Cruceños* have been concerned about the impact of his economic policies, perceived as favouring the highlands. There is considerable local opposition to the national government and Santa Cruz has spearheaded the eastern lowland departments' drive for greater autonomy from La Paz. The city is modern and bustling, far removed from most travellers' perceptions of Bolivia. The centre still retains a bit of its former air however, and the main plaza – 24 de Septiembre – is well cared for and a popular meeting place. During the extended lunchtime hiatus locals (who call themselves *cambas*) take refuge in their homes from the heat or rain, and the gridlock traffic eases. December to March is the hottest and rainiest time of the year.

Arriving in Santa Cruz

Getting there The international **airport** is at **Viru-Viru**, 13 km from the centre, taxi US$10, micro from Ex-Terminal (see Transport, below), or El Trompillo, US$1, 45 min. From airport take micro to Ex-Terminal then taxi to centre. Regional flights operate from **El Trompillo** airport, south of the centre on the Segundo Anillo, taxi US$1.50, many micros. Long distance and regional **buses** leave from the combined bus/train terminal, **Terminal Bimodal**, Avenida Montes on the Tercer Anillo, T348 8382; police check passports and search luggage here; taxi to centre, US$1.50. The city has eight ring roads, Anillos 1, 2, 3, 4 and so on, the first three of which contain most sites of interest to visitors. The neighbourhood of Equipetrol, where many upscale hotels, restaurants and bars are situated, is northwest of the centre in the Tercer (3rd) Anillo.

Tourist information There is a **departmental tourist office**ⓘ *Junín 22 on main plaza, T334 6776, Mon-Fri 0800-1200, 1500-1800; also a desk at Viru-Viru airport, 0700-2000.* **InfoTur**

ⓘ *Sucre y Potosí, inside the Museo de Arte, T339 9581, Mon-Fri 0800-1200, 1500-1900.* **APAC**
ⓘ *Av Busch 552 (2nd Anillo), T333 2287, www.festivalesapac.com,* has information about cultural events in the department of Santa Cruz. See also **www.destinosantacruz.com**.

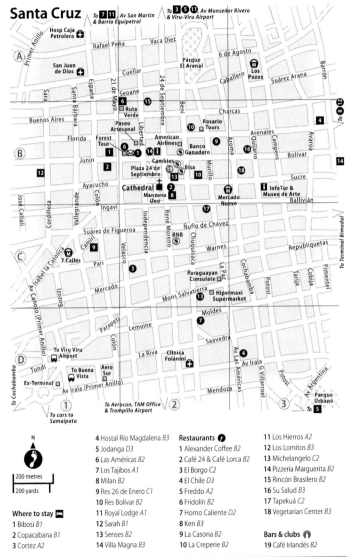

Santa Cruz

N

200 metres
200 yards

Where to stay 🛏
1 Bibosi *B1*
2 Copacabana *B1*
3 Cortez *A2*
4 Hostal Río Magdalena *B3*
5 Jodanga *D3*
6 Las Américas *B2*
7 Los Tajibos *A1*
8 Milan *B2*
9 Res 26 de Enero *C1*
10 Res Bolívar *B2*
11 Royal Lodge *A1*
12 Sarah *B1*
13 Senses *B2*
14 Villa Magna *B3*

Restaurants 🍴
1 Alexander Coffee *B2*
2 Café 24 & Café Lorca *B2*
3 El Borgo *C2*
4 El Chile *D3*
5 Freddo *A2*
6 Fridolín *B2*
7 Horno Caliente *D2*
8 Ken *B3*
9 La Casona *B2*
10 La Creperie *B2*
11 Los Hierros *A2*
12 Los Lomitos *B3*
13 Michelangelo *C2*
14 Pizzería Marguerita *B2*
15 Rincón Brasilero *B2*
16 Su Salud *B3*
17 Tapekuá *C2*
18 Vegetarian Center *B3*

Bars & clubs 🍸
19 Café Irlandés *B2*

Health and safety Dengue fever outbreaks are common during the wet season (Jan-Mar), take mosquito precautions. Crime is on the rise in Santa Cruz. Be especially careful in crowds and market areas, and take only radio taxis at night. ►► *See also Safety, page 12.*

Places in Santa Cruz

The Plaza 24 de Septiembre is the city's main square with the huge **Cathedral** (also a basilica) ① *museum, T332 4683, Mon-Fri 1500-1800, US$1.50.* You can climb to a mirador in the cathedral **bell tower** ① *daily 0800-1200, 1500-1900, US$0.50,* with nice views of the city. **Manzana Uno,** the block behind the Cathedral, has been set aside for rotating art and cultural exhibits. **El Casco Viejo,** the heart of the city, with its arcaded streets and buildings with low, red-tiled roofs and overhanging eaves, retains a slight colonial feel, despite the profusion of modern, air-conditioned shops and restaurants. The **Museo de Historia** ① *Junín 141, T336 5533, Mon-Fri 0800-1200, 1500-1830, free* has several displays includingarchaeological pieces from the Chané and Guaraní cultures and explorers' routes. **Museo de Arte Contemporáneo** ① *Sucre y Potosí, T334 0926, Mon-Fri 0900-1200, 1500-2000, Sat-Sun 1500-1900, free,* houses contemprary Bolivian and international art in a nicely restored old house.

Some 12 km on the road to Cotoca are the **Botanical Gardens** ① *micro or trufi from C Suárez Arana, 15 mins, open daily 0800-1700, entry US$0.50,* a bit run-down but with many walking trails, birds and several forest habitats. **Las Lomas de Arena del Palmar** ① *18 km south of the city, off the road to Palmasola, taxi (4WD may be required in wet season), US$32 return with 2 hrs' wait, entry US$1.50,* are impressive sand dunes with great views. **Parque Ecológico Yvaga Guazu** ① *Km 12.5 Doble Vía a La Guardia, taxi US$5, T352 7971, www.parqueyvagaguazu.org, daily 0800-1600, US$9 for 2-hr guided tour in Spanish (more for English-speaking guide),* 14 ha of tropical gardens with native and exotic species, plants for sale, restaurant serves Sunday buffet lunch. **Biocentro Güembé** ① *Km 7 Camino a Porongo, taxi US$7, T370 0700, www.biocentroguembe.com, daily 0830-1800, US$13 includes guided tour in Spanish or English,* is a resort with accommodation (**$$$** range), restaurant, butterfly farm, walk-in aviary, swimming pools and other family recreation.

Santa Cruz listings

For hotel and restaurant price codes and other relevant information, see pages 9-10.

⬤ Where to stay

Santa Cruz *p114, map p115*
$$$$ Los Tajibos, Av San Martín 455, Barrio Equipetrol, T342 1000, www. lostajiboshotel.com. Set in 6 ha of lush gardens, one of the city's most traditional luxury hotels, all facilities including a/c, business centre, art gallery, restaurants and spa. Weekend discounts.
$$$ Cortez, Cristóbal de Mendoza 280 (Segundo Anillo), T333 1234, www. hotelcortez.com. Traditional tropical hotel

with a/c, restaurant, pool, gardens, meeting rooms, Wi-Fi, parking, good location for dining and nightlife.
$$$ Royal Lodge, Av San Martín 200, Equipetrol, T343 8000. With restaurant and bar, pool, Wi-Fi, airport transfers. Excellent option for its location and price range.
$$$ Senses, Sucre y 24 de Septiembre, just off main plaza, T339 6666. Self-styled boutique hotel in the heart of the city, minimalist decor, includes buffet breakfast, a/c, Wi-Fi.
$$$ Villa Magna, Barrón 70, T339 9700, www.villamagna-aparthotel.com. Fully furnished apartments with a/c, small pool, Wi-Fi, parking, attentive owner and staff,

English and German spoken, monthly rates from US$770.

$$-$ Hostal Río Magdalena, Arenales 653 (no sign), T339 3011, www.hostalrio magdalena.com. Comfortable rooms, downstairs ones are dark, includes breakfast, a/c, cheaper with ceiling fan, small yard and pool, Wi-Fi, popular.

$$ Bibosi, Junín 218, T334 8548, htlbibosi@ hotmail.com. Includes breakfast, private bath, electric shower, a/c, cheaper with fan, Wi-Fi in lobby, good value.

$$ Copacabana, Junín 217, T336 2770, hotelcopacabanascz@hotmail.com. Includes breakfast, restaurant, a/c, cheaper with fan, very good, popular with European tour groups.

$$ Jodanga, C El Fuerte 1380, Zona Parque Urbano, Barrio Los Chóferes, T339 6542, www.jodanga.com. Good backpacker option 10 mins' walk from Terminal Bimodal, a/c, cheaper with fan and without bath, cheaper in dorm, kitchen, bar, swimming pool, billiards, DVDs, nice communal areas, internet, laundry, helpful owner and multilingual staff.

$$ Las Américas, Seoane 356 y 21 de Mayo, T336 8778, www.lasamericas-hotel.com. bo. A/c, buffet breakfast, Wi-Fi, discount for longer stays, indoor parking, restaurant, bar. Starting to show its age but still OK.

$ Milán, René Moreno 70, T339 7500, www.hotelmilan.web.bo. Includes breakfast, private bath, some rooms with a/c, hot water, Wi-Fi, central location.

$ Res 26 de Enero, Camiri 32, T332 1818. In a busy market area. Cheap basic rooms with private bath, even cheaper without, nice courtyard.

$ Res Bolívar, Sucre 131, T334 2500, www.residencialbolivar.com. Includes good breakfast, private bath, cheaper with shared bath and in dorm, lovely courtyard with hammocks, rooms can get hot, alcohol prohibited, popular.

$ Sarah, C Sara 85, T332 2425, hotel.sarah@ hotmail.com. Includes breakfast, simple rooms with a/c, cheaper with fan, screened windows, small patio, good value.

🍴 Restaurants

Santa Cruz *p114, map p115*
Santa Cruz has the best meat in Bolivia, try a local *churrasquería* (grill). Av San Martín in Barrio Equipetrol, and Av Monseñor Rivero are the areas for upmarket restaurants and nightlife. Both are away from the centre, take a taxi at night. Some restaurants close Mon. Restaurants also listed in www.restobolivia.com.

$$$-$$ La Creperie, Arenales 135. Mon-Sat 1900-2400, serves good crêpes, fondues and salads.

$$$-$$ Los Hierros, Av Monseñor Rivero 300 y Castelnau, daily 1200-1500, 1900-2400. Popular upmarket grill with salad bar.

$$$-$$ Michelangelo, Chuquisaca 502, Mon-Fri 1200-1430, 1900-2330, Sat evenings only. Excellent Italian cuisine, a/c.

$$ El Borgo, Velasco 256, T330-1625, daily 1100-2400. Good Italian and light European fare.

$$ Ken, Uruguay 730 (1er Anillo), T333 3728, 1130-1430, 1800-2300, closed Wed. Sushi and authentic Japanese food, popular.

$$ La Casona, Arenales 222, T337 8495, 1130-1500, 1900-2400. German-run restaurant, very good food.

$$ Pizzería Marguerita, Junín y Libertad, northwest corner of the plaza. A/c, good service, coffee, bar, 0830-2400. Popular with expats, Finnish owner speaks English and German.

$$ Rincón Brasilero, Libertad 358, daily 1130-1430,1930-2330. Brazilian-style buffet for lunch, pay by weight, very good quality and variety, popular; pizza and à la carte at night. Recommended.

$$ Tapekuá, Ballivián y La Paz, T334 5905. French and international food, good service, live entertainment some evenings.

$$-$ El Chile, Av Las Américas 60, daily 1200-1500, 1700-2400. Mexican and Bolivian food, good set lunch with salad bar, à la carte at night.

$$-$ Los Lomitos, Uruguay 758 (1er Anillo), T332 8696, daily 0800-

2400. Traditional *churrasquería* with unpretentious local atmosphere, excellent Argentine-style beef.

$$-$ Vegetarian Center, Aroma 64, entre Bolívar y Sucre, Mon-Sat 1200-1500. Set lunch or pay-by-weight buffet.

$ Pizzería El Horno, 3er Anillo, frente a Hospital Oncológico, Equipetrol, T342 8042; also Av Roque Aguilera 600, Las Palmas; and Lagunillas 134, Braniff; daily 1100-2300. True Italian pizza, very popular.

$ Su Salud, Quijarro 115, Mon-Thu 0800-2100, Fri and Sun 0800-1700. Tasty vegetarian food, filling lunches, sells vegetarian products.

Cafés

There are lots of very pleasant a/c cafés where you can get coffee, ice cream, drinks, and snacks.

Alexander Coffee, Junín y Libertad near main plaza, and Av Monseñor Rivero 400 y Santa Fe. For good coffee and people watching.

Café 24, downstairs at René Moreno y Sucre, on the main plaza, daily 0830-0200. Breakfast, juices, international meals, wine rack, nice atmosphere, Wi-Fi.

Café Lorca, upstairs at René Moreno y Sucre, on the main plaza, Mon-Thu 0900-0100, Fri-Sat 0900-0300, Sun 1800-2400. Meals and drinks, Spanish wines, small balcony with views over plaza, live music Tue-Sat from 2100, part of a cultural project, see www.lorcasantacruz.org.

Freddo, Monseñor Rivero 245, good expensive ice cream imported from Argentina.

Fridolín, 21 de Mayo 168, Pari 254, Av Cañoto y Florida, and Monseñor Rivero y Cañada Strongest. All good places for coffee and pastries.

Horno Caliente, Chuquisaca 604 y Moldes, also 24 de Septiembre 653. Salteñas 0730-1230. Traditional local snacks and sweets 1530-1930, popular and very good.

🎵 Bars and clubs

Santa Cruz *p114, map p115*
Bar Irlandés Irish Pub, 3er Anillo Interno 1216 (between Av Cristo Redentor and Zoológico). Irish-themed pub, food available, Irish owner, live music Wed, Fri and Sat evenings. Also *Café Irlandés*, Plaza 24 de Septiembre, overlooking main plaza. Popular.
Kokopelli, Noel Kempff Mercado 1202 (3er Anillo Interno), bar with Mexican food and live music.

❂ Festivals

Santa Cruz *p114, map p115*
Cruceños are famous as fun-lovers and their music, the *carnavalitos*, can be heard all over South America. Of the various festivals, the brightest is **Carnival**, renowned for riotous behaviour, celebrated for the **15 days before Lent**: music in the streets, dancing, fancy dress and the coronation of a queen. Water and paint throwing is common – no one is exempt. **24 Sep** is the local holiday of Santa Cruz city and department.

The Festival de Música Renacentista y Barroca Americana "Misiones de Chiquitos" is held in **late April through early May** every even year (next in 2014) in Santa Cruz and the Jesuit mission towns of the Chiquitania. It is organized by **Asociación Pro Arte y Cultura** (APAC), Av Busch 552, Santa Cruz, T333 2287, www.festivalesapac. com, and celebrates the wealth of sacred music written by Europeans and indigenous composers in the 17th and 18th centuries. APAC sells books, CDs, and videos and also offers – in both Santa Cruz and the mission towns – a schedule of musical programmes. The festival is very popular: book hotels at least 2-3 weeks in advance. Every odd year the city of Santa Cruz APAC holds a **Festival Internacional de Teatro**, and every Aug and Dec a **Festival de la Temporada** in Santa Cruz and major towns of Chiquitania, featuring *música misional* with local performers.

For art exhibits and other cultural events see Cultural Centres, page 121. For cinema, **Cine Center**, Av El Trompillo (2do Anillo) entre Monseñor Santiesteban y René Moreno, www.cinecenter.com.bo.

○ Shopping

Santa Cruz *p114, map p115*
Bookshops Librería El Ateneo, Independencia 365 y Mercado, T333 3338. Books in English, access to internet. **Los Amigos del Libro**, Ingavi 14, T332 7937, sells foreign language books and magazines, expensive but good selection.
Handicrafts Bolivian Souvenirs, Shopping Bolívar, loc 10 & 11, on main plaza, T333 7805; also at Viru-Viru airport. Expensive knitwear and crafts from all over Bolivia. **Paseo Artesanal La Recova**, off Libertad, ½ block from Plaza. Many different kiosks selling crafts. **Vicuñita Handicrafts**, Ingavi e Independencia, T333 4711. Wide variety of crafts from the lowlands and the altiplano, very good.
Jewellery Carrasco, Velasco 23, T336 2841, and other branches. For gemstones. **RC Joyas**, Bolívar 262, T333 2725. Jewellery and Bolivian gems.
Markets Always beware of theft and bag-snatching. **Los Pozos**, between Quijarro, Campero, Suárez Arana and 6 de Agosto; is a sprawling street market for all kinds of produce. **Siete Calles**, Isabel la Católica y Vallegrande, mainly clothing. **Mercado Nuevo**, at Sucre y Cochabamba, rebuilt in 2012. **Hipermaxi** and **Fidalga** are two well-stocked supermarket chains; several locations including Florida y 21 de Mayo, and Monseñor Salvatierra y La Paz.

○ What to do

Santa Cruz *p114, map p115*
Bird Bolivia, T358 2674, www.birdbolivia. com. Specializes in birding tours.
Forest Tour, Galería Casco Viejo, upstairs, No 115, T337 2042, www.forestbolivia.com.

Environmentally sensitive tours to Refugio los Volcanes, birdwatching, national parks, Chiquitania and Salar de Uyuni. English spoken.
Fremen Tours, Beni 79 y Bolívar, T333 8535, www.frementours.com. Offers tours throughout the country, including resort at Villa Tunari and the *Reina de Enín* riverboat.
Magri Turismo, Velarde 49 y Irala, T334 4559, www.magriturismo.com. Long-established agency for airline tickets and tours.
Misional Tours, Los Motojobobos 2515, T360 1985, www.misionaltours.com. Covers all of Bolivia, specializing in Chiquitania, Amboró, and Santa Cruz. Tours in various languages.
Rosario Tours, Arenales 193, T336 9977, www.rosariotours.com. Highly regarded, with English-speaking staff, tours throughout Bolivia.
Ruta Verde, 21 de Mayo 318, T339 6470, www.rutaverdebolivia.com. Offers national parks, Jesuit missions, Amazonian boat trips, Salar de Uyuni, and tailor-made tours, Dutch/Bolivian owned, English and German also spoken, knowledgeable and helpful.

○ Transport

Santa Cruz *p114, map p115*
Air Viru-Viru, 13 km from the centre, open 24 hrs, airline counters from 0600; *casa de cambio* changing cash US$ and euros at poor rates, 0630-2100; various ATMs; luggage lockers 0600-2200, US$5.50 for 24 hrs; ENTEL for phones and internet, plus a few eateries. Domestic flights with **Aero Sur**, **Boliviana de Aviación** (BoA) and **TAM** (Bolivia), to **La Paz**, **Cochabamba**, **Sucre**, **Tarija** and **Cobija**. International flights to **Asunción**, **Buenos Aires**, **Salta**, **Lima**, **Madrid**, **Miami**, **Washington**, **Santiago** and **São Paulo**.
El Trompillo is the regional airport operating daily 0500-1900, T352 6600, located south of the centre on the Segundo Anillo. It has a phone office and kiosk selling drinks, but no other services. **TAM** has

flights throughout the country, different destinations on different days. **Aerocon** flies via **Trinidad** to various towns in the northern jungle.

Bus Most long distance buses leave from the ageing **Terminal Bimodal**, departing in the evening and travelling overnight. Terminal fee, US$0.50, left luggage US$0.50, there are ATMs and cambios. Regional buses and vans leave either from behind the Terminal Bimodal (use pedestrian tunnel under the rail tracks) or from near the Ex-Terminal (the old bus station, Av Irala y Av Cañoto, 1er Anillo, which is no longer functioning). To **Cochabamba**, via the lowland route, many depart 0600-0930 and 1630-2130, US$8-16, 8-10 hrs, also **Trans Carrasco** vans leave when full across the street from the Terminal Bimodal, US$15; via the old highland route, **Trans Carrasco**, depart from the main plaza in El Torno, 30 km west of Santa Cruz, daily at 1200 (from Mairana daily at 0800 and 1500), US$6, 14 hrs. Direct to **Sucre** via Aiquile, around 1600, US$7.50-15, 12-13hrs. To **Oruro**, US$11-20, 14-15 hrs, and **La Paz** between 1630-1900, US$11-25, 15-16 hrs; change in Cochabamba for daytime travel. To **Camiri** (US$4, 4-5 hrs), **Yacuiba** (border with Argentina), US$7-16, 8 hrs and **Tarija**, US$13-26, 17-24 hrs. To **Trinidad**, several daily after 2000, 9 hrs, US$7-15. To **San José de Chiquitos**, US$7-10, 5 hrs, **Roboré**, US$7-10, 7 hrs, and **Quijarro** (border with Brazil), at 1030 and between 1700-2000, US$10-20, 11-12 hrs. Also vans to San José, leave when full, US$10, 4½ hrs. To **San Ignacio de Velasco**, US$10, 10 hrs; Jenecherú bus-cama US$18; also **Expreso San Ignacio** vans leave when full, US$20, 8 hrs.

International: Terminal fee US$1.50. To **Asunción**, US$50-60, 20-24 hrs via Villamontes and the Chaco, at 1930, with **Yacyretá**, T362 5557, Mon, Tue, Thu, Sat; **Stel Turismo**, T349 7762, daily; and **Pycazú**, daily. Other companies are less reliable. See page 124 for the route to Paraguay across the Chaco. To **Buenos Aires** daily

departures around 1900, US$70-90, 36 hrs, several companies. To São Paulo via Puerto Suárez, with **La Preferida**, T364 7160, Mon, Wed, Fri, US$140, 2 days.

Taxi About US$1-1.50 inside 1er Anillo (more at night), US$2 inside 3er Anillo, fix fare in advance. Use radio-taxis at night (eg **Matico**, T335 6666).

Train Ferroviaria Oriental, at Terminal Bimodal, T338 7300, www.ferroviaria oriental.com, runs east to **San José de Chiquitos**, **Roboré**, **Puerto Suárez** and **Quijarro** on the Brazilian border. The **Ferrobus** (a rail-car with the fastest most luxurious service) leaves Santa Cruz Tue, Thu, Sun 1830, arriving Quijarro 0756 next day, US$43; **Expreso Oriental** (an express train), Mon, Wed, Fri 1600, arriving 0800, US$21; **Tren Regional** (the slowest and most run-down), Tue, Thu, Sat 1145, arriving 0620, US$9-19. There is also little-used weekly train service south to **Yacuiba** on the Argentine frontier, but buses are much faster. Passport required to board trains.

ⓘ Directory

Santa Cruz *p114, map p115*
Airline offices Amazonas, Aeropuerto El Trompillo, T357 8988. **Aerocon**, Aeropuerto El Trompillo, T351 1200. **Aero Sur**, Irala 616, T336 7400, and 24 de Septiembre 46 on main plaza, T335 8413. **Aerolíneas Argentinas**, Junín 22 y Libertadm on main plaza, Edif Banco de la Nación Argentina, T333 9776. **American Airlines**, Beni 167, T334 1314. **BoA**, Prolongación Aroma 20, Edificio Casanova, T312 1343. **COPA/ Continental**, Sucre y 24 de Septiembre, T332 2222. **GOL**, T800-100121 or 385 2200. **TAM** (Mercosur), Velasco 700 y La Riva, T337 1999. **TAM** (Militar), El Trompillo airport, T352 9669. **Car hire** Avis, Av Cristo Redentor Km. 3.5, T343 3939, www.avis.com.bo. **Barron's**, Av Alemana 50 y Tajibos, T342 0160, www.rentacarbolivia. com. Outstanding service and completely trustworthy. IMBEX, C El Carmen 123, entre

Av Suárez Arana y Av Charcas, T311 1000, www.imbex.com. **Localiza**, Cristo Redentor entre 2do y 3er Anillo, T341 4343; also at airport, T341 4343; www.localiza.com.

Cultural centres Asociación Pro Arte y Cultura, see Festivals, page 118. **Centro Boliviano Americano**, Cochabamba 66, T334 2299, www.cba.com.bo. Library with US papers and magazines, English classes, some cultural events. **Centro Cultural Feliciana Rodríguez**, Ñuflo de Chávez 21, T337 3657, www.amerida.org. Art exhibits and events. **Centro Cultural Franco Alemán**, 24 de Septiembre on main plaza, T335 0142, www.ccfrancoaleman.org. Joint cultural institute with language courses, cultural events, library (internet access), both open Mon-Fri 0900-1200, 1530-2000. **Centro Cultural Santa Cruz**, René Moreno 369, T335 6941, www.culturabcb.org.bo. Rotating art exhibits and events. **Centro de Formación de la Cooperación Española**, Arenales 583, T335 1311, www.aecid-cf. bo (concerts, films, art exhibitions, lectures, etc), very good. **entro Simón I Patiño**, Independencia y Suárez de Figueroa 89, T 337 2425, www.fundacionpatino.org. Exhibitions, galleries, and bookstore on Bolivian cultures. **Medical services** Santa Cruz is an important medical centre with many hospitals and private clinics. **Clínica Foianini**, Av Irala y Chuquisaca, is among the better regarded and more expensive; **San Juan de Dios**, Cuellar y España, is the public hospital. **Useful addresses** Immigration, Av El Trompillo (2do Anillo) near El Deber newspaper, T351 9574, Mon-Fri 0830-1200, 1430-1800; busy office, give yourself extra time. **Fundación Amigos de la Naturaleza (FAN)**, Km 7.5 Vía a La Guadria, T355 6800, www.fan-bo.org. SERNAP, Calle 9 Oeste 138, frente a la Plaza Italia, Barrio Equipetrol, T339 4310, Mon-Fri 0800-1200, 1400-1800.

Southeastern Bolivia

The highlights of this area known as Los Valles Cruceños, are southwest of Santa Cruz: the Inca site of El Fuerte by the pleasant resort town of Samaipata, nearby Parque Nacional Amboró and the Che Guevara Trail, on which you can follow in the final, fatal footsteps of the revolutionary.

Samaipata → *Phone code: 03. Population 3000. Altitude: 1650 m.*

From Santa Cruz the spectacular old mountain road to Cochabamba runs along the Piray gorge and up into the highlands. Some 100 km from Santa Cruz is Samaipata, a great place to relax midweek, with good lodging, restaurants, hikes and riding, and a growing ex-pat community. A two-hour walk takes you to the top of Cerro de La Patria, just east of town, with nice views of the surrounding valleys. Local *artesanías* include ceramics, paintings and sculpture. At weekends the town bursts into life as crowds of Cruceños come to escape the city heat and to party. See www.samaipata.info and www.guidetosamaipata. com. There are no ATMs in Samaipata, take cash.

The **Museo de Arqueología** houses the tourist information office and a collection of ceramics with anthropomorphic designs, dating from 200 BC to AD 300, and provides information on the nearby pre-Inca ceremonial site commonly called **El Fuerte** ① *daily 0900-1700, museum Mon-Fri 0830-1200, 1400-1800, Sat-Sun AM only, US$7 for El Fuerte and Museum, US$0.85 for museum only, ticket valid 4 days. Spanish- and English-speaking guides available at El Fuerte, US$12.* This sacred structure (altitude 1990 m) consists of a complex system of channels, basins, high-relief sculptures, etc, carved out of one vast slab of rock. Some suggest that Amazonian people created it around 1500 BC, but it could be later. There is evidence of subsequent occupations and that it was the nethermost outpost of the Incas'

Kollasuyo (their eastern empire). Behind the rock are poorly excavated remains of a city. It is not permitted to walk on the rock, so visit the museum first to see the excellent model. El Fuerte is 9 km from Samaipata; 3 km along the highway to Santa Cruz, then 6 km up a rough, signposted road (taxi US$6 one way, US$13 return with two hours wait); two to three hours' walk one way. Pleasant bathing is possible in a river on the way to El Fuerte.

In addition to tours to El Fuerte and the Ruta del Che (see below), many other worthwhile excursions can be made in the Samaipata area. Impressive forests of giant ferns can be visited around **Cerro La Mina** and elsewhere in the Amboró buffer zone. Also **Cuevas**, 20 km east of town, with waterfalls and pools, often visited together with El Fuerte. Further east are forest and sandstone mountains at **Bella Vista/Codo de los Andes**. There is a wonderful hike up to the **Mirador de Cóndores**, with many condors and nearby the the 25-m high **La Pajcha** waterfall, 40 km south of Samaipata. **Postrervalle** is a quaint hamlet with many interesting walks and mountain bike trails. There is good birdwatching throughout the region, especially around Mataral (see below), and tour operators in Samaipata can arrange all of the above trips.

The little village of **Bermejo**, 40 km east of Samaipata on the road to Santa Cruz, provides access to the strikingly beautiful **Serranía Volcanes** region, abutting on Parque Nacional Amboró. Here are the upmarket **Laguna Volcán Eco-Resort** (www.ecolagunavolcan.com) and the excellent **Refugio Los Volcanes** (www.refugiovolcanes.net, recommended). Also near Bermejo is **Ginger's Paradise** (www.gingersparadise.com), a simple country inn popular with backpackers.

Samaipata

Where to stay
1 Andoriña
2 El Jardín
3 El Pueblito Resort
4 Hostal Siles
5 Landhaus
6 La Posada del Sol
7 La Víspera
8 Res Kim
9 Res Paola

Restaurants
1 Café 1900
2 Chakana
3 El Descanso en Las Alturas
4 El Turista
5 La Bohème
6 La Oveja Negra & Ben Verhoef Tours
7 La Ranita
8 Latina Café
9 Tierra Libre

Comarapa and the highland road to Cochabamba

Past Samaipata the road from Santa Cruz continues west 17 km to **Mairana**, a hot dusty roadside town where long-distance buses make their meal stops and there is daily service to Cochabamba (see Santa Cruz transport, page 120). It is 51 km further to **Mataral**, where there are petroglyphs and the road to Vallegrande branches south. Another 57 km west is **Comarapa** (altitude 1800 m), a tranquil agricultural centre half-way between Santa Cruz and Cochabamba. The town provides access to several lovely natural areas including **Laguna Verde** (12 km, taxi US$11.50 with two hours wait, or walk back over the hills), surrounded by cloud forest bordering Parque Nacional Amboró; and the **Jardín de Cactáceas de Bolivia**, where the huge *carpari* cactus and 25 other endemic species may be seen (entry US$0.75, take a *trufi* from Comarapa to Pulquina Abajo, US$1). The Jardín itself is run-down but there are many more impressive cactii, good walking and birdwatching throughout the area. The tourist office at El Parquecito in Comarapa can arrange local guides. Beyond Comarapa the road is unpaved and very scenic. It climbs through cloud forest past the village of **La Siberia** to the pass at El Churo and enters the department of Cochabamba (see page 98).

Parque Nacional Amboró

This vast (442,500 ha) protected area lies only three hours west of Santa Cruz. Amboró encompasses four distinct major ecosystems and 11 life zones and is home to thousands of animal, plant and insect species (it is reputed to contain more butterflies than anywhere else on earth). The park is home to over 850 species of birds, including the blue-horned curassow, quetzal and cock-of-the-rock, red and chestnut-fronted macaws, hoatzin and cuvier toucans, and most mammals native to Amazonia, such as capybaras, peccaries, tapirs, several species of monkey, and jungle cats like the jaguar, ocelot and margay, and the spectacled bear. There are also numerous waterfalls and cool, green swimming pools, moss-ridden caves and large tracts of virgin rainforest. The park itself is largely inaccessible, but there is good trekking in the surrounding 195,100-ha buffer zone which is where most tours operate. The best time of year to visit the park is during April to October. There are two places to base yourself: Samaipata (see above) to access the southern highland areas of the park, and Buena Vista (see below) for northern lowland sections. You cannot enter the park without a guide, either from a tour operator, or from a community-based project. The park is administered by SERNAP, for their Santa Cruz office see page 121. There are also park offices in Samaipata and Buena Vista. Note that there are many biting insects so take repellent, long-sleeved shirts, long trousers and good boots.

Buena Vista → *Phone code: 04.*

This sleeply little town is 100 km northwest of Santa Cruz by paved road (see www. buenavistabolivia.com). No ATM in town, but US$ cash can be changed. There is an interpretation office one block from the plaza, T932 2055. Three kilometres from town is **Eco-Albergue Candelaria** ① *T7781 3238 or contact in advance through Hacienda El Cafetal (page 126)*, a community tourism project offering cabins in a pleasant setting, activities and tours. From Buena Vista there are five tourist sites for entering the national park: **Villa Amboró** (T03-343 1332, www.probioma.org.bo), good for hiking; the community can arrange horse riding. Get there either by 4WD, or take a taxi-trufi to Las Cruces (35 km from Buena Vista) and then hike to the refuge (about two hours). **Macuñucu**, about 2 km from Villa Amboró, is an entrance favoured by tour operators. **La Chonta**, a community-based ecotourism lodge (T6773 5333, www.lachontaamboro.wordpress.com), offers tours to the forest and to farming communities with local guides. Take a taxi-trufi via Haytú to the Río Surutú and from there walk or horse ride 2½ hours. Further along the road to Cochabamba is **Mataracú**, used by the operators, with natural pools, waterfalls and dinosaur fossils. It has the private **Mataracú Tent Camp** (T03-342 2372) and other camping options. At **Cajones de Ichilo**, a community lodge 70 km from Buena Vista (T0763 02581, 0600-0900, 1800-2200) in mountainous scenery with a large river, there are trails which offer a good chance of seeing mammals and, with luck, the horned currassow, one of the most endangered species of bird in Bolivia.

Vallegrande and La Higuera

Some 115 km south of the Santa Cruz-Cochabamba road is La Higuera, where Che Guevara was killed. On 8 October each year, people gather there to celebrate his memory. La Higuera is reached through the town of **Vallegrande** where, at **Hospital Nuestro Señor de Malta** ① *no fee, but voluntary donation to the health station*, you can see the old laundry building where Che's body was shown to the international press on 9 October 1967. Near Vallegrande's air strip you can see the results of excavations carried out in 1997 which finally unearthed his physical remains (now in Cuba), ask an airport attendant to see the site. Vallegrande has a small archaeological museum *US$1.50*, above which is the **Che Guevara Room** ① *free.*

The schoolhouse in La Higuera (60 km south of Vallegrande) where Che was executed is now a museum. Another **museum** (T03-942 2003), owned by René Villegas, is open when he is in town. Guides, including Pedro Calzadillo, headmaster of the school, will show visitors to the ravine of El Churo (or Yuro), where Che was captured on 8 October 1967.

A **'Che Guevara Trail'**, which would follow the last movements of Che and his band as they tried to flee the pursuing Bolivian Army, has been proposed as a way of attracting tourism to the area. It is an ambitious 815-km circuit, winding its way along dirt roads in the sub-tropical area bordering Santa Cruz and Chuquisaca departments. Tours are organized by agencies in Santa Cruz and Samaipata. Adventurous tourists with sufficient time and interest can also reach the area by public transport and arrange for local guides.

To Paraguay and Argentina

South of Santa Cruz a good paved road passes through Abapó, Camiri, Boyuibe, Villamontes – access for the Trans-Chaco route to Paraguay – and Yacuiba, on the border with Argentina.

Villamontes → *Phone code: 04.*

Villamontes, 500 km south of Santa Cruz and 280 km east of Tarija, is renowned for fishing. It holds a Fiesta del Pescado in August. It is a hot, friendly, spread-out city on the north shore of the Río Pilcomayo, at the base of the Cordillera de Aguaragüe, the easternmost range. The river cuts through this range (Parque Nacional Aguaragüe) forming **El Angosto**, a beautiful gorge. The road to Tarija is cut in the cliffs along this gorge. At Plaza 6 de Agosto is the **Museo Héroes del Chaco** ① *Tue-Sun 0800-1200, 1400-1800, US$0.30*, with photographs, maps, artefacts, and battle models of the 1932-1935 Chaco War. There is no ATM, but banks, **Prodem** and various *cambios* change US$ cash (**Cambios San Bernardo** also changes guaraníes and Argentine pesos). They are all on Av Méndez Arcos. There are many internet cafes and *cabinas* for phone calls in the centre.

From Villamontes, the road to Paraguay runs east to **Ibibobo** (70 km). The first 30 km is paved, thereafter it's gravel and further paving is in progress. Motorists and bus travellers should carry extra water and some food, as climatic conditions are harsh and there is little traffic in case of a breakdown. Bolivian exit stamps are given at Ibibobo. If travelling by bus, passports are collected by driver and returned on arrival at Mcal Estigarribia (Paraguay), with Bolivian exit stamp. Paraguayan immigration and thorough drugs searches take place in Mcal Estigarribia. See Santa Cruz Transport (page 119) for international bus services. From Ibibobo to the Bolivian frontier post at Picada Sucre is 75 km, then it's 15 km to the actual border and another 8 km to the Paraguayan frontier post at **Fortín Infante Rivarola**. There are customs posts, but no police, immigration nor any other services at the border.

Yacuiba → *Population: 11,000.*

Yacuiba is a prosperous city (reported less-than-safe due to drug running) at the crossing to Pocitos in Argentina. There is a train service from Santa Cruz to Yacuiba but this is slow and poor, road travel is a better option, or **Aerocon** flights to Santa Cruz (Santa Cruz 1336, T468 3841). In Yacuiba, there are ATMs on Campero, **Entel** and Correos. Argentine consul at Comercio y Sucre. The border crossing is straightforward. Passengers leaving Bolivia must disembark at Yacuiba, take a taxi to Pocitos on the border (US$0.40, beware unscrupulous drivers) and walk across to Argentina.

Southeastern Bolivia listings

For hotel and restaurant price codes and other relevant information, see pages 9-10.

🛏 Where to stay

Samaipata *p121, map p122*
Rooms may be hard to find at weekends in high season.
$$$-$$ El Pueblito Resort, camino a Valle Abajo, 20 mins' walk uphill from town, T944 6383, www.elpueblitoresort.com. Fully-equipped cabins and rooms, includes breakfast, pool, restaurant and bar set around a mock colonial plaza, with shops and meditation chapel.
$$ La Víspera, 1.2 km south of town, T944 6082, www.lavispera.org. Dutch-owned organic farm with accommodation in 4 cosy cabins with kitchen, camping US$4-7 pp, breakfast and lunch available in **Café-Jardín** (0800-1500 daily), book exchange, maps for sale. A peaceful slow-paced place; owners Margarita and Pieter are very knowledgeable and can arrange excursions. They also sell medicinal and seasoning herbs. Highly recommended.
$ Andoriña, C Campero, 2½ blocks from plaza, T944 6333, www.andorinasamaipata. com. Tastefully decorated hostel, cheaper

without bath, includes good breakfast, kitchen, bar, good views, volunteer opportunites. Dutch-Bolivian run, enthusiastic owners Andrés and Doriña are very knowledgeable, English spoken.
$ El Jardín, C Arenales, 2 blocks from market, T7311 4461. With electric shower, cheaper in dorm, ample grounds, camping US$3pp, kitchen facilities, Belgian-Bolivian run.
$ Hostal Siles, C Campero, T944-6408. Simple rooms, cheaper with shared bath electric shower, kitchen and laundry facilities, good value.
$ Landhaus, C Murillo uphill from centre, T944 6033, www.samaipata-landhaus.com. Cabins and rooms in nice ample grounds, small pool, hammocks, parking, sauna (extra), craft shop, good breakfast available. Older rooms are cheaper and good value.
$ La Posada del Sol, C Arteaga, 3 blocks north of plaza, T7211 0628, www.laposada delsol.net. Most rooms with private bath, electric shower, nice grounds, includes breakfast, restaurant, views, US-Bolivian run.
$ Paola, C Terrazas, diagonal to the plaza, T944 6093. Simple rooms, cheaper without bath, electric shower, restaurant serves set meals, internet (extra), kitchen and laundry facilities.

$ Res Kim, C Terrazas, near plaza, T944 6161. Cheaper with shared bath, family-run, spotless, good value.

Comarapa *p123*
$ El Paraíso, Av Comarapa 396 (main road to Cochabamba), T946 2045. Pleasant economical hotel, private electric shower, nice garden, parking, decent restaurant, popular.

Buena Vista *p123*
$$$-$$ Hacienda El Cafetal, 5.5 km south of town (taxi from plaza US$3), T935 2067. Comfortable suites for up to 5 people, double rooms, breakfast included, restaurant, bar, birdwatching platform, on a working coffee plantation (tours available), with shade forest.
$$ Buenavista, 700 m out of town, T03-932 2104, www.buenavistahotel.com.bo. Pretty place with rooms, suites and cabins with kitchen, viewing platform, pool, sauna, very good restaurant, horse riding.
$ La Casona, Av 6 de Agosto at the corner of the plaza, T03-932 2083. Small simple rooms with fan, shared bath, electric shower, courtyard, hammocks, good value.
$ Quimori, 1 km east of Buena Vista, T03-932 2081. Includes breakfast, others meals with advance notice, pool, nice grounds, tours in dry season, family-run.
$ Res Nadia, T03-932 2049. Cheaper without bath, simple, small, family run.

Vallegrande and La Higuera *p124*
$ Hostal Juanita, M M Caballero 123, Vallegrande, T942 2231. Cheaper without bath, electric shower, good value, Doña Juanita is kind.
$ La Casa del Telegrafista, La Higuera, T6773 3362, www.lacasadeltelegrafista. com. Small, welcoming French-owned posada, rooms with shared bath, lovely garden, great views, meals on request, camping (US$2), horseback and mountain bike tours, US$15, also bikes for hire.
$ Res Vallegrande, on the plaza, Vallegrande. Basic accommodation.

To Paraguay *p124*
Camiri
$$-$ Hotel JR, Tte Coronel Sánchez 247 y Comercio, T952 2200, jrhotelcamiri@yahoo. es. Includes buffet breakfast, a/c, parking.
$ Premier, Av Busch 60, ½ block from plaza, T952 2204. A/c, cheaper with fan, spacious, comfortable, welcoming owners. Recommended.

Villamontes *p124*
$$ El Rancho, Av Méndez Arcos opposite the train station, 15 blocks from the centre, T672 2059, rancho@entelnet.bo. Lovely rooms, a/c, includes full breakfast, frigobar, nice grounds and pool, parking, excellent restaurant.
$ Gran Hotel Avenida, Av Méndez Arcos 3 blocks east of Plaza 15 de Abril, T672 2106. A/c, includes breakfast, helpful owner, parking.
$ Res Raldes, Cap Manchego 171, 1½ blocks from Plaza 15 de Abril, T672 2088, fernandoarel@gmail.com. Well maintained family run hotel, a/c, electric shower, cheaper with shared bath and fan, nice courtyard, small pool, parking.

Yacuiba *p125*
$$ París, Comercio 1175 y Campero, T04-682 2182. The best, with breakfast, a/c.
$$ Valentín, San Martín 1153, T04-682 2645, valentinhotel@hotmail.com. With breakfast, a/c (cheaper with fan), restaurant, pool, sauna (extra).
$ Rojas, Comercio 1025, T04-682 2883. With bath, a/c, hot water, cheaper with fan.

🍴 Restaurants

Samaipata *p121, map p122*
$$ El Descanso en Las Alturas, C Arteaga, uphill from plaza, opens mostly on weekends. Wide choice including good steaks and pizzas.
$$ La Oveja Negra, Campero 217, open from 1800, closed Tue. Rustic decor, good vegetarian dishes, nice bar.

$$ Latina Café, Bolívar, 3 blocks from plaza, Fri-Tue 1800-2200, Sat-Sun also 1200-1430. Nice upmarket restaurant/bar with very good Bolivian and international food including vegetarian, try the *ensalada orgásmica*. French-Bolivian run and recommended.
$$-$ Chakana, Terrazas on plaza, daily 0800-2300. Bar/restaurant/café serving *almuerzos*, good snacks, salads, cakes and ice cream, outside seating, book exchange, Dutch-owned.
$$-$ Tierra Libre, Sucre ½ block from plaza, open 1200-2200, Sun 1200-1500, closed Wed. Nice terrace with outdoor seating, good meat and vegetarian, pleasant atmosphere. Recommended.
$ Café 1900, Sucre on plaza, daily 0800-2300. Good set lunch, sandwiches and crepes. Same owners as Latina Café.
$ El Turista, opposite the gas station on the highway. Good local dishes.
La Boheme, Sucre y Terrazas, diagonal to plaza, daily 1200-2400. Trendy Australian-run bar for drinks and snacks, opened in 2012.
La Ranita, Arce near plaza, daily 0800-1230, 1430-1830. Tea house and bakery, French specialities.

Buena Vista *p123*
$$-$ La Plaza, on the plaza. Elegant restaurant/bar with a terrace, wide range of international dishes, good service.
$ El Patujú, on the plaza. The only café in town, serving excellent local coffee, teas, hot chocolate and a range of snacks. Also sells local produce and crafts.

⚙ What to do

Samaipata *p121, map p122*
Cycling
Club de Ajedrez, Bolivar near the museum, rents bikes.
Robert's Biking Tours, same location and opening hours as Zen-tro massage, T7368 0229. Cycling and walking tours.

Horse riding
Horses are available from **La Vispera**, see Where to stay, above.

Massage
Zen-tro, Bolivar opposite the museum, T7708 2055, Wed-Sat 0900-1200, 1500-1800. Alexanda Thomas offers massage (US$22 for 1 hr), reflexology and other therapies.

Tour operators
Except as noted, all tour agencies are on C Bolívar near the museum. Most day-trips cost about US$20-25 pp in a group of 4.
Ben Verhoef Tours, Campero 217, T944 6365, www.benverhoeftours.com. Dutch-owned, English, German and Spanish also spoken. Offer tours along La Ruta del Che and throughout the area.
Jucumari Tours, T944 6129, erwin-am@hotmail.com. Run by Edwin Acuña, who has a 4WD vehicle.
Michael Blendinger, T944 6227, www.discoveringbolivia. com. German guide raised in Argentina who speaks English, runs fully equipped 4WD tours, short and long treks, horse rides, specialist in nature and archaeology.
Road Runners, T944 6193. Olaf and Frank speak English, German and Dutch, enthusiastic, lots of information and advice.
Tucandera Tours, T7316 7735, sa.cossio@hotmail.com. Saul Arias and Elva Villegas are biologists, excellent for nature tours and birdwatching, English spoken, competitive prices. Recommended.

Buena Vista *p123*
Amboró Travel & Adventure on the plaza, T7160 0691, amborotravel@hotmail.com. Prices include transport to and from the park, guide and meals. Recommended.
Puertas del Amboró, corner of the plaza, T03-932 2059. They also offer full packages.

☉ Transport

Samaipata *p121, map p122*

Bus From **Santa Cruz** to Samaipata, only
Sucre-bound buses leave from the Terminal
Bimodal. **Taxis Expreso Samaipata** in Santa
Cruz at Av Omar Chávez 1147 y Soliz de
Holguín, T333 5067 (Samaipata T944 6129),
leave when full Mon-Sat 0530-2030 (for
Sun book in advance), US$4.50 per person
shared; or US$20 in private vehicle, 2½ hrs.
Returning to Santa Cruz, they pick you up
from your hotel in Samaipata. Buses leaving
Santa Cruz for **Sucre** and other towns pass
through Samaipata between 1800 and
2000; tickets can be booked with 1 day's
notice through **Hotel El Turista**, at main road
opposite petrol station. To get to **Samaipata**
from **Sucre**, buses leave at night and arrive
0500-0600 (set your alarm in case the driver
forgets to stop for you), stopping in Mataral
or Mairana for breakfast, about half an hour
before Samaipata.

Comarapa *p123*

To/from **Santa Cruz** with Turismo
Caballero (T350 9626) and **Trans Comarapa**
(T7817 5576), both on Plazuela Oruro, Av
Grigotá (3er Anillo), 3 daily each, US$4.50,
6 hrs. To **Cochabmaba**, 2 buses a day pass
through from Mairana.

Buena Vista *p123*

Sindicato 10 de Febrero in Santa Cruz at
Izozog 668 y Av Irala, 1er Anillo behind
ex-terminal, T334 8435, 0730-1830, US$3 pp
(private vehicle US$15), 2½ hrs. Also another
shared taxi company nearby, and 'Linea 102'
buses from regional section of Terminal
Bimodal. From Buena Vista, the access to
the park is by gravel road, 4WD jeep or
similar recommended as rivers have to
been crossed. All operators and community
eco-lodge coordinators offer transport.

Vallegrande and La Higuera *p124*

Bus Flota Vallegrande has 2 daily buses
morning and afternoon from Santa Cruz to
Vallegrande via **Samaipata** (at 1130 and
1630), 5 hrs, US$5. Best to book in advance.
From Vallegrande market, a daily bus
departs 0815 to **Pucará** (45 km), from where
there is transport (12 km) to **La Higuera**.
Taxi Vallegrande-La Higuera US$25-30.

Villamontes *p124*

Bus To **Yacuiba**, Coop El Chaco, Av
Méndez Arcos y Ismael Montes, hourly
0630-1830, US$1.35, 1½ hrs. Cars from
Av Montenegro y Cap Manchego, hourly
or when full, 0630-1830, US$2, 1½ hrs. To
Camiri, cars from Av Montenegro y Méndez
Arcos, leave when full 0530-1800, US$3.50,
2 hrs. Long distance buses from terminal on
Av Méndez Arcos, 13 blocks east of Plaza
15 de Abril (taxi US$0.40 pp). To **Tarija** via
Entre Ríos, mostly unpaved and extremely
scenic (sit on the right for best views),
US$5-6, 10-11 hrs, several companies
1730-1930; for day travel, **Copacabana**
may depart at 1030, 2-3 per week from the
terminal; Guadalupana, Wed and Sat at
0930, from Coop El Chaco office. To **Santa
Cruz**, several companies daily, US$4.50-
8.50, some bus cama, 7-8 hrs.

To **Asunción**, buses from Santa Cruz pass
through 0200-0300, reserve a day earlier,
US$35, about 15 hrs. 5 companies, offices
all on Av Montenegro, either side of Av
Méndez Arcos. Best are **Stel**, T672 3662,
or Vicky Vides T7735 0934; Yaciretá, T672
2812, or Betty Borda, T7740 4111.

Yacuiba *p125*

Bus To **Santa Cruz**, about 20 companies
run daily services, mostly at night, 14 hrs,
US$8-15. To **Tarija**, daily morning and
evening. To **La Paz**, via Tarija, 32 hrs, US$23.
To **Sucre** with **Trans Chaqueña**, Tue, Sat
1000, US$23, 20 hrs.

Eastern Bolivia

The vast and rapidly developing plains to the east of the Eastern Cordillera are Bolivia's richest area in natural resources. For the visitor, the beautiful churches and rich traditions of the former Jesuit missions of Chiquitos are well worth a visit. Here too are some of the country's largest and wildest protected natural areas. This combination of natural beauty, living indigenous culture and Jesuit heritage make the region one of Bolivia's hidden gems.

Jesuit Missions of Chiquitos

Nine Jesuit missions survive east of Santa Cruz, six of which – San Javier, Concepción, San Rafael, Santa Ana, San Miguel and San José de Chiquitos – have churches which are UNESCO World Heritage Sites. Many of these were built by the Swiss Jesuit, Padre Martin Schmidt and his pupils. Besides organizing *reducciones* and constructing churches, for each of which he built an organ, Padre Schmidt wrote music (some is still played today on traditional instruments) and he published a Spanish-Chiquitano dictionary based on his knowledge of all the dialects of the region. He worked in this part of the then-Viceroyalty of Peru until the expulsion of the Jesuits in 1767 by order of Charles III of Spain. One of the best ways to appreciate this region is at the bi-annual Festival de Música Renacentista y Barroca Americana, held every even year (next in 2014, see page 118), but the living legacy of the missions can be appreciated year-round. Church services are exceptionally well attended, with Chuiquitano musicians and choirs sometimes performing at Sunday mass. The centres of the towns have been beautifully refurbished and are a pleasure to stroll around.

Access to the mission area is by bus or train from **Santa Cruz**: a paved highway runs north to San Ramón (180 km) and on north, to San Javier (40 km further), turning east here to Concepción (60 km), then to San Ignacio de Velasco (160 km, of which the first 30 are paved). A rough road (scheduled for improvement in 2012-13) runs south from San Ignacio either through San Miguel, or Santa Ana to meet at San Rafael for the continuation south to San José de Chiquitos. Access is also possible by the mostly-paved Santa Cruz-Puerto Suárez highway, which goes via San José de Chiquitos. By rail, leave the Santa Cruz-Quijarro train at San José and from there travel north by bus. The most comfortable way to visit is by jeep, in about five days. The route is straightforward and fuel is available. For jeep hire, see Directory, page 120. For information see **www.chiquitania.com** for extensive historical and practical information; also **www.mancochiquitana.org**, **www.misionesjesuiticas.com.bo** and http://chiquitos.santacruz.gob.bo.

San Javier (or San Xavier) The first Jesuit mission in Chiquitos (1691), its church built by Padre Schmidt between 1749 and 1752. Some of the original wooden structure has survived more or less intact and restoration was undertaken between 1987 and 1992 by the Swiss Hans Roth, himself a former Jesuit. Subtle designs and floral patterns cover the ceiling, walls and carved columns. One of the bas-relief paintings on the high altar depicts Martin Schmidt playing the piano for his indigenous choir. It is a fine 30-minute walk (best in the afternoon light) to **Mirador El Bibosi** and the small **Parque Piedra de Los Apóstoles**. There is also good walking or all-terrain cycling in the surrounding countryside (no maps, ask around), thermal swimming holes at **Aguas Calientes**, and horse riding from several hotels. Patron saint's *fiesta*, 3 December. Tourist guides' association has an office in the **Alcaldía** ① *T7761 7902, or 7763 3203 for a guide*. Information also from the **Casa de Cultura** ① *on the plaza, T963 5149*.

Concepción The lovely town is dominated by its magnificent cathedral, completed by Padre Schmidt and Juan Messner in 1756 and totally restored by Hans Roth (1975-1986) ① *0700-2000, tours 1000, 1500, donation invited*. The interior of this beautiful church has an altar of laminated silver. In front of the church is a bell-cum-clock tower housing the original bells and behind it are well-restored cloisters. On the plaza, forming part of the Jesuit complex, is the **Museo Misional** ① *Mon-Sat 0800-1200, 1430-1830, Sun 1000-1230, US$3.50*, which has an *artesanía* shop. The ticket also gives entry to the **Hans Roth Museum**, dedicated to the restoration process. Visit also the **Museo Antropológico de la Chiquitania** ① *16 de Septiembre y Tte Capoblanco, 0800-1200, 1400-1800, free*, which explains the life of the indigenous peoples of the region. It has a café and guesthouse. Fiesta de la Inmaculada Concepción: 8 December. An orchid festival is held in the second week of October. The **Municipal tourist office** ① *Lucas Caballero y Cabo Rodríguez, one block from plaza, T964 3057*, can arrange trips to nearby recreational areas, ranches and communities. An **Asociación de Guías Locales** ① *south side of plaza, contact Ysabel Supepi, T7604 7085; or Hilario Orellana, T7534 3734*, also offers tours to local communities many of which are developing grass-roots tourism projects: eg **Santa Rita**, **San Andrés** and **El Carmen**. With advance notice, they can also organize private concerts with 30 to 40 musicians. Various restaurants in town. Many places sell wood carvings, traditional fabrics and clothing. **Estancia La Fortaleza** (T7607 5789, www.lafortaleza.ch), 44 km south of Concepción, is a Swiss-run 2500 ha forest reserve and working ranch, oferring upmarket accommodation with full board and farm tours.

San Ignacio de Velasco This is the main commercial and transport hub of the region, with road links to Brazil. A lack of funds for restoration led to the demolition of San Ignacio's replacement Jesuit church in 1948, the original having burnt down in 1808. A modern replica contains the elaborate high altar, pulpit and paintings and statues of saints. Tourist information office at **Casa de la Cultura** ① *La Paz y Comercio, on the plaza, T962 2056 ext 122, culturayturismo.siv@gmail.com, Mon-Fri 0800-1200, 1430-1830*, can help organize guides and visits to local music schools. The **Centro Artesanal** ① *Santa Cruz entre Bolívar y Oruro, Mon-Sat 0800-1930, Sun 0800-1200*, sells lovely textile and wood crafts. There is community tourism in the villages of **San Juancito**, 18 km from San Ignacio, where organic coffee is grown, and **San Rafael de Sutuquiña**, 5 km; both have artisans. **Laguna Guapomó** reservoir on the edge of San Ignacio is good for swimming and fishing. Patron saint's day, preceded by a cattle fair, 31 July. There is only one ATM in town, best take some cash.

Santa Ana, San Rafael and San Miguel de Velasco These three small towns are less visited than some others along the missions circuit. Allow at least two days if travelling independently from San Ignacio: you can take a bus to Santa Ana in the afternoon, stay overnight, then continue to San Rafael the next afternoon and return to San Ignacio via San Miguel on Tuesday, Thursday or Sunday (see Transport, page 136). A day trip by taxi from San Ignacio costs about US$65 or an all-inclusive tour can be arranged by **Parador Santa Ana** (see Where to stay, page 134). An entry fee of US$1-2 is charged to visit the churches and local guides are available, US$10.

The church in **Santa Ana** (founded 1755, constructed after the expulsion of the Jesuits), is a lovely wooden building. It is the most authentic of all the Jesuit *templos* and Santa Ana is a particularly authentic little village. The tourist office on the plaza can provide guides. Simple economical accommodation at 11 different **Ecoalbergues Familiares**, which have been recommended. Fiesta de Santa Ana: 26 July.

San Rafael's church was completed by Padre Schmidt in 1748. It is one of the most beautifully restored, with mica-covered interior walls and frescoes in beige paint over the exterior. Patron saint's day, with traditional dancing, 24 October; Christmas pageant is worth seeing. **$ Hotel Paradita**, T962 4008, and others; restaurants near the plaza; tourist information office T962 4022.

The frescoes on the façade of the church (1766) at **San Miguel** depict St Peter and St Paul; designs in brown and yellow cover all the interior and the exterior side walls. The mission runs three schools and a workshop; the sisters are very welcoming and will gladly show tourists around. There is a **Museo Etnofolclórico**, off the Plaza at C Betania; next door is the Municipalidad/Casa de la Cultura, with a tourist information office, T962 4222. San Miguel has many worksops and rivals San Ignacio for the quality of its Jesuit-inspired art. Patron saint's day: 29 September.

San José de Chiquitos → *Phone code: 03.*

One complete side of the plaza is occupied by the superbly restored frontage of the Jesuit mission complex of four buildings and a bell tower, begun in the mid-1740s. Best light for photography is in the afternoon. The stone buildings, in Baroque style, are connected by a wall. They are the 18th century chapel; the church (1747) with its triangular façade; the four-storey bell-tower (1748) and the mortuary (*la bóveda* – 1750), with one central window but no entrance in its severe frontage. The complex and **Museo** ① *Mon-Fri 0800-1200, 1430-1800, Sat-Sun 0900-1200, 1500-1800, entry US$3,* are well worth visiting. Behind are the *colegio* and workshops, which house the **Escuela Municipal de Música**, visits to rehersals and performances can be arranged by the tourist office. **InfoTur** ① *in the Municipio, C Velasco, ½ block from plaza, T972 2084, Mon-Fri 0800-1200, 1430-1830,* has information and arranges various tours; there is internet upstairs. On Mondays, Mennonites bring their produce to San José and buy provisions. The colonies are 50 km west and the Mennonites, who speak English, German, plattdeutsch and Spanish, are happy to talk about their way of life. Fiesta de San José is 1 May, preceded by a week of folkloric and other events. There is only one ATM in town, best take some cash.

About 2 km south from San José is the 17,000 ha **Parque Nacional Histórico Santa Cruz la Vieja**. It has a monument to the original site of Santa Cruz (founded 1561) and a *mirador* with great views. The park's heavily forested hills contain much animal and bird life. There is a *mirador* and various trails for hiking; guides can be organized by the tourist office in San José. It gets very hot so start early, allow over one hour to get there on foot (or hire a vehicle) and take plenty of water and insect repellent. There is also good walking with lovely views at **Cerro Turubó** and the **Serranía de San José**, both outside San José.

East of San José de Chiquitos

Paving of the highway from Santa Cruz east to Brazil in 2011 opened up this once isolated region of friendly villages surrounded by natural wonders. The **Serranía de Chiquitos** is a flat-topped mountain range running east-west, north of the highway and railroad. It is filled with rich vegetation, caves, petroglyphs, waterfalls, birds and butterflies. These hills are part of the 262,000 ha **Reserva Valle de Tucavaca** which protects unique Chiquitano dry forest and offers great hiking opportunities. Various community tourism projects are underway in the area and local guides are available in the towns.

The village of **Chochis**, 80 km east of San José de Chiquitos, is known for its sanctuary of the Virgen Asunta built by Hans Roth in 1988 (one of his few major works not connected with restoring Jesuit missions). The large sanctuary is built at the foot of an impressive red sandstone outcrop called **La Torre,** 2 km from town. Along the rail line from Chochis toward La Torre is a signed trail leading to the **Velo de Novia** waterfall, a pleasant one- to two-hour walk. A much more challenging hike climbs 800 m to the flat top of **Cerro de Chochis,** where you can camp or return to town in a long day; guide required.

Sixty kilometres east of Chochis is **Roboré**, the regional centre and transport hub. The **Oficina Municipal de Turismo** ① *Rubén Terrazas, one block from plaza, T974 2276, www.gobiernomunicipalrobore.com,* has information about local excursions including **Los Helechos** and **Totaisales**, two lovely bathing spots in the forest. Roboré is an old garrison town dating back to the Chaco War and retains a strong military presence. The local fiesta is 25 October.

Seven kilometres east of Roboré, a secondary road (being improved in 2012) branches northeast and in 14 km reaches the particularly friendly village of **Santiago de Chiquitos**. Founded in 1754, Santiago was one of the last missions built in Chiquitania. There is an impressive church here, excellent accommodations and more good walking to a fine *mirador*, natural stone arches and caves with petroglyphs; guides available in town. A poor road continues 150 km past Santiago to **Santo Corazón**, a still-isolated Jesuit mission town (the last one built, 1760) inside **Parque Nacional San Matías**.

Aguas Calientes is 32 km east of Roboré along the rail line and highway to Brazil. The hot little village is unimpressive but nearby is a river of crystal-clear thermal water, teeming with little fish and bird life. There are several spots with facilities for bathing and camping, which is preferable to the basic accommodations in town. There are many tiny biting sand-flies, so your tent should have good netting. Soaking in the thermal water amid the sights and sounds of the surrounding forest at dawn or on a moonlit night is amazing.

Parque Nacional Noel Kempff Mercado

In the far northeast corner of Santa Cruz Department, **Parque Nacional Noel Kempff Mercado** (named after a Bolivian conservation pioneer who was killed while flying over the park) ① *park office in San Ignacio de Velasco, C Oruro y Cochabamba, T962 2747, Mon-Fri 0830-1200, 1430-1800, no park entry fee in 2012 (subject to change); additional information from SERNAP and FAN, both in Santa Cruz (page 121),* is one of the world's most diverse natural habitats. This World Heritage site covers 1,523,446 ha and encompasses seven ecosystems, within which are 139 species of mammals (including black jaguars), 620 species of birds (including nine types of macaw), 74 species of reptiles and 110 species of orchids. Highlights include the **Huanchaca** or **Caparú Plateau**, which with its 200-500 m sheer cliffs and tumbling waterfalls is a candidate for Sir Arthur Conan Doyle's *Lost World* (Colonel Percy Fawcett, who discovered the plateau in 1910, was a friend of Conan Doyle).

This outstanding natural area received fewer than 200 visitors in 2011 and organizing a trip requires time, money and flexibility. The authorities sometimes restrict access, enquire in advance. Operators in Santa Cruz (see page 119) may be able to arrange all-inclusive tours. Otherwise, the best base is San Ignacio (page 130), which has some provisions but more specialized items should be brought from Santa Cruz.

The southwestern section of the park is reached from the village of **Florida**, where there is a ranger station and a community tourism project offering basic accommodation and guides (guide compulsory, US$25 per day, www.parquenoelkempffmercado.blogspot.com). It is 65 km from Florida to the trailhead (pickup US$60 one way), which provides access to the 80-m high **El Encanto** waterfall and the climb to the plateau; allow 5-6 days for the return excursion. To reach Florida from San Ignacio, either hire a 4WD (US$100 per day), or there is one bus a week in the dry season (Jun-Nov, see Transport page 137).

In the northeastern section of the park are the great **Arco Iris** and **Federico Ahlfeld** waterfalls, both on the Río Paucerna and accessible mid-Dec to May when water levels are sufficiently high. Access is either from the Bolivian village of **Piso Firme** or the Brazilian town of **Pimenteiras do Oeste**; in all cases you must be accompanied by a Bolivian boatman/guide, available in Piso Firme and organized by the park office in San Ignacio. It is 6-7 hours by motorized canoe from Piso Firme to a shelter near the Ahlfeld waterfall, and a full day's walk from there to Arco Iris. There is, in principle, one bus a week to Piso Firme from Santa Cruz and another from San Ignacio in the dry season (see Transport page 137).

To Brazil
There are four routes from Santa Cruz: by air to Puerto Suárez, by rail or road to Quijarro (fully paved except for 40 km between Santa Cruz and San José de Chiquitos), by road to San Matías (a busy border town reported unsafe due to drug smuggling), and via San Ignacio de Velasco to either Vila Bela or Pontes e Lacerda (both in Brazil). Puerto Suárez is near Quijarro and this route leads to Corumbá on the Brazilian side, from where there is access to the southern Pantanal. The San Matías and Vila Bela/Pontes roads both link to Cáceres, Cuiabá and the northern Pantanal in Brazil. There are immigration posts of both countries on all routes except Vila Bela/Pontes. If travelling this way get your Bolivian exit stamp in San Ignacio (immigration office near **Jenecherú** bus station) and Brazilian entry stamp in Cáceres or Vilhena. There may be strict customs and drugs checks entering Brazil, no fresh food may be taken from Bolivia.

Quijarro and Puerto Suárez → *Phone code: 03.*
The eastern terminus of the Bolivian road and railway is **Quijarro**. It is quite safe by day, but caution is recommended at night. The water supply is often unreliable, try the tap before checking-in to a hotel. Prices are much lower than in neighbouring Brazil and there are some decent places to stay. **Rossy Tours**, C Costa Rica, four blocks toward river from train station, T978 2022, offers 4WD tours to **Parque Nacional Otuquis** in the Bolivian Pantanal, and various boat trips. ATMs and and bank are at the border, see below.

On the shores of Laguna Cáceres, 8 km west of Quijarro, is **Puerto Suárez**, with a shady main plaza. There is a nice view of the lake from the park at the north end of Avenida Bolívar.

Border with Brazil
The municipality by the border is known as Arroyo Concepción. You need not have your passport stamped if you visit Corumbá for the day. Otherwise get your exit stamp at Bolivian immigration (see below), entry stamp at Brazilian border complex. Yellow Fever vaccination is compulsory to enter Bolivia and Brazil, have your certificate at hand when you go for your entry stamp, otherwise you may be sent to get revaccinated. Bolivian immigration is at the border at Arroyo Concepción (0800-1200, 1400-1730 daily), or at Puerto Suárez airport, where Bolivian exit/entry stamps are also issued. There are ATMs at Arroyo Concepción, on the border. Money changers right at the border offer the worst rates, better to ask around in the small shops past the bridge. There are Brazilian consulates in Puerto Suárez and Santa Cruz. See Transport, below, for taxis from the border.

Eastern Bolivia listings

For hotel and restaurant price codes and other relevant information, see pages 9-10.

🛏 Where to stay

Jesuit Missions of Chiquitos *p129*
San Javier
$ Alojamiento San Xavier, C Santa Cruz, T963 5038. cheaper without bath, electric shower, garden, nice sitting area. Recommended.
$ El Reposo del Guerrero, C Tte Busch Becerra, T963 5022. Includes breakfast, a/c, restaurant.
$ Residencial Chiquitano, Av Santa Cruz (Av José de Arce), ½ block from plaza, T963 5072. Simple economical rooms, fan, large patio, friendly atmosphere, good value.

Concepción
$$ Gran Hotel Concepción, on plaza, T964 3031. Excellent service, including buffet breakfast, pool, gardens, bar, very comfortable. Highly recommended.
$$ Hotel Chiquitos, end of Av Killian, T964 3153. Colonial style construction, ample rooms, frigobar, internet, pool, gardens and sports fields, orchid nursery, parking. Includes breakfast, tours available. Recommended.
$ Colonial, Ñuflo de Chávez 7, ½ block from plaza, T964 3050. Economical place, hammocks on ample veranda, parking, breakfast available.
$ Las Misiones, C Luis Caballero, 1 block from church, T964 3021. Small rooms, nice garden, small pool, also has an apartment, good value.
$ Oasis Chiquitano, C Germán Bush, 1½ blocks from plaza. Includes buffet breakfast, a/c, pool, nice patio with flowers.
$ Residencial Westfalia, Saucedo 205, 2 blocks from plaza, T964 3040. cheaper without bath, German-owned, nice patio, good value.

San Ignacio de Velasco
$$$ La Misión, Libertad on plaza, T962 2333, www.hotel-lamision.com. Upmarket hotel, includes buffet breakfast, restaurant, meeting rooms, a/c, pool, parking, dowstairs rooms have bath tubs.
$$ Apart Hotel San Ignacio, 24 de Septiembre y Cochabamba, T962 2157, www.aparthotel-sanignacio.com. Includes breakfast, comfortable rooms, a/c, nice grounds, pool, hammocks, parking. Despite the name, no apartments or kitchenettes.
$$ Parador Santa Ana, Libertad entre Sucre y Cochabamba, T962 2075, www.paradorsantaana.blogspot.com. Beautiful house with small patio, very clean and tastefully decorated, 5 comfortable rooms, includes good breakfast, a/c, Wi-Fi, knowledgeable owner arranges tours, credit cards accepted. Recommended.
$$ San Ignacio, Libertad on plaza, T962 2283. In a beautifully restored former episcopal mansion, non-profit (run by diocese, funds support poor youth in the community), a/c, breakfast.
$ Res Bethania, Velasco y Cochabamba, T962 2367. Simple clean rooms with shared bath, electric shower, small patio, economical and good value.

San José de Chiquitos *p131*
$$$ Villa Chiquitana, C 9 de Abril, 6 blocks from plaza, T7315 5803, www.villachiquitana.com. Charming hotel built in traditional style, includes breakfast, restaurant open to public, a/c, frigobar, pool (US$3 for non-guests), garden, parking, craft shop, tour agency. French run.
$ Turubó, Bolívar on the plaza, T972 2037, hotelturubo@hotmail.com. With a/c, cheaper with fan, electric shower, variety of different rooms, ask to see one before checking-in, good location, friendly owners.

East of San José de Chiquitos *p131*
Chochis
$ Ecoalbergue Comunitario, 1 km west of town along the rail line, T7263 9467; Santa Cruz contact: **Probioma**, T343 1332, www.probioma.org.bo. Simple community-run lodging in 2 cabins, shared bath, cold water, small kitchen, screened hammock area, camping US$3.50 pp, meals on advance request.
$ El Peregrino, on the plaza, T7313 1881. Simple rooms in a family home, some with fan and fridge, shared bath, electric shower, ample yard, camping possible.

Roboré
$$ Anahí, Obispo Santiesteban 1½ blocks from plaza, T974 2362. Comfortable rooms with a/c, electric shower, nice patio, parking, kitchen and washing facilities, friendly owner runs tours.
$$ Choboreca, C La Paz, T974 2566. Nice hotel, rooms with a/c.
Several other places to stay in town.

Santiago de Chiquitos
$$ Beula, on the plaza, T313 6274, pachecomary@hotmail.com. Comfortable hotel in traditional style, includes good breakfast, a/c, frigobar. Unexpectedly upmarket for such a remote location.
$ El Convento, on plaza next to the church, T6890 2943. Former convent with simple rooms, one has private bath, lovely garden, hot and no fan but clean and good value.
$ Panorama, 1 km north of plaza, T313 6286, katmil@bolivia.com. Simple rooms with shared bath and a family farm, friendly owners Katherine and Milton Whittaker sell excellent home-made dairy products and jams, they are knowledgeable about the area and offer volunteer opportunities. There are also various *alojamientos familiares* around town, all simple to basic.

Aguas Calientes
$$ Cabañas Canaan, across the road from Los Hervores baths, T7467 7316. Simple wooden cabins, cold water, fan, restaurant, rather overpriced but better than the basic places in town.
$ Camping Miraflores, 1 km from town on the road to Los Hervores baths, T7215 1188, www.aguascalientesmiraflores.com.bo. Lovely ample grounds with clean bathrooms, electric showers, barbeques, small pier by the river. Recommended.

Quijarro and Puerto Suárez *p133*
Quijarro
$$$-$$ Bibosi, Luis Salazar s/n, 4½ blocks east of train station, T978 2044. Variety of rooms and prices, some with a/c, fridge, cheaper with fan and shared bath, breakfast, pool, patio, restaurant, upscale for Quijarro.
$$ Tamengo, Costa Rica 57, Barrio Copacabana, 6 blocks toward river from train station, T978 3356, www.tamengo.com. Located by the river, all rooms with a/c (cheaper with shared bath and in dorm), includes breakfast, restaurant and bar, pool, sports fields, Wi-Fi and book exchange. Day-use of facilities by visitors US$8.50. Arranges tours and volunteer opportunities.
$ Gran Hotel Colonial, Av Luis de la Vega, 2 blocks east of train station, T978 2037. With a/c (cheaper with fan and private bath; even cheaper with shared bath). Restaurant serves good set lunch.
Willy Solís Cruz, Roboré 13, T978 2204, wiland_54@hotmail.com. For years Willy has helped store luggage and assists with ticket purchases, he also has internet, laundry, cooking facilities and clothes and shoe mending; and plans to offer rooms for tourists (date and price unspecified). He speaks English, very helpful.

Puerto Suárez
$ Beby, Av Bolívar 111, T976 2270. Private bath, a/c, cheaper with shared bath and fan.
$ Casa Real, Vanguardia 39, T976 3335, www.hotelenpuertosuarez.com. A/c, frigobar, Wi-Fi, parking, tours.

🍴 Restaurants

Jesuit Missions of Chiquitos *p129*
San Javier
\$\$ Ganadero, in Asociación de Ganaderos on plaza. Excellent steaks. Others eateries around the plaza.

Concepción
\$ El Buen Gusto, north side of plaza. Set meals and regional specialties.

San Ignacio de Velasco
\$ Club Social, Comercio on the plaza, daily 1130-1500, decent set lunch.
Panadería Juanita, Comercio y Sucre, good bakery.
Mi Nonna, C Velasco y Cochabamba. 1700-2400, closed Tue, café serving cappuccino, sandwiches, salads and pasta.

San José de Chiquitos *p131*
\$\$ Sabor y Arte, Bolívar y Mons Santisteban, by the plaza, Tue-Sun 1800-2300. International dishes, for innovation try their coca-leaf ravioli, nice ambience, French-Bolivian run.
\$\$-\$ Rancho Brasilero, by main road, 5 blocks from plaza, daily 0900-1530. Good Brazilian-style buffet, all you can eat grill on weekends.

East of San José de Chiquitos *p131*
Roboré
\$ Casino Militar, on the plaza, daily for lunch and dinner. Set meals and à la carte. Several other restaurants around the plaza.

Santiago de Chiquitos
\$ Churupa, ½ block from plaza. Set meals (go early or reserve your meal in adavance) and à la carte. Best in town.

🎉 Festivals

The region celebrates the **Festival de Música Renacentista y Barroca Americana** every even year (next in 2014).

Many towns have their own orchestras, which play Jesuit-era music on a regular basis. **Semana Santa** (Holy Week) celebrations are elaborate and interesting throughout the region.

🚌 Transport

Jesuit Missions of Chiquitos *p129*
San Javier
Trans Guarayos, T346 3993, from Santa Cruz Terminal Bimodal regional departures area, 7 a day, 4 hrs, US\$4.50, some continue to **Concepción**. Several others including Jenecherú, T348 8618, daily at 2000, US\$6, *bus-cama* US\$10, continuing to **Concepción** and San Ignacio. Various taxi-*trufi* companies also operate from regional departures area, US\$5, 3½ hrs.

Concepción
Bus To/from **Santa Cruz**, Trans Guarayos, US\$5, 5 hrs, and Jenecherú, as above, US\$6; various others. To **San Ignacio de Velasco**, buses pass though from Santa Cruz (many at night); also **Flota 31 del Este** (poor buses) from C Germán Busch in Concepción, daily at 1700, 5-6 hrs, US\$4.25. Concepción to **San Javier**, 1 hr, US\$1.50.

San Ignacio de Velasco
Bus From **Santa Cruz**, many companies from Terminal Bimodal depart 1900-2000, including Jenecherú (most luxuriuos buses, see above), US\$10, bus cama US\$17-30, 11 hrs; returning 1800-1900. For daytime service **31 del Este** (slow and basic) at 1100. Also *trufis* from regional departures area 0900 daily (with minimum 7 passengers), US\$17, 8 hrs. To **San José de Chiquitos**, see San José Transport, below. To **San Rafael** (US\$3, 2½ hrs) via **Santa Ana** (US\$1.50,1 hr) **Expreso Baruc**, 24 de Septiembre y Kennedy, daily at 1400; returning 0600. To **San Miguel**, *trufis* leave when full from Mercado de Comida, US\$1.75, 40 min. To **San Matías** (for Cáceres, Brazil) several daily passing

through from Santa Cruz starting 0400, US$12, 8 hrs. To **Pontes e Lacerda** (Brazil), **Rápido Monte Cristo**, from Club Social on the plaza, Wed and Sat 0900, US$22, 8-9 hrs; returning Tue and Fri, 0630. All roads to Brazil are poor. The best option to Pontes e Lacerda is via Vila Bela (Brazil), used by **Amanda Tours** (T7608 8476 in Bolivia, T65-9926 8522 in Brazil), from **El Corralito** restaurant by the market, Tue, Thu, Sun 0830, US$28; returning Mon, Wed, Fri 0600.

San José de Chiquitos *p131*

Bus To **Santa Cruz** many companies pass through starting 1700 daily, US$6. Also *trufis*, leave when full, US$10, 4 hrs. To **Puerto Suárez**, buses pass through1600-2300, US$10, 4 hrs. To **San Ignacio de Velasco** via San Rafael and San Miguel, **Flota Universal** (poor road, terrible buses), Mon, Wed, Fri, Sat at 0700, US$7, 5 hrs, returning 1400; also **31 de Julio**, Tue, Thu, Sun from San Ignacio at 0645, returning 1500.

Train Westbound, the **Ferrobus** passes through San José Tue, Thu, Sat at 0231, arriving Santa Cruz 0755; **Expreso Oriental**, Mon, Wed, Fri 0153, arriving 0800; **Tren Regional**, Mon, Wed, Fri 2308, arriving 0638 next day. Eastbound, the **Ferrobus** passes through San José Tue, Thu, Sun 2339, arriving Quijarro 0756 next day; **Expreso Oriental** Mon, Wed, Fri 2150, arriving 0800 next day; **Tren Regional**, Tue, Thu, Sat 1828, arriving 0620 next day. See Santa Cruz Transport (page 120) and www.ferroviariaoriental.com for fares and additional information.

East of San José de Chiquitos *p131*

Bus To **Chochis** from San Jose de Chiquitos, with **Perla del Oriente**, daily 0800 and 1500, US$3.50, 2 hrs; continuing to **Roboré**, US$1, 1 hr more; Roboré to San José via Chochis 0815 and 1430. Roboré bus terminal is by the highway, a long walk from town, but some buses go by the plaza before leaving; enquire locally. From

Santiago de Chiquitos to Roboré, Mon-Sat at 0700, US$1.50, 45 min; returning 1000; taxi Roboré-Santiago about US$15. Buses to/from Quijarro stop at **Aguas Calientes**; taxi Roboré-Aguas Calientes about US$22 return. From Roboré to **Santa Cruz**, several companies, US$7-20, 7-9 hrs; also *trufis* 0900, 1400, 1800, US$14.50, 5 hrs. From Roboré to **Quijarro** with Perla del Oriente, 4 daily, US$4.50, 4 hrs; also *trufis* leave when full, US$8, 3 hrs.

Train All trains stop in Roboré (see www. ferroviariaoriental.com). Only the **Tren Regional** stops in Chochis and Aguas Calientes to pick up passengers, but the **Ferrobus** and **Expresso Oriental** might let you off at these stations if you ask the conductor in advance.

Parque Nacional Noel Kempff Mercado *p132*

Road/Bus All overland journeys are long and arduous, take supplies. The following are subject to frequent change and cancellation, always enquire locally. **San Ignacio-Florida**, Trans Velasco, Av Kennedy y 24 de Septiembre, T7602 3269, dry season only (Jun-Nov), Sat 0900, US$10, at least 10 hrs; same company runs **San Ignacio-Piso Firme**, dry season only, Fri 1000, US$18, 24 hrs or more, returning Sun 1400. **Santa Cruz-Piso Firme** (via Santa Rosa de la Roca, not San Ignacio), **Trans Bolivia**, C Melchor Pinto entre 2do y 3er Anillo, T336 3866, Thu morning, US$24, 24 hrs or more; returning Sun. For **Pimenteiras do Oeste** (Brazil) see San Ignacio Transport (above) to Pontes e Lacerda and make connections there via Vilhena.

Quijarro and Puerto Suárez *p133*

Air **Puerto Suárez** airport is 6 km north of town, T976 2347; airport tax US$2. Flights to **Santa Cruz** with TAM, 3 times a week, US$85. Don't buy tickets for flights originating in Puerto Suárez in Corumbá, these cost more.

Bus Buses from Quijarro pick up passengers in Puerto Suárez on route to **Santa Cruz**, many companies, most after 1800 (**Trans Bioceanico** at 1030), US$12-22, 11-12 hrs.

Taxi Quijarro to the border (**Arroyo Concepción**) US$0.50 pp; to **Puerto Suárez** US$1 pp, more at night. If arriving from Brazil, you will be approached by Bolivian taxi drivers who offer to hold your luggage while you clear immigration. These are the most expensive cabs (US$5 to Quijarro, US$15 to Puerto Suárez) and best avoided. Instead, keep your gear with you while your passport is stamped, then walk 200 m past the bridge to an area where other taxis wait (US$0.50 to Quijarro). Colectivos to Puerto Suárez leave Quijarro when full from Av Bolivar corner Av Luiz de la Vega, US$1.

Train. With paving of the highway from Santa Cruz train service is in less demand, but the better classes of service remain comfortable and convenient options. Ticket office in Quijarro station Mon-Sat 0730-1200, 1430-1800, Sun 0730-1100. Purchase tickets directly at the train station (passport required) and avoid touts (do not buy train tickets for Bolivia in Brazil). The **Ferrobus** leaves Quijarro Mon, Wed, Fri 1830, arriving Santa Cruz 0755 next day; **Expreso Oriental**, Tue, Thu, Sun 1600, arriving 0800 next day; **Tren Regional**, Mon, Wed, Fri 1100, arriving 0638 next day. See Santa Cruz Transport (page 120) and www.ferroviariaoriental. com for fares and additional information.

Contents

Footnotes

Basic Spanish for travellers

Learning Spanish is a useful part of the preparation for a trip to Latin America and no volumes of dictionaries, phrase books or word lists will provide the same enjoyment as being able to communicate directly with the people of the country you are visiting. It is a good idea to make an effort to grasp the basics before you go. As you travel you will pick up more of the language and the more you know, the more you will benefit from your stay.

General pronunciation

Whether you have been taught the 'Castilian' pronunciation (z and c followed by i or e are pronounced as the th in think) or the 'American' pronunciation (they are pronounced as s), you will encounter little difficulty in understanding either. Regional accents and usages vary, but the basic language is essentially the same everywhere.

Vowels

a	as in English cat
e	as in English best
i	as the ee in English feet
o	as in English shop
u	as the oo in English food
ai	as the i in English ride
ei	as ey in English they
oi	as oy in English toy

Consonants

Most consonants can be pronounced more or less as they are in English. The exceptions are:

g	before e or i is the same as j
h	is always silent (except in ch as in chair)
j	as the ch in Scottish loch
ll	as the y in yellow
ñ	as the ni in English onion
rr	trilled much more than in English
x	depending on its location, pronounced x, s, sh or j

Spanish words and phrases

Greetings, courtesies

hello	hola	please	por favor
good morning	buenos días	thank you (very much)	(muchas) gracias
good afternoon/ evening/night	buenas tardes/noches	I don't speak Spanish	no hablo español
		do you speak English?	¿habla inglés?
goodbye	adiós/chao	I don't understand	no comprendo
pleased to meet you	mucho gusto	please speak slowly	hable despacio por favor
see you later	hasta luego		
how are you?	¿cómo está? ¿cómo estás?	I am very sorry	lo siento mucho
		what do you want?	¿qué quiere? ¿qué quieres?
I'm fine, thanks	estoy muy bien, gracias	I want	quiero
I'm called...	me llamo...	I don't want it	no lo quiero
what is your name?	¿cómo se llama? ¿cómo te llamas?	leave me alone	déjeme en paz/ no me moleste
yes/no	sí/no	good/bad	bueno/malo

Questions and requests

Have you got a room for two people?
¿Tiene una habitación para dos personas?
How do I get to_? *¿Cómo llego a_?*
How much does it cost?
¿Cuánto cuesta? ¿cuánto es?
I'd like to make a long-distance phone call
Quisiera hacer una llamada de larga distancia
Is service included? *¿Está incluido el servicio?*
Is tax included? *¿Están incluidos los impuestos?*

When does the bus leave (arrive)?
¿A qué hora sale (llega) el autobús?
When? *¿cuándo?*
Where is_? *¿dónde está_?*
Where can I buy tickets?
¿Dónde puedo comprar boletos?
Where is the nearest petrol station?
¿Dónde está la gasolinera más cercana?
Why? *¿por qué?*

Basics

bank	*el banco*	market	*el mercado*
bathroom/toilet	*el baño*	note/coin	*el billete/la moneda*
bill	*la factura/la cuenta*	police (policeman)	*la policía (el policía)*
cash	*el efectivo*	post office	*el correo*
cheap	*barato/a*	public telephone	*el teléfono público*
credit card	*la tarjeta de crédito*	supermarket	*el supermercado*
exchange house	*la casa de cambio*	ticket office	*la taquilla*
exchange rate	*el tipo de cambio*	traveller's cheques	*los cheques de*
expensive	*caro/a*		*viajero/los travelers*

Getting around

aeroplane	*el avión*	insured person	*el/la asegurado/a*
airport	*el aeropuerto*	to insure yourself against	*asegurarse contra*
arrival/departure	*la llegada/salida*	luggage	*el equipaje*
avenue	*la avenida*	motorway, freeway	*el autopista/la*
block	*la cuadra*		*carretera*
border	*la frontera*	north, south, west, east	*norte, sur,*
bus station	*la terminal de*		*oeste (occidente),*
	autobuses/camiones		*este (oriente)*
bus	*el bus/el autobús/*	oil	*el aceite*
	el camión	to park	*estacionarse*
collective/		passport	*el pasaporte*
fixed-route taxi	*el colectivo*	petrol/gasoline	*la gasolina*
corner	*la esquina*	puncture	*el pinchazo/*
customs	*la aduana*		*la ponchadura*
first/second class	*primera/segunda clase*	street	*la calle*
left/right	*izquierda/derecha*	that way	*por allí/por allá*
ticket	*el boleto*	this way	*por aquí/por acá*
empty/full	*vacío/lleno*	tourist card/visa	*la tarjeta de turista*
highway, main road	*la carretera*	tyre	*la llanta*
immigration	*la inmigración*	unleaded	*sin plomo*
insurance	*el seguro*	to walk	*caminar/andar*

Index

Titles available in the Footprint *Focus* range

Latin America	UK RRP	US RRP
Bahia & Salvador	£7.99	$11.95
Buenos Aires & Pampas	£7.99	$11.95
Costa Rica	£8.99	$12.95
Cuzco, La Paz & Lake Titicaca	£8.99	$12.95
El Salvador	£5.99	$8.95
Guadalajara & Pacific Coast	£6.99	$9.95
Guatemala	£8.99	$12.95
Guyana, Guyane & Suriname	£5.99	$8.95
Havana	£6.99	$9.95
Honduras	£7.99	$11.95
Nicaragua	£7.99	$11.95
Paraguay	£5.99	$8.95
Quito & Galápagos Islands	£7.99	$11.95
Recife & Northeast Brazil	£7.99	$11.95
Rio de Janeiro	£8.99	$12.95
São Paulo	£5.99	$8.95
Uruguay	£6.99	$9.95
Venezuela	£8.99	$12.95
Yucatán Peninsula	£6.99	$9.95

Asia	UK RRP	US RRP
Angkor Wat	£5.99	$8.95
Bali & Lombok	£8.99	$12.95
Chennai & Tamil Nadu	£8.99	$12.95
Chiang Mai & Northern Thailand	£7.99	$11.95
Goa	£6.99	$9.95
Hanoi & Northern Vietnam	£8.99	$12.95
Ho Chi Minh City & Mekong Delta	£7.99	$11.95
Java	£7.99	$11.95
Kerala	£7.99	$11.95
Kolkata & West Bengal	£5.99	$8.95
Mumbai & Gujarat	£8.99	$12.95

Africa & Middle East	UK RRP	US RRP
Beirut	£6.99	$9.95
Damascus	£5.99	$8.95
Durban & KwaZulu Natal	£8.99	$12.95
Fès & Northern Morocco	£8.99	$12.95
Jerusalem	£8.99	$12.95
Johannesburg & Kruger National Park	£7.99	$11.95
Kenya's beaches	£8.99	$12.95
Kilimanjaro & Northern Tanzania	£8.99	$12.95
Zanzibar & Pemba	£7.99	$11.95

Europe	UK RRP	US RRP
Bilbao & Basque Region	£6.99	$9.95
Granada & Sierra Nevada	£6.99	$9.95
Málaga	£5.99	$8.95
Orkney & Shetland Islands	£5.99	$8.95
Skye & Outer Hebrides	£6.99	$9.95

North America	UK RRP	US RRP
Vancouver & Rockies	£8.99	$12.95

Australasia	UK RRP	US RRP
Brisbane & Queensland	£8.99	$12.95
Perth	£7.99	$11.95

For the latest books, e-books and smart phone app releases, and a wealth of travel information, visit us at: www.footprinttravelguides.com.

footprinttravelguides.com

Join us on facebook for the latest travel news, product releases, offers and amazing competitions: www.facebook.com/footprintbooks.com.